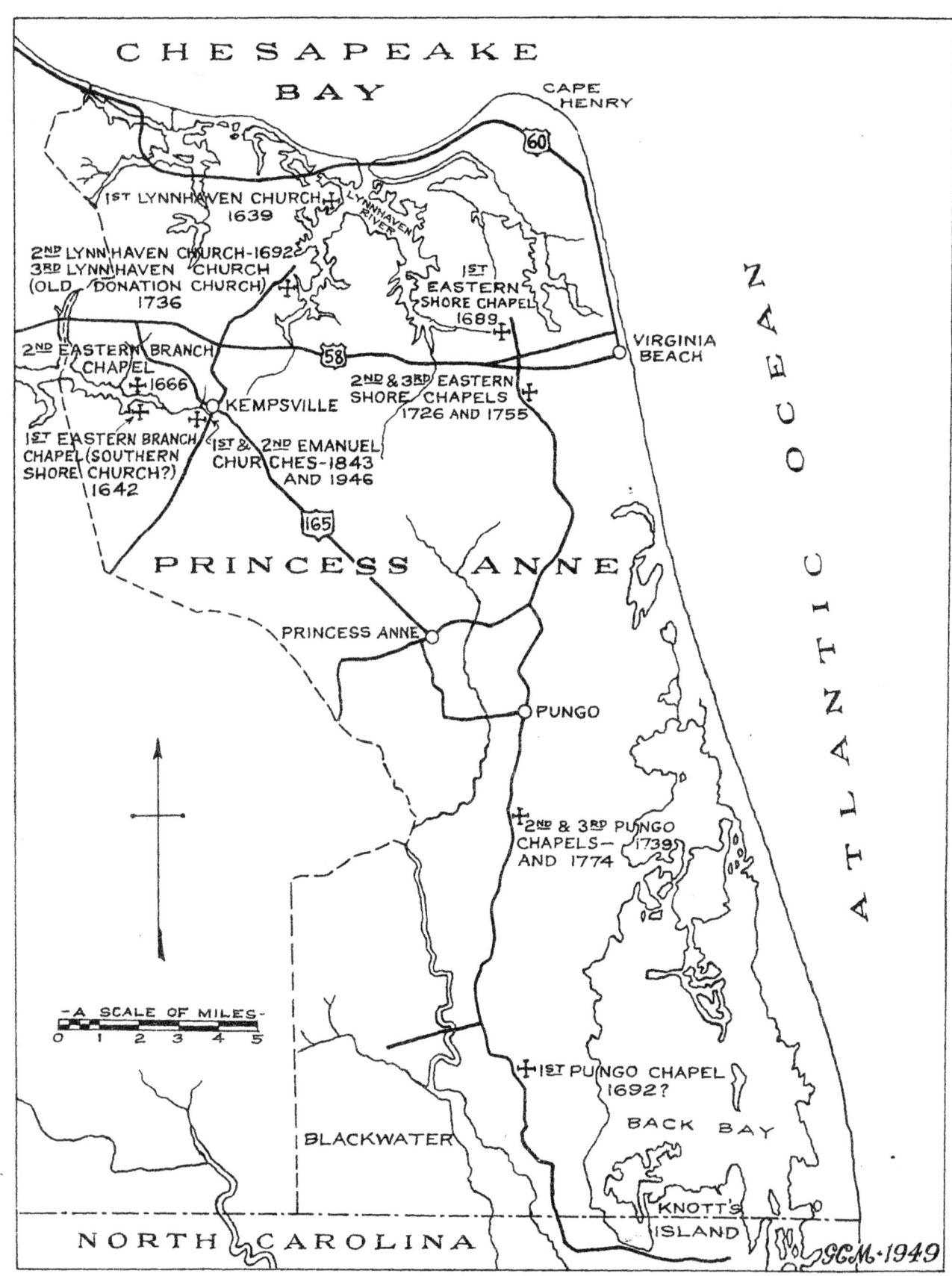

Map of Princess Anne County, showing colonial church sites.

The Colonial Vestry Book of Lynnhaven Parish, Princess Anne County, Virginia, 1723-1786

Transcribed and Edited by
GEORGE CARRINGTON MASON
Historiographer, Diocese of Southern Virginia.

Southern Historical Press, Inc.
Greenville, South Carolina

This volume was repropuced from
a personal copy located in the
Publisher's private library
Greenville, South Carolina

All rights reserved. No part of this publication may be
reproduced, stored in a retieval system, Transmitted in
any form, posted on to the web in any form or by any
means without the prior permission of the publisher.

Please direct ALL correspondence and book orders to:
www.southernhistoricalpress.com
or
**Southern Historical Press, Inc.
PO Box 1267
Greenville, SC 29602-1267
southernhistoricalpress@gmail.com**

Originally published: Newport News, VA 1949
ISBN #0-89308-737-8
All Rights Reserved
Printed in the United States of America

PREFACE

The publication of this work, as the first of a projected series of several such publications, has been prompted by the realization that, out of more than fifty surviving parish records of colonial Virginia, only about fifteen have as yet been published in printed form. The rest of these invaluable manuscripts are unavailable to researchers generally, without a trip to the repositories in which they are kept.

Lithoprinting of a typewritten transcript of the original vestry book text has been adopted as the medium for this publication, in order to demonstrate that the historical and genealogical information contained in the text can be made available to students in this simple and inexpensive format, exactly as well or even better than in the more elaborate and costly one hitherto considered necessary for such volumes.

In order to facilitate the reader's use of this book for research purposes, all obscure abbreviations have been extended, thus doing away with the superior letters and special symbols used generally by colonial scribes to form such abbreviations.[1] To preserve to the full the antique flavor of the original text, no change was made in the spelling, capitalization, punctuation, or wording of the vestry minutes, of which this work is therefore a faithful transcript, with the exception noted above.

The choice of the Lynnhaven Parish vestry book as the first publication of this series is based on its exceptional interest and historical value among surviving Virginia parish records, and on the additional fact that it is the one most familiar to the editor, as the first manuscript of this kind to be examined by him, at the beginning of his extended study of the Virginia colonial churches, later published serially in the historical quarterlies and in book form.

Since further publications in this series are to be of the colonial period, the present volume includes only the colonial and post-Revolutionary portions of this long vestry record, which is actually continuous to the year 1892, with minor lapses due to war. The present publication covers the proceedings of the Lynnhaven Parish vestry down through its reorganization after the disestablishment of the Church of England in 1785, and its replacement by the Protestant Episcopal Church in Virginia, and terminates in 1786, when the vestry's duty of supporting paupers was surrendered to the Overseers of the Poor.

The vestry record for many years after 1786 does not possess the same interest that is found in the minutes published herein, since the vestry had then been shorn of all its principal functions, except as trustees of the parish free school, and was seriously handicapped in the performance of the important duty of securing a rector for the parish by the lack of any practical means of paying his salary.

A brief history of the parish and its churches, based on the study already mentioned, precedes the actual vestry book text. The illustrations showing probable interior arrangements of the parish church and lower chapel at various periods of the vestry book record, are not fanciful, but based solidly on specifications, vestry minutes, and physical features of the existing buildings.

The text is followed by an appendix containing lists of the colonial rectors, churchwardens, vestrymen, and presiding officers of the vestry, as well as of the many county sheriffs mentioned in the vestry book. There is a thorough index, with nearly 5000 references, but no attempt has been made to distinguish between "Senior" and "Junior" persons of the same name, or to give military titles, because the juniors become seniors and the captains turn into colonels, later on in the book. Geographical names of the various precincts of the parish have generally not been indexed, since they occur so often in the vestry minutes as to have no significance.

Although the first syllable of the parish name is spelt with a single "n" throughout the entire vestry book text, the form "Lynnhaven" is used in the title of this work, as being the accepted modern spelling and the correct form of the name of the English locality after which this parish was named.

---

[1] This simplification of the original text was made at the suggestion of Dr. E. G. Swem, Librarian Emeritus, William and Mary College, Williamsburg, Virginia.

INTRODUCTION

The colonial parish vestry functioned in so many ways which vitally affected the people's daily existence that the vestry book, recording as it does every transaction of the vestry, furnishes an unique cross section of the community life of the period.

Composed of the most prominent and able men of the parish, the vestry was first elected by popular vote at the formation of the parish, but thereafter was self-perpetuating, as it filled all vacancies due to death or resignation by electing new members as required. Membership was so nearly hereditary that junior members of leading families were sometimes added to the vestry without a recorded election by that body, and always joined it without opposition. The vestry served without pay and the legal number of vestrymen was twelve, although the membership often stood below that number for several years at a time. Once elected, a vestry could only be dissolved by act of assembly, for misconduct sufficient to justify a petition by the parishioners to the colonial council.

The colonial vestry has been aptly termed "a government within a government", for the parish was an ecclesiastical unit of area within the county as a civil unit, and just as the county commissioners, or justices of the peace, had power to levy taxes to meet the expenses of civil government in the county, so the vestry "laid the levy" for the collection of tithes to meet the civil and religious expenses of the parish.

The resulting tithe, usually figured in pounds of tobacco per poll, as the colonial medium of exchange, had to be paid for every tithable person, or male aged sixteen years or over. A collector, often the county sheriff, was charged with the duty of collecting these tithes and had the legal power to "distrain" or levy on the goods of a delinquent, in order to do so.

There was the closest possible co-operation between the vestry and county court, for the leading men in the county were members of both bodies, and this was especially true in parishes that were coterminous with the county, like Lynnhaven. Although the various functions of court and vestry were prescribed by law, the actual division between the civil duties performed by the two organizations seems to have been made by agreement between their memberships, or according to custom, and varied in different counties and parishes.

For example, the county commissioners were obligated to appoint surveyors of the county highways, while the vestry was legally required to designate the hands who should assist each surveyor in clearing and maintaining the roads, yet the Lynnhaven vestry did neither, and the Petsworth vestry in Gloucester appointed surveyors of the highways, but neglected the duty of supplying hands.

The most important duties of a vestry, in addition to levying tithes, were to employ a minister, purchase and maintain a "glebe" or parish farm, for his residence and support, erect and repair the parish church and chapels, and appoint clerks (readers) and sextons for their operation and upkeep, but the obligation for which the most tithes were levied, after the minister's salary was paid, was the support of the parish poor.

Payments for this last purpose were designated by the modern-sounding name of "relief". Aged paupers and orphan children were assigned to various members of the parish to be supported for a sum allotted in the annual parish levy, and sons and daughters were paid to maintain their indigent parents and widows to care for their own children, apparently in preference to allowing such duties to be performed by strangers. The vestry's provision for care of the poor included large sums paid to doctors for treatment of constitutional disorders, "salivation" by administration of mercury compounds being the most costly of such treatments.

The Lynnhaven vestry also maintained a workhouse and poor farm to reduce the expense of pauper care. Some vestry books contain evidence of schooling given to poor children at the poorhouse or elsewhere, but the Lynnhaven vestry's only recorded project of this sort was not undertaken until the close of the colonial era, and then only as the result of a liberal bequest to the parish by its last colonial rector, the Reverend Robert Dickson. The post-Revolutionary vestry record, for many years, is largely concerned with the vestry's efforts to operate this school, called Dickson's Free School, the bequest being known as Dickson's Donation.

Duties periodically performed by the vestry were the designation of persons to count tobacco plants, as required by early crop-control legislation, and the appointment of "procession-masters" to oversee the "processioning" of every man's land, legally required to be performed every four years, the parish being first divided by the vestry into convenient precincts for this purpose.

Having "warned in" the inhabitants of his precinct to be at home on the date set in the vestry's order, the procession-master with the neighboring land-owners then walked around the boundaries of each property, renewing tree-blazes and other landmarks, and in case of dispute the testimony of the oldest inhabitants was usually accepted. Results of this processioning and the reason for any failure to accomplish it were reported to the county court and recorded in an official register book.

An unusual feature of the Lynnhaven Parish vestry's organization was the apparent recognition of one of its senior members as presiding officer, who signed the vestry minutes and orders as entered in the vestry book, which were then attested by the vestry clerk. This presiding officer sometimes served also as a churchwarden, but usually continued to sign the minutes long after ceasing to hold that office. In his absence, the minutes were signed by some other senior vestryman, and when this was done in 1783 by Anthony Walke, Jr., the note was added "John Ackiss being absent".

The rector was ex officio a member of the vestry and legally entitled to preside. The first of Lynnhaven's rectors to assert this right was the Reverend James Simpson, who took office in 1785. Since the minutes designate him as "President" of the vestry, it may be assumed that the previous presiding officers also had that title.

It speaks well for the faithful performance of their duties by Lynnhaven vestrymen that when the vestry was dissolved, under general legislation enacted in 1783 and 1785, the majority of the old vestry was elected to membership in the new body in both cases. It will be noted from the list of vestrymen appended to the text that continuous service records of twenty years, more or less, are not uncommon among members of the Lynnhaven vestry.

The most remarkable of such records are those of the Anthony Walkes, father and son, who served 46 and 22 years, respectively, on the vestry and shared a combined service of 27 years as churchwardens. It is no wonder that this family was awarded a pew in the chancel of the new Donation Church in 1736, as "a benefit for gifts and services". There are actually only a dozen pages of the vestry text on which the name "Anthony Walke" does not occur.

No less than six different members of the Moseley family served at various times on the Lynnhaven vestry during the period of this vestry book, and this record earned them also a chancel pew. Distinguished records of long service on the vestry were also made by members of the Ackiss, Bonney, Boush, Cornick, Dawley, Ellegood, Keeling, Kempe, Land, Nimmo, Sayer, Walker, Whitehead, Whitehurst, and Woodhouse families and many others.

C O N T E N T S

	Page
Preface	v
Introduction	vii
Acknowledgments	ix
History of Colonial Lynnhaven Parish	xi
The Vestry Book of Lynnhaven Parish, 1723-1786	1
Appendix - Lists of Parish and County Officers, 1640-1786	126
Index	129

I L L U S T R A T I O N S

	Page
Map of Princess Anne County, showing Churches	Frontispiece
Old Donation Church and Communion Silver	xiv
Old Donation Church, Interior Arrangements	xvi
Eastern Shore Chapel and Communion Silver; Pungo Chapel Site	xxi
Eastern Shore Chapel, Interior Arrangements	xxiii

A C K N O W L E D G M E N T S

Grateful acknowledgment is made of the editor's indebtedness to the State Library Board and the State Librarian for their generous approval of the publication project and for the extended loan of a photostatic copy of the original manuscript vestry book, which has immensely reduced the labor of its transcription. His thanks are also due to the rector and vestry of Lynnhaven Parish for their ready permission to publish the parish's colonial vestry record.

George Carrington Mason

George Carrington Mason

Editor

HISTORY OF COLONIAL LYNNHAVEN PARISH, PRINCESS ANNE COUNTY, VIRGINIA.

The colonial parish of Lynnhaven included the whole of the existing county of Princess Anne, Virginia. This county had its origin in the early corporation of Elizabeth City, one of the four "ancient boroughs" which, together with the Eastern Shore settlement, comprised the colony of Virginia in 1618.[1]

Upon the colony's division into eight shires or counties in 1634, this area became a part of Elizabeth City County,[2] but was cut off in 1636 with New Norfolk County, the first county created after the original subdivision. New Norfolk was subdivided, a year later, into Upper Norfolk (now Nansemond) County and Lower Norfolk County.[3] Princess Anne County was formed in 1691 out of the eastern part of Lower Norfolk, whose western part became the present county of Norfolk.[4]

The formation of Lower Norfolk County in 1637 carried with it the creation of a coterminous parish of the same name, but by 1640, there had developed within this county two distinct church bodies, one in the upper part of the county, near Elizabeth River and Hampton Roads, and the other in its lower section, near Lynnhaven River and Chesapeake Bay. The former became Elizabeth River Parish and the latter Lynnhaven Parish, and a first vestry was appointed for each parish, respectively, at the county court sessions of July[5] and August,[6] 1640. Since this court held quarterly sessions, a month apart, in the two sections of the county successively, this amounted to simultaneous organization of the two parishes by the county court.

At the petition of its own inhabitants, boundaries for the new parish of Lynnhaven were set by an act of assembly in 1642.[7] This boundary act refers to a third church body in Lower Norfolk County under the name of Southern Shore Parish. This third parish in the county appears to have been named for its location on the southern shore of the Eastern Branch of Elizabeth River, and it was probably of small area, extending only to the contemporary limit of settlement. The county records show that Southern Shore had ceased to exist as a parish by 1645,[8] and no further documentary reference to it has been found.

When Princess Anne County was formed out of the eastern section of Lower Norfolk in 1691, a part of Lynnhaven Parish was left in Norfolk County until four years later, when an act of assembly of 1695 made the new county coterminous with the parish.[9] These boundaries remained unchanged for exactly two centuries, or until 1895, when East Lynnhaven Parish was formed out of the eastern portion of the county.

Lynnhaven Parish derived its name from Lynnhaven River, which was called

Chesopeian or Chesapeake River in the earliest records, but is believed to have been renamed by Adam Thorowgood after his early home at Lynn, England, about 1635, when he patented ten square miles of land upon its shores.

The county records reveal that there were no churches in service in Lower Norfolk County in 1637, since court orders of that year require certain penances, customarily performed during services at the parish church, to be carried out at private homes "during the time of divine service" on the Sabbath. The houses at which these first church services were held were those of Captain Adam Thorowgood at Lynnhaven[10] and of Captain John Sibsey at Seawell's Point,[11] both places being near the sites where the first churches for the county's two parishes were soon afterward erected.

A later county record proves that there was a "Parish Church at Lynnhaven" already in existence in 1639.[12] This first Lynnhaven Church was built on Adam Thorowgood's land, at what has ever since been known as Church Point,[13] on the west side of Lynnhaven River and only a mile from Chesapeake Bay. The remains of this building were still visible as a mound of old brick in 1850, so that it seems probable that it was a brick church and one of the earliest of its type in Virginia.

The churchyard of this first Lynnhaven Church was gradually washed away by heavy waves admitted through enlargement of a narrow channel cut by fishermen to reopen the original Lynnhaven Inlet, shortly before the Revolutionary War.[14] This inlet had been open at the time of first settlement, as proved by early maps,[15] but had long since been closed by sandbars, compelling fishermen to use a roundabout channel, connecting with Little Creek, in order to pass from Lynnhaven River to their fishing grounds in Chesapeake Bay, on the opposite side of the bar.

The old first church had become ruinous by 1691, and the vestry then ordered it to be replaced by "a good and Substantiall Brick Church". This building was specified to be "forty five foot in length and twenty two foot in breadth between the walls", which were to be thirteen feet high. It was required to be completed by the end of June, 1692, under penalty of 100,000 pounds of tobacco, so that this may safely be taken as its date of erection.[16]

The new church's site lay about two and a half miles southwest by south of the first church and was sold to the parish in 1694 by Ebenezer Taylor, who deeded to the vestry two acres of land "whereon the new brick church of Lynnhaven now stands".[17] The building was erected by Jacob Johnson on Taylor's land "neare the road towards the ferry".

The ferry mentioned had been established a few years earlier across the

Western Branch of Lynnhaven River, near the point since named Witch Duck, after the historic witchcraft trial of Grace Sherwood in 1705. Near this ferry was the 50-acre Ferry Plantation, still known as the Ferry Farm.

The association between the colonial church and court-house was always very close and they were frequently built on adjoining sites. In accordance with this old custom, a court-house for the new Princess Anne County was, on the 12th September, 1695, ordered to be erected "Upon the land belonging to the Brick Church",[18] referring to the two-acre site just purchased from Ebenezer Taylor for the second Lynnhaven Church.

This court-house was not the first one in service for Princess Anne County, since it succeeded an earlier frame court-house ordered on 17th September, 1689, to be built on the Eastern Shore of Lynnhaven,[19] near the southern end of Great Neck, as a local court building for Lower Norfolk County, which in 1691 became the first Princess Anne County Court-house.

The building ordered in 1695 was nevertheless the first court-house built for the new county after its creation in 1691, and it was largely constructed out of the timbers of the earlier building, which were shipped by boat across Lynnhaven River to the new site beside the brick church.[20] This earlier court-house itself had been erected near a church, as described later in this account.

With the rapid increase of wealth and population that took place in colonial Virginia at the beginning of the eighteenth century, this little second Lynnhaven Church was soon outgrown and in June, 1733, the vestry ordered a new church to be erected on a one-acre site at the Ferry Plantation.

Colonial government reports show that the county's population, as indicated by the number of tithables, or taxable persons, had more than doubled since the erection of the previous church building. The new church was therefore specified to be 65 feet long by 30 feet wide, inside, with walls 15 feet high, giving more than twice as much interior space as its diminutive predecessor afforded.

The customary close connection between church and court is evident in the vestry's choice of a church site at the Ferry Plantation, since a two-acre lot at the ferry had already been deeded to the county in 1730, "in order that a court house may be there erected",[21] and the vestry seem to have desired to maintain the previous close connection between church and court.

In September, 1733, only three months after the vestry had selected a site at the ferry for their new church building, they nevertheless reversed themselves and "unanimously agreed that the New Church be placed where the old one now stands". The

Suggested exterior appearance of Donation Church in 1776, at the close of the colonial era.

Communion silver service of Old Donation Church, with flagon of 1716, cup of 1712, and paten of 1711. The paten was the gift of Maximilian Boush and bears his arms.

Old Donation Church as it appears today.

later vestry record shows that this order was not followed too literally, since it was evidently carried out by erecting the new structure adjacent to the old one on the two-acre site deeded to the parish in 1694, for only thus could church services be maintained during the long construction period.

Since this adjacent position was already occupied by the old frame court-house of 1695, the vestry's change of front could only have been prompted by this old county building's actual removal from the church property, upon the approaching completion of the new brick court-house at the ferry. It therefore follows that the new church of 1736, which was the same historic structure that is now known as Old Donation Church, was erected upon the exact site of this old court building, the first constructed for the new county of Princess Anne.

No trace of the second Lynnhaven Church of 1692 is visible above ground at the site, but the sounding rod reveals the outlines of its foundation, parallel to the existing church and about 70 feet south and a little west of it, as marked by brick rubble in the soil. These remains lie due west of the present graveyard, which, although stripped of tombstones, is an ancient burial ground, and this would have been the most probable location for an earlier church.

We are by no means dependent upon the sounding rod, however, for evidence that the second church of 1692 was not torn down to make room for its successor, since we have definite proof of this fact in a vestry order giving the old church "as a convenient place to make a public School off for instructing children in learning" and dated 2nd March, 1736/7, when the new church must have been practically complete.

The third Lynnhaven Parish Church was received by the vestry from its builder, Peter Malbone, on the 25th June, 1736. Its identity as the existing Old Donation Church is sufficiently evident from the exact agreement between the present church's dimensions and those specified for the third church, and from the date 1736 cut in a brick to the right of its west doorway.

The stone tablet set in the west end wall of the existing Old Donation Church is therefore incorrect in giving the date of its construction as 1694. The same error appears on the state historical marker at the cross-road leading to the church, which states that Donation Church was "first built before 1694", unless this was meant to refer to the second Lynnhaven Church, on an adjacent site.

It does not appear, however, that the name "Donation Church" was ever applied to the second church, or even that it was applied to the third church during the colonial period, for the first published use of the name, in connection with the present building, seems to have been as late as 1822, when the vestry ordered "the Church called the Donation Church" to be put in repair. The name undoubtedly origin-

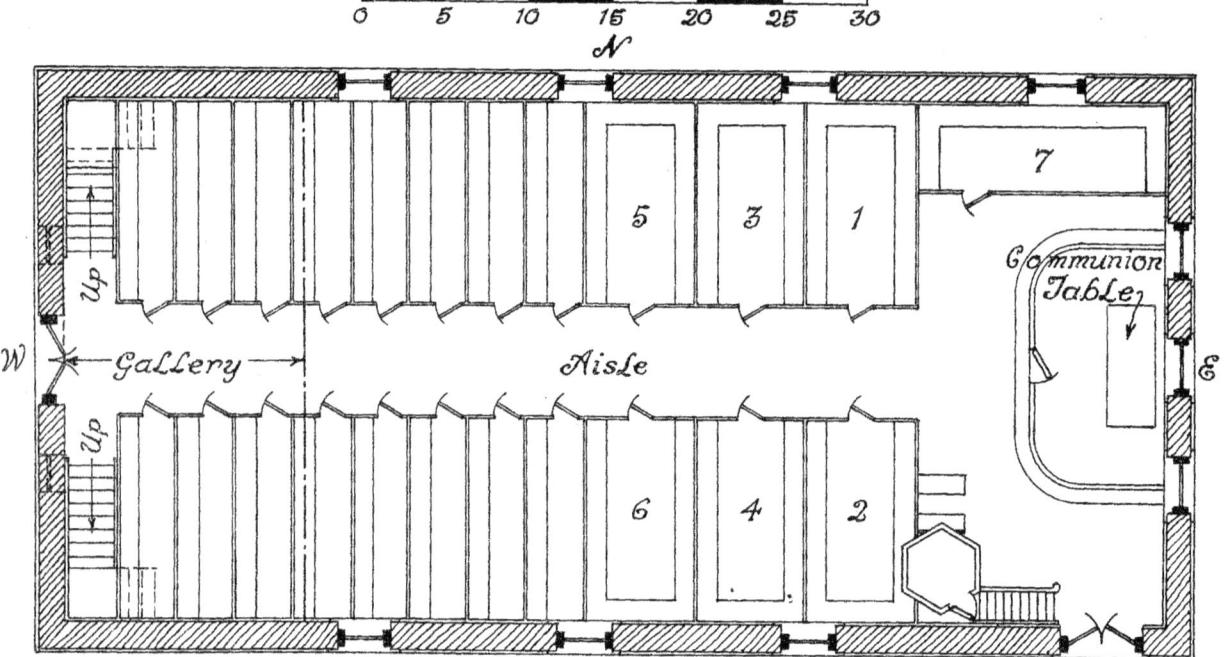

Donation Church in 1736, as originally arranged:

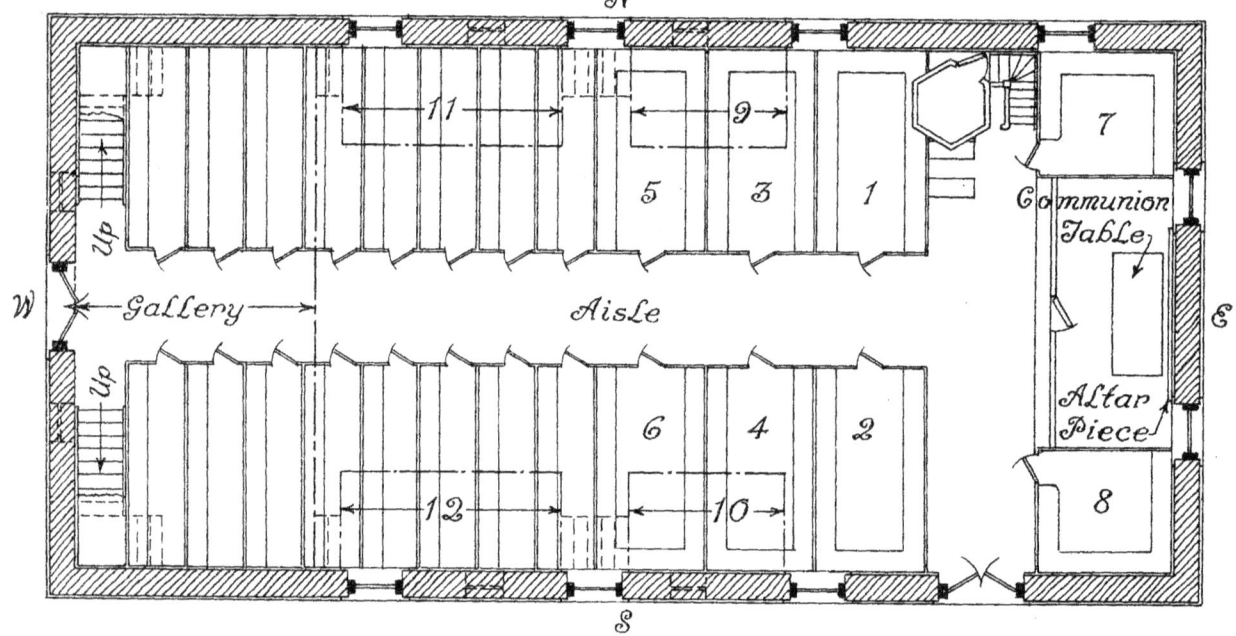

Donation Church in 1776, at end of colonial era:
Assignment of Great Pews by the Vestry: 1. The Magistrates; 2. Their Wives; 3. The family of the Thorowgoods, as their Privilege for the gift of the Glebe; 4. The Elder women of good repute and Magistrates' daughters; 5. Vestrymen and their wives; 6. Such women as the Wardens shall think fitt to place therein; 7. The family and Name of the Walkes, as a Benefit for gifts and Services; 8. The family of the Moseleys. The Hanging Pews granted unto: 9. Kempe; 10. Lyon; 11. Robinson; 12. Hoggard.

·GCM·49·

ated from the gift to the parish of adjoining lands, still known as Donation Farm, by the parish's last colonial rector, the Rev. Robert Dickson, at his death in 1776, for the endowment of a free school for orphan boys.[22]

One of the most interesting features of the Donation Church's original interior arrangement must have been the hanging pews or private galleries built for the family use of wealthy parishioners, at their own expense. These were especially authorized by the vestry and left lasting traces of their presence in the form of small ventilating windows of odd size and shape, high up in the side walls of the church. These little windows are a distinctive feature of Donation Church, not to be found in any other surviving colonial church building in Virginia.

The varying heights of these ventilation openings, which also served to light the private galleries, indicate that the rear hanging pew on each side of the church extended across the tops of the two last regular side windows, adjoining the main gallery, while the front hanging pew, on the north and south sides alike, was placed lower down, between the two middle windows. Access to both sets of hanging pews must have been by steps leading up from the main gallery and down from the rear pew to the front one. A similar hanging pew had been erected by Captain Hillary Moseley over the chancel doorway of the old second church in 1724, for his family's use. The name "hanging pew" was derived from the fact that these little side galleries were literally suspended from the beams above by iron tie-rods, probably of square section and decoratively twisted.

A drastic change in Old Donation's original arrangement was made in 1767, when a private great pew was built by Colonel Edward Hack Moseley, Jr., on the south side of the communion table. Since all the Lynnhaven churches and chapels followed the ancient practice of having the south doorway open directly into the chancel, it was necessary that the pulpit, originally placed on the south side between this doorway and the first great pew, should be moved to a position directly opposite on the north side, to permit the chancel doorway to be shifted clear of the new Moseley pew. Another change of about the same period was the bricking-up of the middle window in the east end wall, to make room for an altar-piece.

In colonial times, when counties were often of vast extent and the parish frequently included the whole county, as it did in Princess Anne, it was recognized as a hardship on the outlying settlers to require them to attend the parish church, for roads were bad and travel was difficult. For their benefit, smaller local churches were built, known as "chapels of ease", at which services were held by the parish minister, whenever possible, and prayers and a sermon were read on Sunday by the clerk of the chapel, at other times. Lynnhaven Parish was no exception to this rule, and early records of both county and parish refer to chapels in various sections of the county remote from the parish church.

Perhaps the earliest chapel of Lynnhaven Parish may have been the same building which served originally as the parish church of the long-vanished parish of Southern Shore, already mentioned as probably named for its location on the southern shore of the Eastern Branch of Elizabeth River.

The existence of an early church in this vicinity is strongly suggested by a grant of 1649 to Richard Whitehurst for 300 acres of land, on the south side of the Eastern Branch of Elizabeth River and bounded easterly on "the Church Creek".[23] An earlier grant of 1637 for this same land locates it five or six miles up the Eastern Branch,[24] and even though the Church Creek is not mentioned in the 1637 grant, this proves that it must have been the second stream east of Indian River. It is mentioned in the land grants that this creek's western bank was marshy, as it is to this day, therefore the church probably stood on the point east of the stream.

In this connection it may be stated that out of scores of references in colonial records to a Church Creek, Church Swamp, Church Point, etc., not one has yet failed to prove a reliable indicator of the former presence of a colonial church building, many of them long-vanished and otherwise unknown.

It is apparent from the bounds set for Lynnhaven Parish by the Act of 1642, that the site of this Southern Shore Parish Church fell within Lynnhaven's limits, which extended beyond the Church Creek to Indian River on the south side of the Eastern Branch. The continued existence of a church at this point is substantiated by the appointment in 1647 of a churchwarden for the Eastern Branch, in addition to the two regularly elected for the parish of Lynnhaven,[25] since the appointment of a churchwarden presupposes the existence of a church building. It is believed that this pioneer Southern Shore Church became the first chapel of ease for Lynnhaven Parish, under the name of the Eastern Branch Chapel.

The above hypothesis of the location of Southern Shore Parish and Church is supported by a Lower Norfolk County court record of 1640, showing that an Episcopal minister, the Reverend Robert Powis, had been receiving tithes from residents of the southern shore of the Eastern Branch, although the Reverend John Wilson had been minister of Elizabeth River at the time and therefore entitled to all tithes from that parish.[26]

The county records also reveal that Parson Powis had become the minister of Lynnhaven Parish by 1645,[27] and after four years of volunteer ministry to the inhabitants of Elizabeth River Parish, then vacant, he was inducted as minister for the

HISTORY OF COLONIAL LYNNHAVEN PARISH

entire Lower Norfolk County in 1648.[28] A county tax list of 1645, giving the total number of tithables in Elizabeth River and Lynnhaven Parishes as exactly equal to the number in the entire county, proves that Southern Shore Parish had ceased to exist by that date.[29]

It appears that Powis was one of the free-lance ministers typical of the earliest period of colonial settlement, who had been trying to build up a following and a parish for himself, but gave up the effort when he was rewarded by the rectorship of the entire county.

The next earliest chapel of Lynnhaven Parish appears to have been the successor of this ancient Southern Shore Church, since it was erected on the north side of the Eastern Branch, nearly opposite to the old Church Creek, in 1661. It is first mentioned in a court order of that year for Lower Norfolk County, entering judgment by jury in "The Difference between Mr. Adam Thorowgood plaintiff and Henry Snaile defendant concerninge buylding a church".[30] Snaile was charged with being so slow about erecting this chapel that some of its timbers had become too rotten for use, and he was ordered to "goe forward with the worke hee hath begun" and complete the building.

This early chapel is further mentioned in the will of William Handcocke of the Eastern Branch of Elizabeth River, dated 4th April, 1687, leaving to his three sons, Simon, William and Samuel, lands adjoining the chapel on the east side of Hoskins' Creek, a tributary of the Eastern Branch.[31] A deed dated October, 1700, to the land next to this church, describes it as the chapel for the Eastern Branch precinct of Lynnhaven Parish, and shows that it was still standing in that year.[32]

This second Eastern Branch Chapel stood close to the site where, in 1697, there was established New Town, one of those transitory villages, typical of colonial times in Virginia, which flourished for a while and then passed away like a dream, leaving no trace behind except a few old bricks turned up by the plow. New Town's span of life was barely a century, but during this time it rose to the dignity of a port of entry, with a custom-house and British garrison; here was located the fourth county court-house, from 1758 to 1778; and here the people of Norfolk took refuge when Dunmore shelled their town and burned it in 1776. The complete absence of further reference to the last Eastern Branch Chapel, in county records and vestry book, indicates that it probably disappeared soon after New Town village was established.

The only colonial vestry book of Lynnhaven Parish, that has survived, opens in 1723 with salary levies for the clerks of the brick church and two chapels. The brick church mentioned is obviously the second Lynnhaven Church of 1692, near the ferry, and the chapels are identified in later entries as the upper and lower chapels of the parish. It is apparent that these chapels were so called from their respective locations in the upper and lower precincts of the Eastern Shore of Lynnhaven. Vestry orders of 1724 and 1725 for the repair of these two buildings name them as Machipongo Chapel and the Eastern Shore Chapel, and there is ample evidence that the first-named structure, later known simply as Pungo Chapel, was the upper chapel of the parish and that the Eastern Shore Chapel was the lower one.

The earliest-known record of the first Eastern Shore Chapel is found in a Lower Norfolk County court order of 17th September, 1689, for the construction of a frame court-house "on Edward Cooper's Land nigh the Chapell of Ease in the Eastern Shore of Linhaven".[33] Repeated allusions to "the chapell" as a boundary feature for lands near Linkhorn Bay, "on the Eastern Shore of Linhaven", in deeds made between 1698 and 1723,[34] prove that this first Eastern Shore Chapel stood near the southern end of Great Neck, at the head of Wolfsnare Creek. These boundary references mention "the great branch that comes up to the chappell" and "the main road leading from Wolfes Snare to the chappell and the eastern shore water mill".

The compass bearings given for these boundaries identify "the great branch" as the north fork of Wolfsnare Creek and the roads as the existing highways adjacent to it. This proves that this first chapel and court-house stood about two miles north of the existing third Eastern Shore Chapel, on the west side of the same highway and in line with Wolfsnare Creek.

In addition to its close connection with the adjacent first Princess Anne County Court-house, this early chapel had another interesting historical association with what may have been the first Presbyterian church in Virginia. This pioneer Presbyterian meeting-house also stood on Edward Cooper's plantation at Great Neck and was registered in 1693 as a place of worship for dissenters from the Established Church. Services in this building, which apparently stood near the first Eastern Shore Chapel and court-house, were held by the Reverend Josias Mackie, a Presbyterian minister who had been dismissed as rector of Elizabeth River Parish in 1692, because of his nonconformist practices.[35] Mackie also had a meeting-house on the Eastern Branch in 1693.

An order for the projected repair of this first Eastern Shore Chapel was cancelled by the vestry in 1724, and they resolved instead, on the 4th August in that year, "that a good, Commodious Chapel be built on the Eastern Shore, fifty foot in Length, twenty five foot in breadth, framed work". A subsequent order of 3rd November, 1726, placing the contract for this new frame chapel, shows that its construction was not actually undertaken until that date. This second Eastern Shore Chapel stood on part of the Cornick family's Salisbury Plains plantation, about two miles south of the site of the first chapel of that name.

The present Eastern Shore Chapel, second church on this site.

Communion silver service of the Eastern Shore Chapel, with date letter for 1759. According to local tradition, this silver was buried under a henhouse in the Civil War, to protect it from Federal raiders.

The Anthony Fentress house, built before 1772 and for many years the home of W. G. Eaton, looking toward site of the second and third Pungo Chapels, which stood on the east side of the Pungo Ridge road, opposite this house.

The building of the third Eastern Shore Chapel, which still exists, on the site of the second one, was ordered by the vestry on 1st October, 1753, when it was "Resolved...That at or near adjoining the place where the present Eastern Shore Chapel now stands is a fit and Convenient place to Erect a New Chapel & that the same be there Erected". The new chapel was specified to be of brick, "Fifty five foot long, Twenty five wide in the Clear...the walls...eighteen feet in height". Further details are given in the vestry book.

In keeping with its character as a simple chapel of ease, the present Eastern Shore Chapel is built of common brick in the usual Flemish bond, but without glazed headers, and it is a foot longer than specified. Above the west doorway there is inset a square brick tile, inscribed with the initials of the builder, Joseph Mitchel, and the date 1754, while the vestry book records its acceptance on the 12th March, 1754.

In connection with these dates, it must be remembered that the old-style dating of records, to suit a legal year ending on the 24th of March, had been abolished in 1752. It nevertheless seems certain that it was still followed in this case, since the vestry-book entry for 12th March, 1754, quoted above, follows the minutes of the vestry meeting of 11th October, 1754, instead of preceding them. Furthermore, it is extremely unlikely that any colonial brick church, even if only a simple chapel of ease, would have been completed in six months. The third Eastern Shore Chapel was therefore actually completed in the year 1755.

The chapel originally had a gallery twelve feet wide in its west end, but this was extended along the entire north side of the building, soon after its completion, and adjoining it on the south side was a hanging pew erected by Captain William Keeling in 1765. The colonial pulpit must also have been on the south side, or it would have prevented the extension of the north gallery.

Machipongo Chapel, the first Upper Chapel of the parish, was still in service at the opening of the vestry book in 1723, and was evidently a simple frame building, without a brick foundation, since a parish levy of 1733 includes payment "for putting blocks under the upper Chapel". This chapel's long Indian name was soon shortened to Pungo, with that of the surrounding region, for which it had been named.

This pioneer chapel is believed to have been the one mentioned in the little-known journal of Philip Ludwell and Nathaniel Harrison, the Virginia commissioners for running the dividing line between Virginia and North Carolina in 1710.[36] According to their journal, the commissioners rode over Pocaty Swamp bridge to the west side of North River (now North Landing River), which they crossed where it was a half mile wide, probably at the present Mundens. After spending the night at Burgess's, they

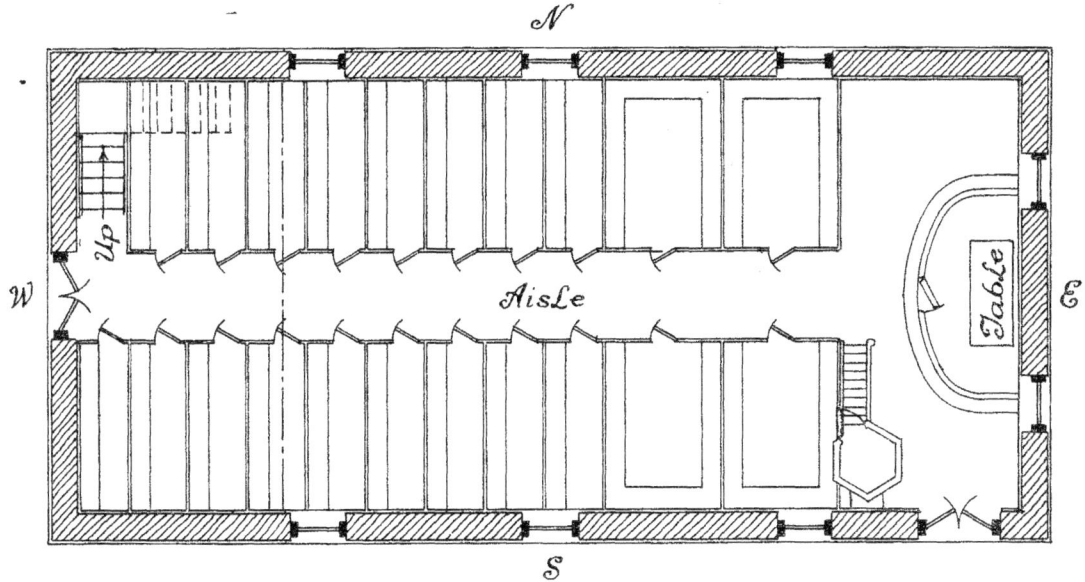

The Third Eastern Shore Chapel, as built originally in 1755.

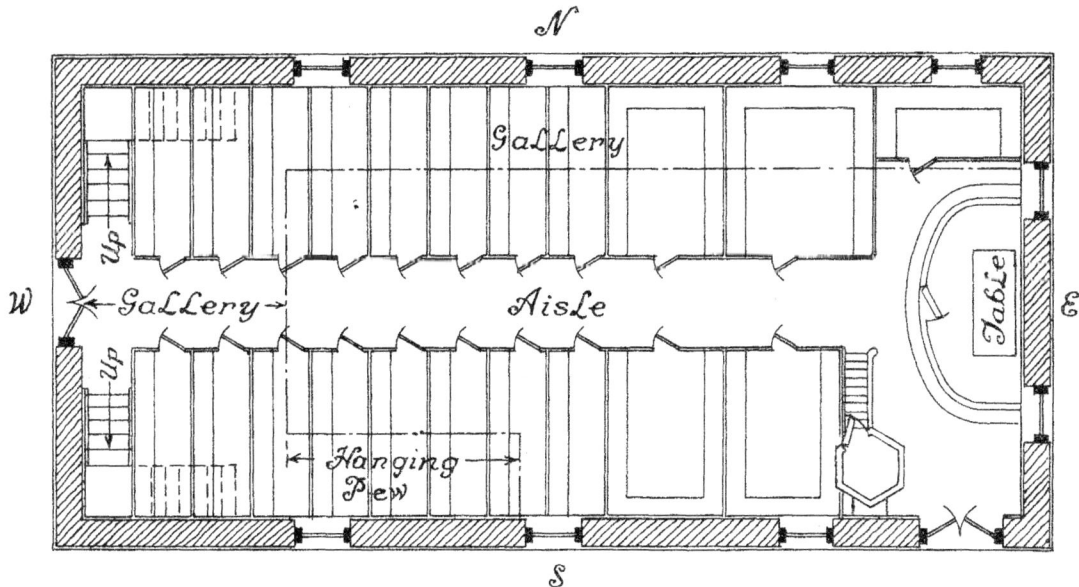

The Third Eastern Shore Chapel, as altered in 1761-1765.

"rode six miles to the Chappell, which was a very wretched one" and "passed by", five miles further, to Captain Francis Moss's [Morse's] plantation, near the present Morse's Point. Their estimated distances are clearly exaggerated and their direction of travel unstated but, since they were on their way to meet the North Carolina commissioners at Knott's Island, this chapel must have been located somewhere on the peninsula between the present North Landing River and Back Bay, possibly in the vicinity of the present Creeds Post Office.

Since this peninsula forms the lower end of Pungo Ridge, it seems certain that this was the first Pungo Chapel of Lynnhaven Parish. Its erection in this remote section of the county at such an early date may be traced to an historic endowment which also caused the erection of early parish chapels in Nansemond and Isle of Wight Counties.[37]

This endowment was in the form of 200 acres of land given in 1692 by a pious philanthropist, Captain Hugh Campbell, for the support of a reader in each of three places remote from church facilities, and the donor also contributed a Bible for each reader's use in holding services. These three places were Somerton in Nansemond County, Blackwater River in Isle of Wight County, and the North River in what had been Lower Norfolk County and is now Princess Anne.

This first Upper Chapel at Pungo was replaced by a new brick chapel, on a different and more suitable site, its erection having been started in 1739 by James James and finished in 1743 by another contractor, after James' death. The second Pungo Chapel was fifty by twenty-five feet in size, within the walls, which were fifteen feet high. It was built on the plantation of William Dyer, who was paid for sinking a well at the chapel and later served as its sexton, his widow and then his son succeeding him after his death.

As there were three successive Lynnhaven Parish Churches and three Eastern Shore Chapels, so we find it recorded that there were also three chapels at Pungo. Although the site of the first Pungo Chapel is not exactly known, the third chapel is recorded as having been built on a one-acre site directly adjoining its predecessor. These last two chapels stood about two and a half miles south of the present Pungo village, on the east side of the Pungo Ridge road and directly opposite the former home of W. G. Eaton, part of which is believed to have been built by Anthony Fentress before 1770.[38] The chapel was built on an acre of Fentress's land, which was purchased by the vestry, and in accordance with the usual custom, he was appointed sexton of the chapel.

The new building was ordered in 1772 and was completed in 1774 by the contractor, Hardress Waller. Its inside dimensions were seventy-five feet by thirty feet by twenty feet high, and it was by far the largest of all the colonial churches of Lynnhaven Parish, being ten feet longer and five feet higher than the Donation Church. This was the Pungo Chapel which survived the colonial period and was still standing shortly before the Civil War, but was later demolished at an unknown date.

Of all the eleven colonial churches and chapels of Lynnhaven Parish, only two survive: the Old Donation Church and the Eastern Shore Chapel. According to the vestry book, the parish had no regular minister from the outbreak of the Revolution until 1785, when the Protestant Episcopal Church of Virginia took the place of the disestablished Church of England. During this interval, the church and chapels were much neglected and they were not put back into repair until 1822-24. After this, the general decline of religion in Virginia left the parish again without a rector of its own, for most of the time.

A reorganization took place in 1842, under the Reverend John G. Hull, and a year later, the former Emmanuel Church was built at Kempsville as the fourth parish church of Lynnhaven. Following the new church's completion, Old Donation was abandoned for general worship and no further services were held there for almost three quarters of a century. After forty years of disuse, its decaying woodwork was completely burned out in 1882 by a woods fire and it became a roofless ruin, with large trees growing up inside its broken walls.

Old Donation was repaired and replaced in service in 1916 as an Episcopal church, and has been in use ever since, although its old position as the parish church was not regained. Its rebuilding was in no sense an exact restoration, since no regard was paid to its original colonial arrangement and appearance, either within or without. The first Emmanuel Church of 1843 was completely destroyed by fire on 12th October, 1943, after almost exactly a century of service, and was rebuilt in 1947.

The present Eastern Shore Chapel seems to have been kept in regular service until the Civil War, during which it suffered the usual desecration by use as an army stable, its interior being badly wrecked. It was replaced in service in 1866, repaired in 1872, and about 1886 its damaged interior trim, with the exception of pews and gallery, was largely replaced. The existing pews appear to date from 1840, when a parochial report to the council by its rector states that the "whole interior, excepting the gallery," was then "replaced with new materials neatly wrought". The chapel is still in active use as the parish church of East Lynnhaven Parish.

For a more complete and detailed account of Lynnhaven Parish and its colonial churches, the reader is referred to the Editor's book "Colonial Churches of Tidewater Virginia", Volume I, pages 128 to 150, inclusive.

A list of the colonial rectors and vestrymen of Lynnhaven Parish, so far as known, is given as an appendix to this volume.

FOOTNOTES FOR "HISTORY OF COLONIAL LYNNHAVEN PARISH"

[1] Kingsbury, Records of Virginia Company of London, III, 100.
[2] Hening, Statutes at Large, I, 224.
[3] Robinson, Virginia Counties, 198.
[4] Hening, Statutes at Large, III, 95.
[5] Lower Norfolk County Minutes, 1637-46, A, 10.
[6] Ibid., 1637-46, A, 42.
[7] Hening, Statutes at Large, I, 250.
[8] Lower Norfolk County Minutes, 1637-46, A, 287.
[9] Hening, Statutes at Large, III, 128.
[10] Lower Norfolk County Minutes, 1637-46, A, 1.
[11] Ibid., 1637-46, A, 2.
[12] Ibid., 1637-46, A, 3.
[13] White, Gleanings in Princess Anne History, 6.
[14] Forrest, Historical Sketches of Norfolk, 457.
[15] See Augustin Herrman's map of Virginia, 1673.
[16] Princess Anne County Deeds, 1691-1708, I, 195.
[17] Princess Anne County Deeds, 1691-1708, I, 68.
[18] Princess Anne County Orders, 1691-1709, I, 87.
[19] Lower Norfolk County Deeds, 1686-95, XV, 146.
[20] Princess Anne County Orders, 1691-1709, I, 119.
[21] Princess Anne County Deeds, 1724-35, IV, 311.
[22] Meade, Old Churches and Families of Virginia, I, 249.
[23] Nugent, Pioneers and Cavaliers, I, 188.
[24] Ibid., I, 57.
[25] Lower Norfolk County Wills, Deeds, 1646-51, B, 36a.
[26] Lower Norfolk County Minutes, 1637-46, A, 39.
[27] Ibid., 1637-46, A, 312.
[28] Lower Norfolk County Wills, Deeds, B, 85.
[29] Lower Norfolk County Minutes, 1637-46, A, 287.
[30] Lower Norfolk County Deeds, Wills, 1666-75, V, fol. 8.
[31] Lower Norfolk County Deeds, Wills, 1666-75, V, fol. 23.
[32] Princess Anne County Deeds, 1691-1708, I, 292.
[33] Lower Norfolk County Deeds, 1686-95, XV, 146.
[34] Princess Anne County Deeds, 1691-1708, I, 349.
[35] William and Mary Quarterly (1), II, 179.
[36] Virginia Historical Magazine, V, 10.
[37] Lower Norfolk Antiquary, I, 65.
[38] Kellam, Old Houses in Princess Anne, 155.

THE VESTRY BOOK
OF
LYNNHAVEN PARISH
Princess Anne County, Virginia: 1723-1786

[1]

Linhaven Parrish

At a Vestery held the 20th of November 1723

Mr: James Tenant minister   Major Maximilian Boush C: warden

Present: Coll: Edward Moseley, Capt: Henry Chapman, Mr: William Ellegood, Capt: John Moseley, Charles Sayer, Capt: Francis Land — Vestrymen

Parish Leavy

	li. Tobo.
The . . Parish . . is . . Debter	
To the reverend mr: James Tenant Convenient	16000
To Mr: James Nimmo clk of the Church & one Chappel	1500
To Mrs: Margret Moseley for keepin an orphan girl 12 months	1200
To Mr: Andrew Peacock Clerk of the Upper Chapel	1500
To the Conveniency of Mr: Tenants Tobacco	4000
To Thos: Wishard for keeping Ann Scott 6 months & finding clothes	750
To a fraction in the County Leavy	386
To Capt: Anthony Walke for parish book &c as Per his account	260
To Walter Vowls for keeping Elizabeth Carrington 12 months	1000
To Charles Sayer Clerk & by his account	561
To Capt: Hillary Moseley for Quitrents of gleeb Land	96
To Mr: John Snaile for keeping the Church Clean	58
" Sallary 10 Per Ct. 2731. for Caske 8 Per Ct. . 2184 . boath is	4915
	32226

The . . Parish . . is . . Cr:		
By Sundry fines as Per orders [of] Court	00315	
" Thomas Brinson for Ditto per bond	00500	
" 1018 Tythables @ 30-3/4 each	31303	
" fraction to the Collectors	108	32226

It is this day agreed & Concluded that the Several vestry men and persons hereafter Named Collect & receive & they are hearby Impowered to Collect & receive of each Tythable person within their Several presincts in this parish the Sum of thirty & three quarter pounds of Tobacco & make payment thereof according to direction of the above Leavy — Persons appointed to Collect the Said Leavy are Capt: Anthony Walke in the Eastern branch and Knots Island: Capt: Henry Chapman in Little Creek; Capt: Francis Land in the western Shore, mr: will: Ellegood in the Lower presinct of the Eastern Shore; mr's: John Bonney's Senior & Junior or either of them in the upper presinct Eastern Shore; mr: willoughby Merchant in black water for this & the Last years Leavy's

[2] Linhaven Parrish

At a Vestry held for Laying the Leavy 15th September [1724]

Mr: James Tenant minister

Major Max: Boush } Church
Mr: John Cornick } wardens

Present:
- Col: Edward Moseley
- Capt: Henry Chapman
- Mr: Chr: Burrowgh
- Capt: Anthony Walke
- Capt: Francis Land
- Mr: John Bonney
- Capt: John Moseley
- Capt: Solomon White
- Mr: John Bolithoe
- Charles Sayer
- Mr: Will: Ellegood
- Capt: Robert Vaughan

} Vestry men

Leavy

The . . Parrish . . is . . Debter	li. Tobo.
To mr: James Tenant, abateing 500: he is to pay: to the Parish	15500
To mr: James Nimmo Clark of the Church	1500
To mr: Andrew Peacock Clark of the Chappel	1500
To the Conveniency of mr: Tenants Tobacco	4000
To Thomas wishard for keeping Ann Scott to this time	1050
To Charles Sayer Clark & by his account	690
To Major Max: Boush for keeping an orphan 9 months	900
To Dorcas Broughton for keeping E: Carrington 3 months	310
To Thomas Creed for keeping a bastard Child 7 months	700
To Lawrence Dawley for keeping John Bishop 5 months	500
To Capt: Anthony Walke for 3 barrels Tarr & Cartage to gleeb	365
To Ditto for 6 Insolvants 1722: [@] 58 Per & 2 Ditto 1723: [@] $30\frac{3}{4}$ Per:	400
10 Per Ct. for Collect 2741: 8 Per Ct. for Cask 2192	4933
	32348

The . . Parrish . . is . . Cr:		
By 1020 Tythables @ $31\frac{1}{2}$ each	32130	
" Fraction to the Collecters	218	32348

Ordered that the Severall vestry men & persons here[after] Named Collect of each Tythable person wi[thin] their Several presincts in this parish the Sum of thirty one [&] a half pounds of Tobacco & that they make payment there[of] according to the Direction of the above Leavy— Persons [ap]pointed to Collect the Said Leavy are Capt: Anthony Walke in the Eastern branch, Capt: Henry Chapman in Little Creek, [Capt:] Francis Land in the western Shore; mr: William Ellegood in the Lower presinct of Eastern Shore; mr: Thomas Haynes in the [upper] presinct for the last & present years; mr: willoughby Merchant in black water; Cornelious Jones in Knots Island

[3]
[Leavy repaid by] Burrough

Whereas there was formerly Leavy'd for mr: Christopher Burrowgh the Sum of Eighteen hundred pounds of Tobacco for him to repair the Eastern Shore Chappel, he having done but Some Small matters towards the Same, it's now Considered that he be allowed two hundred for what is done & thereupon ordered that the Said Burrowgh repay the remainder being Sixteen hundred pounds of Tobo: to the Church wardens for the use of the parrish

Bolithoe [to] shingle Church

Agreed with mr: John Bolitho to Lath & Shingle the South Side of the brick Church [roof] & in Case any of the rafters prove Rotten or unsound — to take them out & put new ones in their room & for his well performing the Said work (the materials being found & brought in place by Major Max: Boush) its ordered that he be paid fifty Shillings by the present Churchwardens

Moseley [to] build [a] pewe

Upon the petition of Capt: Hillary Moseley Liberty is given him to Erect a pewe at his own Cost over the Chancel Doore takeing up as Little room as posable, the Stairs to goe up behind the Said Chancel Doore.

Linhaven Parrish

At a Vestery held the 4th of August 1724

mr: James Tenant minister   Major Max: Boush Church warden

Present {Col: Edward Moseley / Capt: Henry Chapman / Capt: Anthony Walke / Charles Sayer / Capt: Francis Land} {Capt: John Moseley / mr: John Bolithoe / mr: Chris: Burrowgh / mr: John Bonney / mr: william Ellegood} Vestry men

Resolved that Major Maximilian Boush forthwith or as Soon as posable Cause the brick Church to be repaired by Lathing and Shingling thereof that the Same be paid for out of the money in his hands received at Communion times —

Resolved that a good Commodious Chapel be built on the Eastern Shore fifty foot in Length twenty five foot in breadth framed work weather borded with inch pine plank Lathed & Covered with good Cyprus Shingles that the money in the hands of Mrs: Katherine Walke Executrix of Capt: Thomas Walke Deceased being thirty Six pound one Shilling & Sixpence half penny & also that in the hands of Capt: Anthony Walke being seaventeen pound ten Shillings & Seaven pence be appropriated and goe towards the building the aforesaid Chappell

through mistake these orders are recorded after the Leavy   Test Charles Sayer Clerk [of] Vestry

[4]
Linhaven Parrish

At a vestry held the 16th of November 1724

Major Max: Boush Church warden

Present {Coll: Edward Moseley / mr: Christo'r Burrowgh / Capt: Anthony Walke / mr: william Ellegood} {Capt: John Moseley / Capt: Francis Land / Charles Sayer} Vestrymen

Church repaired

Whereas it was agreed with mr: John Bolithoe to repair the South Side of the brick Church [roof] but upon Examination thereof it proved so rotten & unsound that the Same could not be repaired, & thereupon agreed with mr: George Smyth to pull down the whole roof & put up a New one to Lath & Shingle the Same & ceale the inside with half inch plank or boards to get two New plates, & upon his well performing & finishing the Said work having all other materials found & brought in place he is to have & receive the Sum of Six pound fifteen Shillings to be paid him by the Church wardens

Linhaven Parrish

At a Vestery held the Seaventh of July 1725

Lt: Col: Maximilian Boush / mr: John Cornick } Ch: wardens

Present {Col: Edward Moseley / Capt: Henry Chapman / Capt: Anthony Walke / Capt: Francis Land} {Capt: John Moseley / mr: John Bolithoe / " Charles Sayer / mr: william Ellegood} Vestrymen

Counters of Tobacco appointed

Pursuant to the act of assembly Intituled an act for the better & more Effectual Improving the Staple of Tobacco (by which it is Enacted that the vestery of every parish appoint two persons in each presinct to Examine & Inquire of the Names & number of the persons allowed by the Said act to tend Tobacco, & the Crop of the several planters within the Said presinct & the Number of plants growing on any & every plantation or plantations within the Same) the vestery do appoint George Kempe & Am[os] Moseley in the Eastern branch presinct, John wishard & Thomas Hunter in Little Creek, William Poole & Edward Land in the western Shore, Henry woodhouse & Thomas Haynes in the Lower Presinct of the Eastern Shore, Francis woodhouse & Luke Moseley in the upper presinct Cornelious Jones & Mallbone Simmons in Knots Island, W---- Corbell & Adam Tooly in black water, & thereupon ordered that they duly Execute & perform what is Injoyned [upon] them by the Said act

Clerk to read in the presincts

[5]

Whereas Knots Island & black water presincts are very remote from the Chappel & Sermon being there but once in Six weeks the Inhabitants are often disappointed of hearing the word of God, and whereas mr: andrew Peacock Clark of the Said Chappel has for some time past for the benefit and Instruction of the Said Inhabitants read in each of the Said presincts on Certain times in an orderly Course, which is approved by the vestery whereupon its resolved that he Continue to perform the same (according to his usuall method) untill he Shall be otherwayes directed by this vestery

Pungo Chappel repaired

Ordered that Capt: Robert Vaughan agree with Some good workman to repair Machipongo Chappel with such reparation as he thinks fit for the present, that he cause windo Shutters to be made & affixed to the windo's & bring in his accompt of the cost thereof at the Laying the next parish Leavy wherein he Shall be allowed for the Same

Linhaven } Parrish

At a Vestery held the 13th of November 1725

Col: Maximilian Boush } Ch: wardens
mr: John Cornick

Present {
Col: Edward Moseley   Capt: Henry Chapman
Capt: Solomon White   Charles Sayer
Capt: william Ellegood Capt: Robert Vaughan } Vestry men
mr: Chris'r Burrowgh   Major Anthony Walke
Capt: Francis Land
}

Leavy

Linhaven . . Parrish . . is . . Debtor	ll. Tobo.
To mr: James Tenant minister Convenient	16000
To mr: James Nimmo Clark of the Church	1500
To mr: Andrew Peacock Clark of the Upper Chappel	1500
To the Conveniency of mr: Tenants Tobacco	4000
To Thomas wishard for keeping Ann Scott	1000
To Col: Maximilian Boush for keeping two orphans & by account	2563
To Lawrence Dawley for keeping John Bishop	1000
To Thomas Creed for keeping a base born child	1000
To Major Walke for quitrents of the gleeb & Tarr for the Church	288
To Capt: william Ellegood by account for Insolvants	366
To mr: Thomas Haynes by account for Ditto	837
To Capt: Henry Chapman by account for Ditto	246
To Mr: Secretary Carter by account 1724 omited	90
To Edward wood for keeping Eliza: Carrington	100
To Charles Sayer Clark of the vestery & for his account	1064

VESTRY BOOK OF LYNNHAVEN PARISH

To mr: Bolithoe for quitrents of the gleeb and by account	198
To James Linton for 77 foot of plank	77
To Capt: Francis Land by account for Insolvants	166
To mr: Christopher Burrowgh for two arrests	40
To a fraction brought from the County Leavy	62
" 10 Per Ct. for Collect 3209 — 8 Per Ct. for Caske 2567	5776
	37873

The Parrish Cr: By 1046 Tythables @ 36: each   37656

Fraction to the Collector   217   37873

[6] Ordered that the Several persons hereafter named Collect & rec[eive] of each Tythable person within their respective presincts in [this] parish the Sum of thirty Six pounds of Tobacco and in Case of refu[sal] or nonpayment the Said receivers are hereby Impowered to Distra[in] according as the Law in that Case Directs that they make payment thereof to the Several claimors mentioned in the Said Leavy

Persons appointed for Collectors are mr: George Kempe in the Eastern branch, Capt: Henry Chapman in Little Creek, Capt: Francis Land in the western Shore, Capt: william Ellegood in the lower presinct of The eastern Shore, mr: Thomas Haynes in the upper presinct, mr: Solomon White Junior in black water who is also to receive the arrears for 17[23] & 1724: Cornelius Jones in Knots Island

Bolithoe keep orphan   Mr: John Bolithoe this Day agreed & promised to keep an orphan gi[rl] now at Col: Boushe's for Six hundred pounds of Tobacco the Ensui[ng] year & ordered That the Said Boush deliver the Said girl unto him.

Test Charles Sayer Clerk [of] Vestry

Linhaven Parish

At a vestery held the 13th of June Anno 1726

Col: Boush Ch: warden

Present
{ Col: Edward Moseley
Capt: John Moseley   Capt: Henry Chapman
Charles Sayer   Major Anthony Walke
mr: Christo'r Burrowgh Capt: Francis Land } Vestrymen

Tobacco Counters Appointed   Pursuant to the act of assembly intituled an act for improving the Staple of Tobacco & directing & impowering the vestery to appoint persons to count & Number the Tobacco plants growing in each parish, the said vestery doth appoint the following persons to take the Said Number, George Purdy & Amos Moseley for the Eastern branch, Nathaniel Hutchings & John Hunter in Little Creek, william Poole & Thomas Brinson in the western Shore, Horatio woodhouse & william Keeling in the Lower presinct of the Eastern Shore, Denis Dawley & John McLanhan Junior in the uper presinct of the Eastern Shore, James Nickols & adam Tooly in black water, Thomas Dudley & John Ancel in knots Island, & ordered that being first Sworn duly Comply with the Said act in counting the Number of all the Tobo. plants in their divisions & make return thereof as the Said act directs

[7]
Linhaven Parrish

At a vestery held for Laying the Leavy the 3rd November 1726

Col: Boush &
mr: Cornick } Ch: wardens

Present
{ Col: Edward Moseley   Capt: John Moseley
Capt: Henry Chapman   mr: Christo'r Burrowgh
Major Anthony Walke   Charles Sayer
Capt: Francis Land   Capt: Robert Vaughan } Vesterymen

VESTRY BOOK OF LYNNHAVEN PARISH

	The . . Parrish . . is . . Debtor	li. Tobo.
	To mr: James Tenant minister Convenient	16000
	To mr: James Nimmo Clerk of the Church	1500
	To mr: andrew Peacock Clerk of the upper Chappel	1500
	To the Conveniency of mr: Tenants Tobacco	4000
	To Thomas wishard for keeping Ann Scott	1000
	To Max: Boush for keeping two: orphans	2000
	To Lawrence Dawley for keeping John Bishop	1000
	To Thomas Creed for keeping a base born child	900
	To amos Moseley by account	30
Leavy	To George Purdy & amos Moseley for Counting Tobo: plants	205
	To william Poole & Thomas Brinson for Ditto	146
	To Horatio woodhouse & william Keeling for Ditto	161
	To Denis Dawley & John McLanhan for Ditto	116
	To James Nickols & adam Tooly for Ditto	36
	To Capt: Chapman for two Insolvants	250
	To Capt: Robert Vaughan for Insolvants	312
	To mr: william Biddle for physick to mary fitzgerald	1200
	To mr: Robert Sills for Ditto to Courtney	500
	To Joseph walstone for keeping John Courtney 15 months	1000
	To Charles Sayer Clerk & for his account	982
	To Thomas Haynes for insolvants &c: as by account	653
	10 Per Ct. for Collect 4159 — 8 Per Ct. for Casque 3326: boath is	7485
The Parish Cr: — By 1066 Tythables @ 38-1/4 Per pole	40774½	40976
	Fraction to the Collectors	201½

Collectors appointed

Ordered that the Several persons hereafter named Collect & receive of each Tythable person in this parish thirty eight & a quarter pounds of Tobacco for the parish Leavy this year & in case of refusal or nonpayment they are hereby Impowered to distrain as the Law in that case directs that they make payment thereof to the Several Claimors in the above Leavy — Persons appointed to Collect are mr: George Kempe in the Eastern branch, Col: Boush in Little Creek: Capt: Francis Land in the western Shore, mr: Thomas Haynes in the upper & Lower presinct E: Shore. mr: Solomon White Junior in black water, mr: andrew Peacock in Knots Island for this & the last year

A New Chappel to be built

Ordered that Major Anthony Walke & Capt: Francis Land agree with Some good able workman to Erect & build a New Chappel at the Eastern Shore according to the Dementions formerly prescribed that they hereby have power to take into their hands all the ready money belonging to the parish to Enable them to Carry on the said work also that they take bond & Security of the person with whom they Shall agree for Effecting the Said work

VESTRY BOOK OF LYNNHAVEN PARISH

Linhaven Parrish [8]

At a meeting of the Vestery the 2nd February 17[26/7]

       Col: Max: Boush Ch: warden

Present — Col: Edward Moseley, Capt: John Moseley, Capt: Henry Chapman, mr: John Bolithoe, mr: Christo'r Burrowgh, Major Anthony Walke, Charles Sayer, Capt: Francis Land — Vestry men

Mr: Jones to preach

This day agreed with mr: Nicholas Jones minister of the Gosple to preach in the brick Church & Eastern Shore Chappel once Every month for Each Sermon he preaches to be allowed four hundred pounds of Tobacco in casque Convenient to [be] Leavy'd for him in the next parish Leavy

The Clark to read

Ordered that mr: James Nimmo read Constantly every Sunday in the brick Church & John Dawley the Same in the Eastern Shore Chappel for which he Shall be allowed at the next parish Leavy

Linhaven Parrish

At a Vestery held the 29th of June 1727

Present — Col: Edward Moseley, Capt: John Moseley, mr: Christo'r Burrowgh, mr: John Bolithoe, Major Anthony Walke, Charles Sayer, Capt: Francis Land — vestry men

Processioning appointed

Pursuant to an order of Court of princess ann County dated [the] third of this Instant requiring us to Direct processioning of [the] Lands in our parish according to the act of assembly in that behalf made; we Do therefore order that the Several persons hereafter named in their Several presincts warn in the Inhabitants in their Devisions to go & procession all the Lands therein takeing care to Comply with the said act & to Conti[nue] from their begining untill they Shall Compleatly perform [the] Same — Persons appointed to perform the Said processi[oning] are George Smyth & Charles Williamson for the north Side of the Ea[stern] branch who are to begin the first Munday in September, Charles Sm[yth] & George Williamson the South Side to begin the Second munday, James Langley & Thomas Hunter in Little Creek to begin the third munday, William P— & John Thorowgood in the western Shore & william Whitehurst in [the] woods to begin the fourth munday; Jacob Ellegood & william ----- in the Lower presinct of the Eastern Shore to begin the first munday in October: Robert Vaughan & John Dawley in the upper presinct of the Eastern Shore to begin the Second munday & ----- woodhouse & John Cannon in the Lower part to begin the thurd [mun]day: Christopher merchant & adam Tooly in black water to begin the fourth munday, Capt: Solomon White & Robert Dudly in Knots Island to begin the second munday in September

[9]

Tobacco counters appointed

Pursuant to the act of assembly intituled an act for improving the Staple of Tobacco & directing the vestery to appoint person's to Count & Number the Tobacco plants growing in Each parish we do therefore appoint the following persons to take the Said Number — Thomas Spratt & Francis Ackis in the Eastern branch, John Hunter & Thomas wishard Junior in Little Creek, James Dollar & Joseph walstone in the western Shore, Horatio woodhouse Junior and Reod: Malbone Junior in the Lower presinct of the Eastern Shore, Luke Moseley & Thomas Dawley in the upper presinct, James Nickols & Lawrence Dawley in black water, Richard Jones in Knots Island & ordered that they being first Sworn duly Comply with the said act in Counting the Number of all the Tobacco plants in their divisions & make return as the act directs

Linhaven Parrish

At a vestery held for laying the Leavy the 29th September 1727

Present — Col: Edward Moseley, Capt: John Moseley, Major Henry Spratt, Capt: Henry Chapman, mr: Christo'r Burrowgh, Charles Sayer, Capt: Francis Land — vestry men

	li. Tobo.
The . . Parrish . . is . . Debtor	
To mr: Nicholas Jones for preaching 24 Sermons @ 400: each	9600
To mr: James Nimmo Clerk of the Church	1500

Leavy	To mr: Andrew Peacock Clerk of the upper Chapel	1500
	To the Conveniency of Mr: Jones's Tobacco	2375
	To Thomas wishard for keeping Ann Scot	1000
	To Col: Maxim'l: Boush for keeping an orphan girl	1000
	To Lawrence Dawley for keeping John Bishop	1000
	To Capt: Chapman for an Insolvant by account	51
	To Charles Sayer Clerk of the vestry & for his account	999
	To James Linton for cleaning the Church	50
	To Major Anthony Walke & Capt: Francis Land to be appropriated to the building the Eastern Shore Chappell	22000
	Sallary 10 per Cent. 4107: & 8 per Ct. for caske 3286	07393
The Parrish Cr:	By 1147 Tythables at 42-1/4 each 48460	48468
	By the fraction 8	48468

Ordered that the vestry meet this Day four week in order to resolve mr: Nicholas Jones about the time of his preaching

[10]

Linhaven Parrish

At a vestery held according to appointment the 27th October [1727]

Present { Capt: John Moseley, Capt: Henry Chapman, mr: Christ'r: Burrowgh, Major Anthony Walke, Charles Sayer, Capt: Francis Land, Capt: Robert Vaughan } vestery men

agreement with mr: Jones
This day agreed with mr: Nicholas Jones to preach in the brick Church & the two Chappels to begin Tuesday the ninth day of January next & Soe to Continue for Six Turns to the last of October & for each Sermon he Shall preach in the Said Church [&] Chappels to be allowed four hundred pounds of Tobacco in cask Convenient to be Leavyed for him in the next parish Leavy.. if the parish should be Supplyed with a minister before [the] Expiration of the time aforesaid then he is not to be paid for any more Sermons than he has preach'd before the time of entertaining any other minister that Shall or may come

Church wardens chosen
Major Anthony Walke & Capt: Francis Land being this Day Elected and Chosen Church wardens for this parish and ordered to Execute the Said office accordingly

New vestery men
Mr: Thomas Haynes, mr: George Kempe, & mr: Solomon White Junior being chosen for vestery men & haveing taken all the oaths appointed & Enjoyn'd are admitted members of the vestry of this parish & to take their seats accordingly

Linhaven Parrish

At a Vestery held the third of June anno 1728

Major Anthony Walke & Capt: Francis Land   Church wardens

Present { Col: Edward Moseley, Capt: John Moseley, mr: John Bolithoe, Charles Sayer, mr: Thomas Haynes, mr: George Kempe, mr: Solomon White Junior } Vestry men

Nimmo Imployed to go to the Governer
Whereas the vestry has had occasion to Imploy mr: James Nimmo [on] a message to the Governer with a petition for Removeing mr: Thomas Baly who Contrary to the desire of this vestry insisted on being our minister) the Said Nimmo haveing Expended Some money in his Jorney: its therefore ordered that he bee allowed and paid his Expence out of the money received at Cummunion time and that there be Leavyed five hundred pounds of Tobo: in the next parish Leavy for him in consideration of his Trouble going & returning on the message aforeSaid

Nimmo Second message

This day agreed with mr: James Nimmo to goe on a Second Me[ssage] to the Giverner for which he is to be allowed & paid as much [&] after the Same manner as for the first being Soe ordered by the vestry

[11]

Linhaven Parrish

At a Vestery held the 15th Day of June 1728

Major Anthony Walke & Capt: Francis Land   Church wardens

Present
- Capt: John Moseley
- Capt: Henry Chapman
- Charles Sayer
- mr: George Kempe
- Major Henry Spratt
- mr: John Bolithoe
- Mr: Thomas Haynes
- mr: Christo'r Burrowgh

vestry men

Tobacco counters

Pursuant to a late act of assembly for improveing the Staple of Tobacco directing the Vestry to appoint persons to Count and Number the Tobacco plants growing in each parrish, wee Doe therefore appoint the following persons to perform the Said office Anthony Webb & Thomas wiles Senior in the Eastern branch presinct: Samuel Boush & Thomas Wishard Junior in Little Creek presinct: Robert Thorowgood & Thomas Cartwrigh[t] western Shore: James Condon & William Cox in the Lower presinct of the Eastern Shore: John Russel & John Dauge in the upper presinct: John Corprew & Richard Moy in black water: Edward Millian & Bullock Simmons in Knots Island & ordered that they being first Sworn by one of his Majesties Justices duly Comply with the Said act in every thing relating to their Deuty: & make return thereof to the Clarks office of princess ann County as that act Directs

Linhaven Parrish

At a Vestery held the 18th of October 1728

Major Anthony Walke & Capt: Francis Land   Church wardens

Present
- Capt: John Moseley
- Charles Sayer
- mr: George Kempe
- mr: Christo'r Burrowgh
- mr: Thomas Haynes
- Capt: Robert Vaughan

vestrymen

The . . Parrish . . is . . Debtor   li. Tobo.

Leavy

To mr: Nicholas Jones for preaching 20: Sermons	08000
To mr: James Nimmo Clark of the Church	01500
To Ditto for goeing to Williamsburg about mr: Thomas Baily by agrem't	01000
To mr: Andrew Peacock Clark of the upper Chappel	01500
To mr: harald Bly clerk of the Eastern Shore Chappel 6: months	00500
To the Sherrif for the Conveniency of mr: Jones's Tobo.	02000
To Thomas wishard for keeping Ann Scott	01000
To Lawrence Dawley for keeping John Bishop	01000
To Mary Morris for keeping an orphan girl	00600
To Elizabeth Montgomery for keeping Mary Crompton	00700
To Major Anthony Walke for goods &c to Josias Old as per account	00366
To mr: Solomon White for Insolvants as per account	00545
To Charles Sayer Clark of the vestery & for his account	00874
To alexander Hervey for Servis done to the gleeb house	00050
To James Cotton for nursing & Keeping 2 children of Chr: Standly's	01650
	21235

[12]

	Brought Forward	[21285]
	To George Sparrow for dyeting & cureing Josias Old	1300
	To mr: Thomas Haynes for the ballence of 1200: to mr: Jones not leavy'd last year the Said Haynes haveing received of mr: Burrowgh 614: part of his Debt to the parish	00711
	To mr: Christopher Burrowgh 1000: for conveniency of mr: Tenants tobacco by promise of the vestery & now deducted out of his Debt to the parish the ballance is	00214
	To Major Anthony Walke & Capt: Francis Land to buy plank [&] nailes to ceil the Church	02000
	" 10 per Cent for Sallary 2551. 8 per Cent for Caske 2040 is	04591
	Cr: By 1124 Tythables at 26-3/4 each 30067	30101
	fraction carry'd to the County leavy 34	30101

Ordered that mr: Thomas Haynes, Sherrif Collect & receive of each Tythable person in this parish twenty-six & three quarter pounds of Tobacco for the parish Leavy this year & make payment thereof to the Several claimers above Named

Walke to have the rent of the gleeb

Agreed that Major Anthony Walke have & receive the five hundred pounds of Tobacco the rent of the gleeb Land, that he find the parish Six barrels of good Tarr, which is ordered to be used on the Church, Eastern Shore Chappel & gleeb houses

Linhaven Parrish

At a vestery held the Sixth Day of January 1728[/9]

Major Anthony Walke & Capt: Francis Land   Church wardens

Present {Col: Edward Moseley   Major Henry Spratt
         Capt: John Moseley   mr: Chr: Burrowgh   } vestery men
         Charles Sayer   mr: George Kempe

Agreement with mr: Marsden

This day agreed with the reverend mr: Richard Marsden to preach twelve Sermons that is to Say once in every month at the church & cappels to begin at the Easter Shore Chappel the Second wednesday in february & then at the upper Chappel & So to Continue in course round on every Second wednesday in Each month for which there is to be Leavyed for him in the parrish Leavy four hundred pounds of Tobo. in caske for each Sermon & to be paid him Convenient to the Eastern branch, but in case the parrish Should be Supplyed with a minister before the Expiration of the year, then no more Tobacco to be leavyed than for the Sermons he has preached at the time of entertaining a minister as aforesaid

[13]

Linhaven Parrish

At a Vestery held the fourth of June 1729

Capt: Francis Land   Church warden

Present {Col: Edward Moseley   Capt: John Moseley
         Major Henry Spratt   Capt: Henry Chapman
         mr: Christo'r Burrowgh Charles Sayer   } vestry men
         mr: Thomas Haynes   mr: George Kempe
         mr: Solomon White

Tobacco counters

Pursuant to the act of assembly for improving the Staple of Tobo: directing the vestry to appoint persons to count & Number the Tobacco plants growing in each parish we do therefore appoint the following persons to perform the Said office, Nathaniel Nicklis & Thomas wiles Junior in the Eastern branch, George Hancock & George Collins in Little Creek, Richard Poole & James Bannister in the western Shore, Joell Cornick & Henry Moore Junior in the lower presinct of the Eastern Shore, John Morse & John Russell in the upper presinct, William Simmons, & Lawrence Dawley in black water, & ordered that they being first Sworn by one of his Majesties Justices duly Comply with the Said act in every thing releateing to their duty & make return thereof to the Clerks office of princess ann County Court as that act directs

          Test Charles Sayer Clerk [of] Vestry

Linhaven Parish

At a Vestery held for laying the Leavy the 14th November 1729

  Major Anthony Walke & Capt: Francis Land Church wardens

Present:
- Col: Edward Moseley
- Major Henry Spratt
- Charles Sayer
- mr: George Kempe
- Capt: John Moseley
- Capt: Henry Chapman
- mr: Thomas Haynes

} vestry men

Agreement with mr: Barlow

This day agreed with the Reverend mr: Henry Barlow to be minister of this parrish the ensuing year begining the fifth of October Last past & to allow him for his Sallary for the time the Sum of Sixteen thousand pounds of Tobacco in caske to be paid Convenient at the Eastern branch Landing

Leavy

The Parrish . . is . . . . Debtor	li. Tobo:
To mr: James Nimmo Clerk of the Church	1000
To mr: Andrew Peacock clerk of the upper Chapple	1500
To mr: William Keeling clerk of the Eastern Shore Chappel	1000
To Lawrence Dawley for keeping John Bishop	1000
To mary wishard for keeping & burying ann Scott	500
To Elizabeth Montgomery for keeping & burying M: Crompton	250
To mary morris for Keeping an orphan girl	700
To James Cotton for keeping two: of Standlys Children	1200
To the reverend mr: Henry Barlow in consideration of his Expence & some inconvenience removeing to this Parish	2000
To Ditto for 2 months less in his year in the Parish he Came from	2666
To Charles Smyth for makeing Shetters to the Eastern Shore Chappel	1000
To mr: Thomas Haynes per account for Insolvants	521
To Major Walke by attachment for what was due to mr: R: Marsden	1600
To Horatio woodhouse Senior for Tarring Eastern Shore Chappel	100
To Edward Brown for keeping Richard Capps 9½ months to this day	830
To the Conveniency of mr: Barlows Tobacco	932
To Capt: Francis Land per account for Services about the Gleeb house	175
To George Purdy for cleaning the Church	45
To william Keeling for cleaning Eastern Shore Chappel	45
To Charles Sayer Clerk of the vestry & for his account	631
To the fraction brought from the County Leavy	160
" 10 per Cent for receiving 1785 - 8 per Cent for caske 1428 - boath is	3213

Cr: By 1143 Tythables at 18-1/4 each 20859 21068

    fraction   209 21068

VESTRY BOOK OF LYNNHAVEN PARISH

Collectors — Ordered that the Severall persons hereafter Named receive of Each Tythable person in this parish Eighteen & one quarter pounds of Tobacco for the parish leavy this year & in Case of refuseall or nonpayment they are hereby impowered to Distrain as the law in that case directs, that they make payment thereof to the Severall Claimors in the above Leavy, Persons appointed to Collect are, William Poole in the Eastern branch, James Langley in Little Creek, Richard Poole in the western Shore, mr: Thomas Haynes in the Lower & upper presincts of the Eastern Shore & mr: Solomon White in black water.

pungo Chappell new cover'd — Ordered that the Churchwardens agree with Some person as Soone as possable to New Cover the roof of matchipungo Chappell with boards or Shingles as they shall think most proper.

Test Charles Sayer Clerk [of] Vestry

[15] Linhaven Parrish

At a Vestry held for Laying the Leavy the 28th October 1730

mr: Henry Barlow minister

Anthony Walke } Francis Land } gentlemen Church wardens

Present { Edward Moseley, Henry Spratt, Christo'r Burrowgh, George Kempe, John Moseley, Henry Chapman, Charles Sayer, Thomas Haynes } gentlemen vestry men

The . . Parish . . is . . Debtor .   ll. Tobo:

Leavy

	ll. Tobo:
To the reverend mr: Henry Barlow minister Convenient	16000
To mr: James Nimmo Clerk of the Church (Short last year 500)	2000
To mr: William Keeling Clerk of the Eastern Shore Chappel	1500
To mr: Andrew Peacock Clerk of the upper Chappel	1500
To Lawrence Dawley for keeping John Bishop	1000
To mary morris for keeping & burying an orphan girl	449
To william Dyer Junior for making a Table for the upper Chapel	120
To Josiah morris for keeping an orphan child 8 months	800
To Col: Walke for a Large Bible for the upper Chappel	300
To John Key for Rods & Staples for Eastern Shore windo Shutters	100
To George Purdy as by his account	304
To mr: Thomas Haynes assignee of James Cotton	0668
To James Cotton the remainder of 1000: for keeping Standly children	332
To Thomas Oldner for Small windo frames to the Church	50
To Edward Brown for keeping Richard Capps 2 months	166
To Charles Sayer by account for Copias: fines &ca	104
To mrs: Hannah moseley for keeping Dinah Laycock 12 months	1200
To Const: michason in part for burying william Shipp	200
To mr: Thomas Haynes for Insolvants as by account	115
To tobo: to Capt: Jacob Ellegood & mr: Thomas Haynes to be laid out in building & repairing on the gleeb land & houses	4000
To Joel Cornick for Some Convenience to the Eastern Shore Chappel	60
To the Conveniency of mr: Barlows Tobo: (to the Sherrif)	4000

VESTRY BOOK OF LYNNHAVEN PARISH 13

To Lawrence Dawley for keeping Eliza: Day 12 months	1000
To Charles Smyth for work done in the Church by account	100
" 10 per Ct: for Receiving 3606. 8 per Ct: for caske 2885: boath is	6491
Cr: By 1182 Tythables @ 36 Each 42552	42559
fraction is 7	42559

Ordered that Francis Moseley gentleman high Sherrif receive of Each Tythable person in this parish thirty Six pounds of Tobacco for the parish Leavy this year and make payment thereof to the Severall claimers acording to the Above Leavy

Test Charles Sayer Clerk [of] Vestry

[16]
Linhaven Parish:

At a Vestery held for laying the Leavy the 14th October 1731

mr: Henry Barlow minister   Anthony Walke } gentlemen Church wardens
                              Francis Land

Present { John Moseley   Henry Chapman }
        { Chr: Burrowgh   Charles Sayer } gentlemen of the vestery
        { George Kempe   Thomas Haynes }

The . . Parish . . is . . Debtor	ll. Tobo:
To the Reverend mr: Henry Barlow Convenient	16000
To mr: James Nimmo Clerk of the Church & cleaning it	1500
To mr: william Keeling clark of the Eastern Shore Chappel	1500
To mr: Andrew Peacock clark of the upper Chappel	1500
To Lawrence Dawley for keeping John Bishop	1000
To James Cotton for keeping a child of Standlys	1000
To Sarah Aerie for nursing Eliza: Day (assigned to Col: Walke)	806
To Doctor william Happer for Salivating Eliza: Day	1200
To the Sherrif for Conveniency of mr: Barlows Tobo:	3200
To Capt: Anthony Moseley for cleaning the Church & per account	0147
To Charles Sayer clark of the vestry & for his account	0536
To Thomas Oldner as per his account	0200
To John wiggins to cloath his mother Eliza: Day	0500
To the Church wardens for Covering the Upper Chappel Convenient	1600
To Ditto to be Sold & to be imploy'd in building a New Church	12000
To Capt: John Moseley coroner for ballance of his account	166
To the Conveniency of the Tobo for covering the Chappel	320
To Robert Richmond for 1000 bricks for the gleeb	150
4 per Ct. for Caske & 4 per Ct. for accounting	3466

Cr: By 1190 Tythables @ 39-1/4 Each	46707	46791
fraction to the Sherrif	84	46791

Ordered that Francis Moseley gentleman High Sherrif receive of Each Tythable person in this parish thirty nine & one quarter pounds of Tobacco for the parish Leavy this year & make payment thereof to Each Claimer as above Directed

Test Charles Sayer Clerk [of] Vestry

[17]

Munden vs. Holmes platt

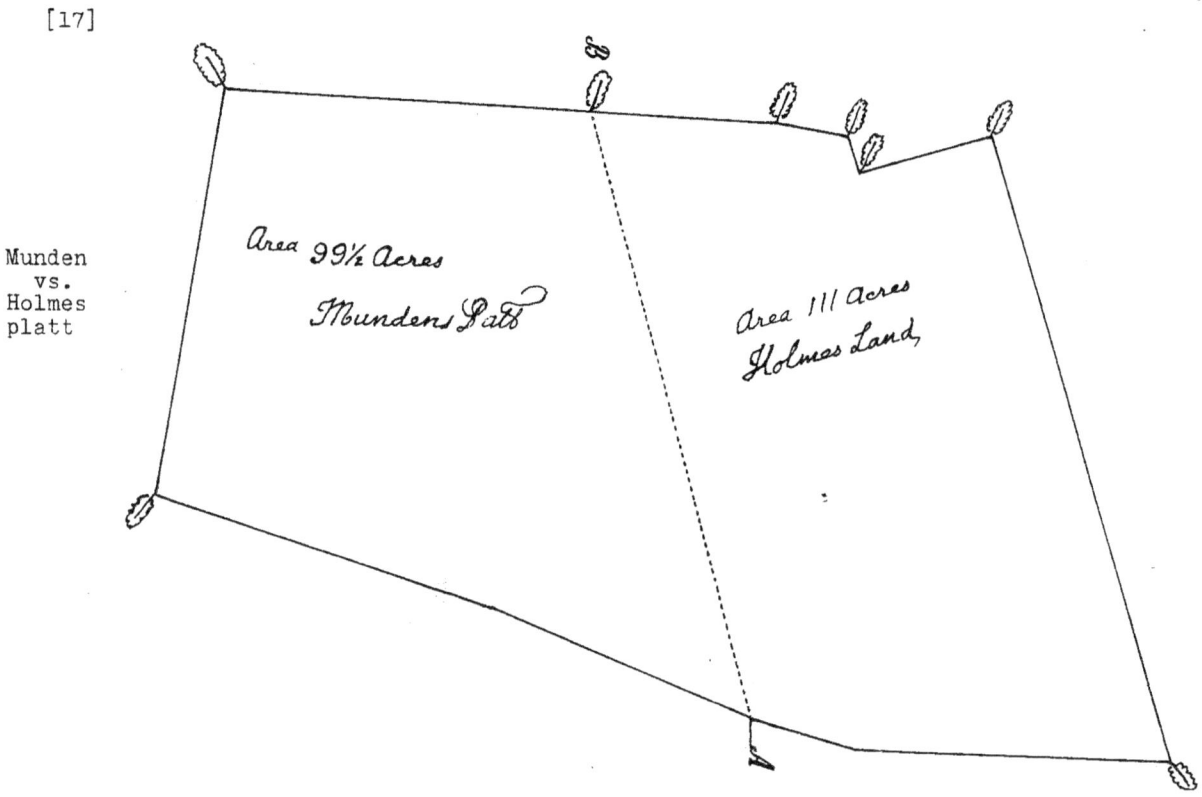

In obedience to an Order of Princess Anne County Court bearing date the 1st day of December 1731, I the Subscriber have binn on the Land in Difference between John Munden and Edward Holmes in Company with a Jury & by their directions have Surveyed the Same & find the Said Land to Contain one hundred & ninty nine & a half acres & have Divided the hundred acres from the ninty nine and a half acres by a prickt line as the above plann Sheweth; the black lines are the bounds of the whole hundred ninty nine and a half acres & the prickt line A & B is the deviding line
January 4th 1731[/2]

per M: Boush Surveyor

Munden vs. Holmes special verdict

Special Verdict Inter John Munden & Edward Holmes by vertue of an order of Princess Anne County Court dated the 1st day of December 1731, by vertue whereof on the day therein appointed wee have laid out the land in Differance according to the Surveyors plott herewith, & Wee find an act of Assembly of this Colony of Virginia made anno 1710, Entituled an act for Settling the Titles & bounds of land etca: & the Severall clauses & provisions therein. Wee find that sometime in February 1728, the plaintiff Munden warned or gave notice to the Defendant Holmes to Survey the land in the presence of two Witnesses vizt: Thorowgood Brinson & James Gittery or that he the Said Munden would Survey the Same. Wee find that the 28th & 29th Aprill 1730, Maximilian Boush gentleman Surveyor of princess Anne County at the request & Charge of the Said Munden Surveyed the land of the Said Holmes reputed one hundred acres & found therein one hundred ninty nine acres & a half & that the Said Holmes was desired to be present & to lay out the Surplus if any where he would & that Holmes answered [that] he would have nothing to Say to it, Munden might take the Surplus if any in what part he would & afterwards vizt: the Same day the Surveyor Survaided that whole Tract
Wee find that the Surveyor the next morning run a Dividing line parting the one hundred acres from the ninty nine acres and a half

[18]

Wee find a pattent granted to the Said Munden for the Said ninty nine acres & a half being the land now in Dispute dated the 28th of September 173 , & that the prick'd line in the Surveyors plott herewith marked A & B, is the Dividing line parting the one hundred acres of Holmes from the ninty nine acres & a half of land granted to Said Munden by the aforesaid pattent out of the Said tract held by Holmes after one hundred devided as aforesaid

Wee find the Surveyors plott herewith & that the black lines Surrounding the whole is the bounds of the hundred acres of Holmes & the ninty nine & a half acres of land now Mundens; Wee find that the Said Holms did not procure rights nor pay the quitrents in arear for the Said One hundred ninty nine acres & a half within one year after notice to Survey by Munden as aforesaid

Wee find that after the notice as aforesaid Holmes paid one years quitrents for the hundred ninty nine acres and a half & no more

Wee find the Said Edward Holmes & Sarah his wife, the 23rd day of May 1730, brought an action of Trespass against the Said John Munden & wee find the Copy of verdict writt declaration & verdict for the Defendant & Judgment for his costs herewith annexed & to which wee refer & that the Trespass therein Complained for was the marking & Surveying the Same land now in Dispute, Wee find a Deed from Fra: Morse & Barbara his wife to Edward Old Senior dated the 28th December 1711, and the Severall Clauses therein & the Indorsement thereon

Wee find the will of Edward Old prov'd November the 5th Anno 1718, & the Severall Clauses therein; Wee find the Depositions of Maximilian Boush, Daniel Barns, William Butler, & Thorowgood Brinson herewith. Wee find the Stake marked A, in the plot to be a Corner Stake in Mundens pattent & the place where Holmes stopp'd the processioners, And if on the whole matter the law be with the Said Munden Wee find the Line A, B, to be the Deviding line between Munden & Holmes otherwise wee find for Holmes the whole tract   In Witness whereof being first Sworn before Jacob Ellegood gentleman one of the Justices of the peace for Princess Anne County wee have hereunto Set our hands & fixed our Seals this 4th day of January 1731[/2]

Henry Snail & Seale	John Saunders foreman & Seale
Thomas Cartwright & Seale	John Jay & Seale
John Gornto & Seale	Richard Poole & Seale
William Mackie & Seale	Francis Ackiss & Seale
James Lamount & Seale	George Williamson & Seale
Charles Smyth & Seale	Robert X Huggins & Seale

Test Charles Sayer Cl Cur

Linhaven Parish

At a Vestry held the 3rd of June Anno Domini 1732

Revd: mr: Henry Barlow minister   Capt: Francis Land & } Church wardens
                                   Col: Anthony Walke   }

Present { Capt: Henry Chapman   Mr: Chr: Burrowgh } Vestry men
        { Charles Sayer   Capt: George Kempe }

processioners appointed

Pursuant to an order of princess ann County Court Dated the   of this Instant requiring us to direct processioning of Lands in our parish according to the act of assembly in that behalf made, we do therefore order that the Severall persons hereafter named in their Severall presincts warn in the inhabitants in their divisions to goe & procession all the lands therein taking care to comply with the Said act— persons appointed to perform processioning are James Kempe & Thomas Spratt [in] the North Side Eastern branch who are to begin the first munday in September: John Nicklis Junior & Thomas wiles Junior South Side begin the 2nd munday in September: James Hunter & Thomas wishard Little creek begin 3rd munday: Robert Thorowgood & Richard Poole Western Shore, Henry Snaile, John Whitehurst Junior up in the woods begin 4th munday: Charles malbone & Joel Cornick lower presinct Eastern Shore, [begin] first munday in october: John Bonney, John Morse, John Dauge & John Gornto upper presinct Eastern Shore, begin the 2nd & 3rd munday in october: Richard Moy & John Corprew in black water to begin the 4th munday

Test Charles Sayer Clerk [of] Vestry

Linhaven Parrish } [19]

At a Vestry held for Laying the Leavy the 29th November 1732

mr: Henry Barlow minister   Capt: Francis Land Church warden

Present { Capt: John Moseley   mr: Christo'r Burrowgh } vestry men
        { Charles Sayer   Capt: George Kempe   }
        { Capt: Robert Vaughan   }

New members chosen

Capt: francis Moseley & mr: James Nimmo Elected new members & haveing taken the oaths of Government appointed by act of parliament and to be conformable to the Doctrines & Decipline of the Church of England are admitted vestry men of this parish

Leavy

The Parish .is .. Debtor	li. Tobo.
To mr: Henry Barlow Minister Convenient	16000
To mr: James Nimmo Clark of the Church	1500
To mr: william Keeling clark of the Eastern Shore Chappel	1500
To mr: Andrew Peacock clark of the upper Chappel	1500
To Lawrence Dawley for keeping John Bishop	1000
To mary wishard for keeping George Griffens orphan to this time	800
To the Collector for the Conveniency of mr: Barlows tobacco	3200
To Capt: Anthony Moseley for makeing 3 horse blocks	150
To James Cotten for keeping of Standlys child	800
To the Church wardens to be by them imploy'd to Support E: Day	600
To mr: william Poole for work done at the Gleeb by account	500
To James Partree for work done on the Gleeb by agreement	1200
To the Church wardens to be imploy'd in procureing plank to be laid in the gleeb house floore &ca:	500
To Charles Sayer Clerk of the vestery & for his account	564
To Capt: John Saunders for 1200 bricks for the gleeb	150
To the fraction brought from the County Leavy	422
" 4 per Ct. for caske: 4 per Ct. for accounting: on 30386 is	2430
	32816

Cr: by 1202 Tythables @ 27-1/4 Each   32754

fraction to the Collector   62   32816

This Day agreed with mr: James Nimmo & mr: William Keeling to Officiate as Clerks of the Church and Chappel the ensuing year for one thousand pounds of Tobacco each to be Leavyed for them in the next parish Leavy

Test Charles Sayer Clerk [of] Vestry

VESTRY BOOK OF LYNNHAVEN PARISH

Linhaven Parish [20]

At a Vestery held the 11th day of August [1733]

mr: Henry Barlow minister

Col: Anthony Walke } Church wardens
Capt: Francis Land

Present:
- Capt: John Moseley
- Major Henry Spratt
- Capt: George Kempe
- mr: James Nimmo
- mr: Christopher Burrowgh
- Capt: Thomas Haynes
- Capt: Francis Moseley

} vestry men

New members chosen: Capt: Henry Moore, Major Maximilian Boush & Capt: Jacob Ellegood Elected new members & haveing taken the oaths of Government appointed by act of parliament and to be conformable to the doctrine & Decipline of the Church of England are admitted vestry men of this parish

New church placed: Resolved by the majority of one voice that at the ferry plantation is a fit and Convenient place to Set a New Church at and that the Same be ther Erected

New members chosen: Mr: John Bonney and mr: John Gornto Chosen New members of this vestery who haveing taken all the oaths of Government and to be conformable to the Doctrines of the Church of England as by Law Established are admitted vestry men of this parish

bricks to be made: Ordered that Col: Anthony Walke Capt: Francis Land & Capt: Francis Moseley & Capt: Jacob Ellegood or any two of them agree with Some person to make Sixty thousand bricks or more this fall towards building the new Church

persons to agree about building the Church: Ordered that Col: Anthony Walke Capt: Francis Land Capt: Francis Moseley & Capt: Jacob Ellegood put Some Estimate or value on one acre of Land at the ferry belonging to Charles Smyth to Erect the new Church on, he the Said Smyth condesending thereto; & agreeing to take the price by them Set as a full Satisfaction for the Said Land

Test Charles Sayer Clerk [of] Vestry

[21]

Linhaven Parish

At a Vestry held for Laying the Leavy the 5th October 1733

mr: Henry Barlow minister

Col: Anthony Walke } Church wardens
Capt: Francis Land

Present:
- Major Henry Spratt
- Charles Sayer
- Capt: Francis Moseley
- Capt: Henry Moore
- Mr: John Bonney
- mr: Christopher Burrowgh
- Capt: George Kempe
- Capt: Jacob Ellegood
- Major Maximilian Boush

} vestry men

Leavy

The . . Parish . . is . . Debtor	ll. Tobo.
To the Reverend mr: Henry Barlow Convenient	16000
To mr: James Nimmo clerk of the Church	1000
To mr: william Keeling clerk of the Eastern Shore Chapel	1000
To mr: Andrew Peacock clerk of the upper Chapel	1500
To Lawrence Dawley for keeping John Bishop	800
To James Cotten for keeping Standlys child	800
To mary wishard for keeping George Griffens child	800
To Sarah Arie for nursing Katherine Knowland	400
To mr: william Happer for Salivating Katherine Knowland	1375
To the Sherrif for the Conveniency of mr: Barlows tobo:	4000
To Ditto Short Last year on Ditto	800
To william Harvey for keeping & Burying William Burrowgh	750

To Josiah Morris for puting blocks under the upper Chapel		150
To the Church wardens to be imployed in building the new Church		40000
To Joseph Harman for keeping William Burrowgh per account		50
To the widow Sparrow for accomadating Josias Old &ca:		500
To Thomas Oldner for mending the church & Pews per account		175
To Charles Sayer clerk of the vestry & for his account		494
To the fraction brought from the County Leavy		447
" 4 per Cent for caske & 4 per Cent for accounting on 71041		5683
		76724
Cr: By 1233 Tythables at 62 Each	76446	
fraction to be accounted for	278	76724

Ordered that Capt: Jacob Ellegood high Sherrif receive from each Tythable person in this parish Sixty two pounds of Tobacco for the parish Leavy this year and make payment thereof to the Severall claimors above Named

Bigness of the Church Resolved that the New Church be Sixty five foot Long & thirty foot wide from inside to inside, The walls fifteen foot high three bricks thick from the foundation to the water Table & two bricks to the Top

Test Charles Sayer Clerk [of] Vestry

[22]

[Linhaven] Parish

At a Vestry held the 13th of November 17[33]

mr: Henry Barlow minister   Col: Anthony Walke } Church wardens
                                          Capt: Francis Land }

Present:
- Col: Edward Moseley
- Capt: John Moseley
- Charles Sayer
- mr: James Nimmo
- Major Maximilian Boush
- Major Henry Spratt
- mr: Christopher Burrowgh
- Capt: Francis Moseley
- Capt: Jacob Ellegood
- mr: John Gornto

vestrymen

Brook clerk of the Church Mr: Ezra Brook haveing had a Tryall of his ability to per[form] the office of a clerk is approved of and now voted that he [be] admited clerk of the Church the Ensuing year that th[ere] be Leavied for him one thousand pounds of Tobo: in the next [parish] Leavy as a reward for his performing the Deuty aforesaid

New Church placed This Day unanimously resolved by the whole vestry [that] the new Church be built and placed where the old one [now] stands & that the Same be there Erected & Set

persons to agree about building the Church Ordered that Col: Anthony Walke Capt: Francis Land & Capt: Jacob Ellegood or any two [of them] agree with mr: Peter malbone on what Terms to build and finish the new Church & make articles with him and take bond for his compleating the Said work

Test Charles Sayer Clerk [of] Vestry

Linhaven Parrish

At a Vestery held for laying the Leavy the 31st October 17[34]

mr: Henry Barlow Minister   Col: Anthony Walke & } Church wardens
                                        Capt: Francis Land }

Present:
- Capt: John Moseley
- Charles Sayer
- Capt: Henry Moore
- mr: John Gornto
- mr: Christopher Burrowgh
- Capt: Jacob Ellegood
- Major Maximilian Boush

Vestry men

VESTRY BOOK OF LYNNHAVEN PARISH 19

	The . . Parish . . . . . Debtor	ll. Tobo:
	To the Reverend Mr: Henry Barlow Minister	16000
	To mr: Ezra Brooke Clerk of the Church	1000
	To mr: William Keeling clerk of the Eastern Shore Chappel	1000
	To mr: Andrew Peacock clerk of the upper Chappel	1000
	To Lawrence Dawley for keeping John Bishop	600
	To Katherine Cotton for keeping Standlys child	[600]
	To mary wishard for keeping George Griffens child	[600]
	To the Sheriff [for the] Conveniency of [Mr:] Barlows Tobo:	[4000]
[23]	To John Griffen for keeping Leaversage's child 2½ months & cloaths	125
	To the Church wardens to be imployed in building the New Church	30000
	To the Conveniency for Ditto	07500
	To Charles Sayer Clerk of the Vestry and by accompt	00635
	To will: Oakham for Tarr and Taring the upper Chappel	00130
	" 4 per Cent for cask & 4 per Cent for accounting on 63190 is	5055
		68245

Cr: By 1166 Tythables at 58½ Each   68211

The fraction carryed to the County Leavy   34   68245

Ordered that Major Maximilian Boush Sheriff Collect & Receive from Every Tythable person in this Parish fifty Eight and a half pounds of Tobacco for the parish Leavy this year & make payment thereof to Each Claimer as above Directed

Test Charles Sayer Clerk [of] Vestry

Linhaven Parish

At a Vestery held the 13th of May 1735

Col: Anthony Walke
Capt: Francis Land } Church wardens

Present { mr: Christo'r Burrowgh   Charles Sayer
Major Maximilian Boush   Capt: Francis Moseley
Capt: Henry Moore   Capt: Jacob Ellegood
mr: John Gornto } vestry men

Prosessioners appointed

Pursuant to an order of princess ann County Court dated the 7th Instant requireing us to direct processioning of lands in our parish according to the act of assembly in that behalf made we do therefore order that the Severall persons hereafter named in their Severall presincts warn in the inhabitants in their divisions to go & prosession all the lands therein taking care to comply with the Said act— persons appointed to perform prosessioning are John Nicholas the South Side Eastern branch & amos moseley North Side to begin the first munday in September: John Hunter & Samuel Boush little creek to begin 2nd munday in September: John Thorowgood western Shore on this Side the ferry James Bannister the other Side, Henry Snail & John whitehurst in the woods to begin 3rd munday, matthew Ellegood William Consaul Lower presinct Eastern Shore, Henry Leamont upper part Same presinct to begin 4th munday in September: John Henly Senior, James Whitehurst, Henry Da[uley], James Spratt upper presinct Eastern Shore [to begin the 1st & 2nd munday in October], ----
------ [in black water to begin the] 3rd munday in October [and that they make return thereof as the] act Directs

[24]

Test Charles Sayer Clerk [of] Vestry

Linhaven Parish

At a vestery held for laying the leavy the 30th Oc[tober 1735]

Mr: Henry Barlow minister   Col: Anthony Walke } Church wardens
                                 Capt: Francis Land

Present:
- Capt: John Moseley
- Charles Sayer
- mr: James Nimmo
- Major Maximilian Boush
- mr: John Bonney
- mr: Christo'r Burrowgh
- Capt: Francis Moseley
- Capt: Jacob Ellegood
- Capt: Henry Moore
- mr: John Gornto

vestry [men]

Note at head of Page 24 of Vestry Book, inadvertently omitted in transcription: "Henry Dauley being Gon to Sea by a verball direction of Some of the vestrymen William Cornick is appointed in the room of the Said Dauley." "Charles Sayer Clerk [of] Vestry"

The . . Parish . . is . . Debtor	ll. Tobo:
To the reverend mr: Henry Barlow minister Convenient	16000
To mr: Ezra Brook clerk of the Church	[1000]
To mr: William Keeling clerk of the Eastern Shore Chappel	[1000]
To mr: Andrew Peacock clerk of the upper Chappel	[1000]
To Lawrence Dawley for keeping John Bishop	[600]
To Katherine Cotton for keeping Standleys child 5 months	[250]
To the Collector for Convenience of mr: Barlows Tobo:	[4000]
To mary wishard for keeping George Griffens child	[400]
To mr: Christopher Burrowgh for burying Thomas Phillips	[150]
To Cockroft for keeping Glode Witchards child	[300]
To adam Tooly for keeping Dennis Care's child 5 months	[165]
To John Rudd for keeping another of Said Cares children 5 months	[225]
To Col: Anthony Walke for Tarr oyle & paint for new Church	[1000]
To william Hancock for keeping Mary Kelly 7 weeks	[65]
To Benjamine Burrowgh for his relief	[250]
To Eve Etheridge for keeping Horshay's child 5 months	[165]
To the Church wardens to be imployed in finishing new Church	20[000]
To Charles Sayer clerk of the vestry & by accompt	[586]
To Elizabeth Day for her releif	[250]
To James Langley for keeping cares child	[160]
To the Church wardens to be imployed in repairing gleeb houses	[1500]
To the fraction brought from the county leavy	[248]
4 per Ct: for casque & 4 per Ct: for accounting on 48981	[3918]
	[53147]
Cr: By 1231 Tythables at 43: each 52933	
By a fraction to the Collector [214]	[53147] .

[25]   [Ordered that ---------- ----- Collect & receive from each Tythable person in this] parish fourty three pounds of Tobacco being [the] parish leavy this year that he make payment thereof [to] every Claimor as above Directed

This day agreed with John Griffen to keep Mary Griffen the Ensuing year for three hundred and fifty pounds of Tobacco to be leavied for him in the next parish leavy.

On the motion of Col: Edward Moseley 'tis unanimusly agreed & Liberty given him to Erect a hanging Pewe on the north Side of the New Church at his own cost for himself his grandson mr: Edward Hack Moseley Captain Anthony & Capt: francis Moseley's

            Charles Sayer Clerk [of] Vestry

Linhaven Parish

At a Vestry held the 25th of June 1736

Reverend Henry Barlow minister   Col: Anthony Walke Church warden

Present { Capt: francis Moseley   Charles Sayer
     mr: James Nimmo   Capt: Jacob Ellegood } vestry men

mr: James Kempe being chosen a vestry man of this parish and haveing taken all the Oaths Enjoin'd and Subscrib'd the Test is admited a member of the Said vestry

This day Received from mr: Peter malbone the New Church and Do discharge him from his obligation of building & finishing the same, he hereby obleiging himself to Stop the punk holes in the wall & fasten the Tyle if they want dureing the Said malbones life

Agreed with francis Moseley to Clean the New Church for which he is to have two hundred pounds of Tobacco per year leavy'd in the parish Leavy to commence from the 9th July next

            Charles Sayer Clerk [of] Vestry

[26]

Linhaven Parish

At a Vestry held the 10th of July 1736

Reverend Henry Barlow minister   Col: Anthony Walke Church warden

Present {
mr: Christopher Burrowgh   Charles Sayer
Capt: francis Moseley   mr: James Nimmo
Capt: Henry Moore   Major Maximilian Boush
Capt: Jacob Ellegood   mr: John Bonney
mr: John Gornto   mr: James Kempe
} vestry men

Gleeb house repaired &ca: Resolved that 'tis necessary to repair the dwelling house on the Gleeb by puting brick [walls] thereto mending & Stoping the leaks in the roof, also that an addition be made On the garden Side Sixteen foot long twelve foot wide brick walls & chimney, and agreed with mr: James Langley to make the repair for eight thousand pounds of Tobo: to be leavyed this year: & for the new addition the Sum of Seven thousand pounds of Tobo: to be Leavyed next year

Robinson build a Pew On the motion of mr: William Robinson Liberty is given him to build a hanging Pew on the north Side of the new Church (& in case the family of the moseleys who have had the first liberty refuse to accept thereoff then the Said Robinson to have the liberty of building the first Pew as aforeSaid not obstructing the light of the windows

Church wardens Resolved that Col: Anthony Walke be continued Church warden for the Ensuing year & Capt: Jacob Ellegood being Elected in the room of Capt: francis Land 'tis therefor ordered they Execute the said office particularly in placeing & Seating the people in the New Church

Assignment of pews For preserving order desency peace & Harmony in the New Church 'tis resolved & the vestry doe hereby assign & appoint the two upper opposite great Pews for the Magestrates & their wives: the next adjoyning pew on the north Side of the Church to the family of the Thorowgoods as their privilege in consideration of the gift of our gleeb by that family: the third great pew on the north Side for the vestry men & their wives— the pew on the north side of the Communion Table is assign'd to the family & Name of the Walkes as a benefit formerly granted them in Consideration of gifts & Services made & done by Col: Thomas Walke deceased & Col: Anthony Walke the Senior: the next great pew on the South Side for the Elder women of good repute & magestrates daughters: the other great pew on the Same Side for Such women as the Churchwardens with the approbation of the vestry Shall think fit to place therein

[27]

Persons apointed to keep order &ca:

Resolved that mr: Patrick Hackett is a fitt person to Sett up in the gallery to keep everybody in order & if boy's or any other person will not be restrained but doe any indecency he is hereby required to report Same to the Church wardens who are Desired to take proper measures to punish Such disorderly person: Likewise mr: francis Moseley is appointed to look out of doors & if any person or persons are Siting & talking or Commiting any indecency dureing divine Service, he is hereby Impowered to Commit them to the care of the Constable & inform the Churchwardens thereof to be Dealt with as the Law requires

Charles Sayer Clerk [of] Vestry

Linhaven Parish }

At a vestry held the 2nd of August 1736

Reverend Henry Barlow minister   Col: Anthony Walke / Capt: Jacob Ellegood } Church wardens

Present { Major Henry Spratt, Capt: francis Moseley, Major Maximilian Boush, mr: James Kempe, Charles Sayer, mr: James Nimmo, Capt: Henry Moore } vestry men

Alteration of the New addition

Resolved that the former agreement with mr: Langley for the new addition on the Gleeb Land be altered as to the biggness of the Said building & instead thereof agreed that the Said Langley make the addition fourteen foot Square within the walls which are to be of brick a chimney Starecase, two sash windows, two doors & compleatly finish the outside and lower Roome of the Said house in every respect as mentioned in the former agreement for which he is to have & receive the Same reward and in the Same manner as in the Said agreement mentioned

Charles Sayer Clerk [of] Vestry

[28]

Linhaven Parish }

At a Vestry held for laying the Leavy the 16th October 17[36]

Reverend Henry Barlow minister   Col: Anthony Walke / Major Jacob Ellegood } Church wardens

Present { Capt: James Nimmo, Capt: Henry Moore, Capt: James Kempe, Charles Sayer, mr: John Gornto } vestry men

Leavy

The . . Parish . . is . . Debtor	li. Tobo:
To the Reverend Henry Barlow minister Convenient	16000
To mr: Ezra Brook clark of the Church	1000
To mr: william Keeling clark of the Eastern Shore Chappel	1000
To mr: Andrew Peacock clark of the upper Chappel	1000
To Lawrence Dawley for keeping John Bishop	600
To the Collector for the Conveniency of the ministers Tobo:	4000
To John Griffen for keeping his brothers child	350
To Cockroft old for keeping Glode witchards child	500
To adam Tooly for keeping Dennis Cares child	400
To John Rudd for keeping another of Said Cares children	550
To mr: william Happer by account for Sallivating 3 persons	3200
To Sarah Airy for keeping Dobbs in Sallivating	300
To Eve Etheridge for keeping Horseys child	700
To Thomas Moore for keeping Edmond Ellegoods child 1 month 10 days	69

To mr: Ezra Brooke per account aboute the register book	300
To William Hancock for burying Mary Kelley per account	140
To Josiah Tainer for burying Patrick Burke per account	200
To the Church wardens to be paid to mr: James Langley for repairing the gleeb house by agreement	8000
To Charles Sayer clark of the vestry & by account	580
To mr: francis Moseley for cleaning the Church &ca:	70
To Joseph Harmon for keeping William Harveys child	250
To mrs: margaret Land for the ballance of Capt: Lands account	135
" 6 per Ct: for accounting & 4 per Cent: for caske on 39404 . is . .	3940
	43344
Cr: By 1256 Tythables at 34½ each 43332	
By the fraction remaining 12	43344

Avers to keep Hough
agreed with Sarah Avers to keep a child belonging to Daniel Hough the Ensuing year for which She is to have five hundred pounds of Tobo: leavyed in the next parish Leavy

Walke to pay Nichalson
Ordered that Col: Anthony Walke pay to mrs: Eliza: Nichalson Six pounds ten shilings & Six pence out of the parish money, it being due to her for boarding & Looking after Elizabeth & Benjamin Burrowgh in the time of their Sallivation

[29]

Condon collect parish leavy
Ordered that Capt: James Condon Collect & Receive from Each Tythable person in this parish the Sum of 34½ pounds of Tobo:— for the parish Leavy this year that he make payment thereof to Each claimer as Directed by the Said Leavy

Whereas Several of the inhabitants of this parish has not thought fit to accept off, & others to keep to the Seats & pews the Church wardens have assigned to & placed them, in the new Church lately built; to the great disturbance & disorder of the congregation; to prevent which Disorder in the Said Church for the future, we the vestry of the Said parish have meet at the parish Church, & after due consideration, have assigned & Register'd the adjacent persons & family's according to their Several Stations, the most proper Seats or pews; & do hereby publish & declare, that who, or whatsoever person or persons Shall assume to themselves a power: or take the Liberty to place themselves or others in any other Seats or pews in the Said Church: Shall be Esteem'd a Disorderly person & may Expect to be dealt with according to Law; and we Doe further impower and appoint the Church wardens for the future to place all persons in the church of the Said parish

Test Charles Sayer Clerk [of] Vestry

At a meeting of the Vestry the 2nd March 1736[/7]

Col: Anthony Walke } Church wardens
Major Jacob Ellegood

Present { Capt: John Moseley   Charles Sayer
         Major francis Moseley Capt: James Nimmo } vestry men
         Capt: James Kempe

The old Church given for a School
On the motion of Col: Anthony Walke that the old Church woo'd be a Convenient place to make a public Schoole off for instructing children in learning, that liberty might be given for applying it to that purpose, the vestry takeing the Same under their consideration & agreeing to the Said proposeall also being of opinion that after it is made Commodious 'twould be an Encouragement to induce a master constantly to attend thereon; doe therefore unanimously Resolve that the Said Church be, and it is hereby given for the use aforeSaid, and to & for no: other use or purpose whatsoever

Test Charles Sayer Clerk [of] Vestry

VESTRY BOOK OF LYNNHAVEN PARISH

Linhaven Parish

At a Vestry held for laying the Leavy the 2nd November 1737

Reverend Henry Barlow Minister   Col: Anthony Walke } Church wardens
                                        Major Jacob Ellegood

Present: Major francis Moseley, Capt: James Nimmo, mr: John Gornto, Charles Sayer, Capt: Henry Moore, Capt: James Kempe — vestry men

The . . Parish . . is . . Debtor	ll. Tobo:
To the Reverend Henry Barlow minister Convenient	16000
To mr: Ezra Brooke clark of the Church	1000
To mr: William Keeling clark of the Eastern Shore Chappel	1000
To mr: andrew Peacock clark of the upper Chappel	1000
To Lawrence Dawley for keeping John Bishop	600
To the Collector for the Conveniency of the ministers Tobo:	4000
To John Griffen for keeping his brothers child	350
To Cockroft Old for keeping Glode witchards child	500
To adam Tooly for keeping Dennis Care's child	400
To John Rudd for keeping another Said Care's children	500
To mr: william Happer for Sallivating Benjamin Burrowgh &ca & per acct:	1665
To Eliza: Jenkins for looking after Mary Brown per account	137
To Eve Etheridge for keeping Horsey's child	600
To Thomas Moore for keeping Edmond Ellegood's child	600
To francis Moseley for cleaning the church &ca: per Agreement	300
To Joseph Harman for keeping William Harveys child	500
To John Buskey for a leavy overcharg'd last year	54
To Thomas Cartwright for keeping Simon franklins child	500
To Thomas Wishard on account Ditto's children as per ballance account	300
To Mary Whitehurst for keeping Rachel Whitehurst child	300
To the Church wardens to be paid to James Langley for the new building on the gleeb Land	7000
To Charles Sayer clark of the vestry & by account	590
To Thomas Moore for keeping Daniel Hough's child	500
To Ditto to carry the Said child to its father per agreement	200
To Joseph Harman for burying Barbara Burrowgh	100
To the Church wardens to pay for the Seller on the gleeb land	1800
To John Harper for cureing Mary Griffen	200
" fraction brought from the county leavy	214
" 6 per Cent for accounting & 4 per Cent for caske on 40910	4091
	45001

Leavy

VESTRY BOOK OF LYNNHAVEN PARISH

Cr: By 1270 Tythables at 35-1/4 each	44767	
By a fraction to be accounted for	234	45001

[31]

Linhaven Parish } At a vestery held the 27th June anno 1738

Reverend Henry Barlow minister   Col: Anthony Walke } Church wardens
                                                          Col: Jacob Ellegood

Present { Capt: James Nimmo   Charles Sayer } vestry men
          { Capt: Henry Moore   Capt: James Kempe

gleeb house repaired — Resolved that the chamber windows of the old house on the gleeb: be glaiz'd & the chambers new plaister'd & whitewash'd the milkhouse covered with good oak boards & the inside plaister'd, that the church wardens agree with Some proper person to perform the Said Service or any other Small thing necessary to the Said repair with liberty to the Said Churchwardens or either of them if they think fit to doe the Said work & bring in their account at the next leavy

                                           Test Charles Sayer Clerk [of] Vestry

Linhaven Parish } At a vestry held for laying the Leavy the 26th October 1738

Reverend Henry Barlow minister   Col: Anthony Walke } Churchwardens
                                                           Col: Jacob Ellegood

Present { Capt: John Moseley   Charles Sayer
          { Capt: James Nimmo   Capt: Henry Moore } vestry men
          { mr: John Bonney   mr: John Gornto
          { Capt: James Kempe

Leavy

The . . Parish . . is . . Debtor	li. Tobo:
To the Reverend Henry Barlow minister Convenient	16000
To mr: Ezra Brooke clark of the Church	1000
To mr: William Keeling clark of the Eastern Shore Chappel	1000
To mr: Andrew Peacock clark of the upper Chappel	1000
To Lawrence Dawley for keeping John Bishop	600
To the Collector for the conveniency of the ministers Tobo:	4000
To Cockroft old for keeping Glod witchards child	400
To adam Tooly for keeping Dennis cares child	400
To John Red for keeping another Said Cares children	500
To Eve Etheridge for keeping Horseys child	600
To Joseph Harman for keeping William Harveys child	500
To francis Moseley for cleaning the Church &ca:	300
To Mary Whitehurst for keeping Rachel Whitehurst child	300
To Thomas Moore for keeping Edmond Ellegoods child	600
To Thomas Cartwright for keeping franklins child	500
To Thomas Moor for Releif of his Sister Ann to this time	200
	27900

Brought forward		27900
[32] To Charles Sayer clark of the vestry & by account		[730]
To Thomas Cartwright for keeping Ann Tainer while Salivated		200
To mr: Henry woodhouse for a leavy overcharg'd last year		48
To mary Broughton for Releife of her 3 children		600
To mary morris for keeping another Said Broughtons children		200
To Capt: James Condon for Insolvants per account		240
6 per Ct: for Collecting & 4 per Ct: for casque on 29718		2971
		32689
Cr: By 1327 Tythables at 24½ Each	32511	
fraction carryed to the county leavy	178	32689

Ordered that Capt: Charles Malbone Sheriff Receive from each Tythable person in this parish the Sum of twenty four & a half pounds of Tobacco being the parish leavy this year & make payment thereof to each Claimor as above directed

Test Charles Sayer Clerk [of] Vestry

Linhaven Parish

At a vestry held the 10th of May 1739

Reverend Henry Barlow minister   Col: Anthony Walke } Churchwardens
                                 Col: Jacob Ellegood

Present { Charles Sayer   Capt: James Nimmo } vestry men
        { Capt: James Kempe   mr: John Gornto

Processioning apptd:

Pursuant to an order of princess ann County Court requiring us to Cause a processioning of land in our parish according to the act of assembly we doe therefore order that the Several persons hereafter named in their Several presincts warn in the inhabtants in their divisions to goe & procession all the lands therein takeing care to comply with the Said act..... Persons appointed to perform processioning are William Hancock & Nathaniel Nicholas on the South Side of the Eastern branch, Tully Robinson Smyth & Charles Smyth the north Side to begin the first Munday in September: Thomas Hunter & George Wishard in little Creek to begin the 2nd munday: Thomas Haynes & James Hunter the lower part of the western Shore: Thomas Langley & John fentris the upper part to begin the 3rd munday: matthew Pallet, Lemuel Cornick & adam Hayes in the Lower presinct of the Eastern Shore to begin the 4th munday: Thomas Spratt & william morris the upper part of the upper presinct of the Eastern Shore, Peter malbone, Thomas morse & Thomas ward Junior the lower part of that presinct to begin the first & Second mundays in october, Kitely Roe & Robert Reed in black water to begin the third munday in october & that they make return thereof as that act Directs

[33] New members elected

Resolved that Capt: Nathaniel Newton, mr: Edward Hack Moseley, mr: John Hunter mr: adam Tooly, mr: John Whitehurst, mr: Job Gasking & & mr: George Wishard be appointed vestry men of this parish if they think fit to Quallify for the Same

Smoke house built

Resolved that a New Smoke house be built on the gleeb Land to be twelve foot Square with good oak boards—— that the Church wardens or either of them agree with a workman to perform the Said work on the best Terms they can for money

Test Charles Sayer Clerk [of] Vestry

VESTRY BOOK OF LYNNHAVEN PARISH

Linhaven Parish

At a vestry held for laying the Leavy the 15th October 1739

Reverend Henry Barlow minister   Col: Jacob Ellegood Church warden

Present: Charles Sayer, Capt: Henry Moore, Major Nathaniel Newton, mr: John Hunter, Capt: James Nimmo, Capt: James Kempe, mr: Job Gasking — vestry men

Leavy

The . . Parish . . is . . Debtor	ll. Tobo:
To the reverend Henry Barlow Convenient	16000
To mr: Ezra Brooke Clark of the Church	1000
To mr: william Keeling clark of the Eastern Shore Chapel	1000
To mr: Andrew Peacock clark of the upper Chappel	1000
To Lawrence Dauley for keeping John Bishop	600
To the Collector for the Conveniency of the ministers Tobo:	4000
To Cockroft Old for keeping Glode witchards child	300
To adam Tooly for keeping Dennis Cares child	400
To John Redd for keeping another Said Cares children	400
To Eve Etheridge for keeping Horsey's child	500
To Eliz: Harmon for keeping Harveys child ass[igned] to John Harper	400
To francis Moseley for Cleaning the Church &ca:	300
To M[ary] Whitehurst for keeping Rachel Whitehurst child	300
To Thomas Moore for keeping Edmond Ellegoods child	600
To Thomas Cartwright for keeping franklins child	400
To Thomas Moore for Releif of his sister	400
To James Brock for keeping E: Milasons Child 8 months	266
To mr: William Happer for Sallivating Broughtons wife	1000
To Mary Scady for keeping Barringtons child 10 months	250
To Anthony Williamson for keeping the Same child 3 months	75
To James fentris for keeping Isdells child 1 year	500
To Henry Moore for cleaning Eastern Shore chapel & Spring	100
To Charles Sayer clark of the vestry & by accompt	520
To John Harper for cureing Ann Goughs foot	200
To willis Nicholas for keeping Barringtons child 6 weeks	150
To wm: fentris Junior for keeping E: Milason when she lay in 1 month	200
To the Churchwardens to be imployed towards a New chappel at pungo	12000
To Ditto to provide pullpit cloth & cussion & cloth for the Table	4000
To a fraction from the county leavy ll& to the Sheriff to acct: for 3:	14
6 per Ct: for accounting & 4 per Ct: for caske on 46861	4686
	51561

Cr: By 1343 Tythables at 38-1/4 per pole   51561

[34]

Ordered that Capt: James Kempe Sheriff Receive from Each Tythable person in this parish 38-1/4 pounds of Tobo: for the parish leavy this year & make payment thereof to each claimor as above Directed

Cribb built

Resolved that a good cribb of twelve foot long be built on the gleeb Land to be made with good mauld popler peices that the Churchwardens agree with Some person to Doe the Same as Soon as posable

Test Charles Sayer Clerk [of] Vestry

Linhaven Parish

At a Vestry held the first day of March 1739[/40]

Reverend Henry Barlow minister   Col. Anthony Walke, Col. Jacob Ellegood } Churchwardens

Present {
Charles Sayer
Mr. John Gornto
Mr. John Hunter
Mr. George Wishart
Capt. Henry Moore
Mr. Job Gasking
Capt. James Condon
Mr. Adam Tooly
} vestrymen

chappel placed

Resolved that at William Dyers is the most convenient place to build a new chappel (Excepting the black water presinct, who are Excluded from paying any part of the Cost or charge of building the same Except what is already Leavyed

Bigness of the Chappel

Resolved that the New chappel be built fifty foot long Twenty five foot wide within the walls, which is to be of brick, & fifteen foot hight, covered with heart cypress Shingles, & a gallery of fifteen foot long; three large sash windows on the north side & two on the south side, two over the communion table, two small ones at the end where the gallery is, three large wainscot pews, two on the north side & one on the south side, the wall to be two & a half bricks thick from the foundation to the water table & two bricks from that to the top of the wall; & round the Communion table to be neatly rail'd & banistred

[35]

agreement with James for cappel

Agreed with James James to build the aboveSaid chappel for the sum of three hundred Twenty two pounds Ten shillings which is to be compleatly finished According to art

Ordered that Anthony Walke, Jacob Ellegood, Nathaniel Newton, John Bonney, & John Gornto gentlemen sometime in this month repair to the plantation of William Dyers, to view & resolve on the place where to Erect the new Chappel

Test Arthur Sayer Clerk [of] Vestry

Linhaven Parrish

At a Vestry held for laying the leavy the 14th October 1740

Reverend Henry Barlow minister   Col. Anthony Walke, Col. Jacob Ellegood } Churchwardens

Present {
Capt. James Kempe
Mr. John Gornto
Mr. John Whitehurst
Mr. Job Gasking
Mr. John Bonney
Mr. John Hunter
Mr. George Wishart
} Vestrymen

The Parrish is . . . . . Debtor	ll. Tobo:
To the reverend Henry Barlow minister convenient	16000
To Mr. Ezra Brooke clerk of the Church	1000
To Mr. William Keeling clerk of the Eastern Shore Chappel	1000
To Mr. Andrew Peacock clerk of the upper Chapel	1000
To Lawrance Dawley for keeping John Bishop	600
To the collector for Conveniency of the ministers Tobo:	4000
To Cockroft Old for keeping Glode Whitchards child	150
To Adam Tooly for keeping Dennis Cares child	400

VESTRY BOOK OF LYNNHAVEN PARISH 29

	To John Red for keeping another of the Said Cares Children	300
	To Eve Etheridge for keeping Horseys child	500
	To Eliza: Harmon for keeping Harvey & Baringtons children	450
	To Francis Moseley for Cleaning the Church &ca:	300
	To Mary Whitehurst for keeping Rachel Whitehursts child	150
	To Thomas Moore for keeping Edmond Ellegoods child	500
	To Thomas Cartwright for keeping Franklins child & Thomas Gilbert 1 mo:	400
	To John Consolvo for keeping Thomas Gilbert	200
	To Anne Moore for releif of Anne Moore	400
	To Iliff Brock for keeping Elizabeth Milasons child	500
	To Mr. William Happer for Sallivating Mrs. Allen &ca:	1720
	To Capt. William Keeling for Cleaning chappel &ca:	159
	To the Church wardens towards building a Chapple at pungo	25000
	To William Clancy for keeping & burying Isdells child	250
	To Ruth Sparks for keeping her own child	300
[36]	Fraction from the County leavy	324-3/4
	6 per Ct. for Accounting & 4 per Ct. for cask on 55279	5527
		61130-3/4
	Cr. By 1282 Tythables at 19½ per pole 24999	
	By 1377 ditto at 26 per pole 35802	
	Fraction to be allowed the sherif next year 329-3/4	61130-3/4

Ordered that Capt. James Kempe Sherif receive from each Tythable person in this parrish nineteen & a half & Twenty six pounds of Tobo: for the parrish leavy this year, & make payment thereof to each claimer as above Directed.

Parrish's agreement with Thorowgood

On the petition of Mr. Francis Thorowgood liberty is given him to take of[f], a house built by the said Francis, on the land belonging to this parrish, & that the Church wardens make a lease to the said Francis for the said land for Twenty one years, & that at the Expiration of the said lease the said Thorowgood is to pay to the said parrish the sum of four pounds ten shillings or build a house of that value on the said parrish land

Test Arthur Sayer Clerk [of] Vestry

Linhaven Parrish

At a Vestry held for laying the Leavy the 15th October 1741

Reverend Henry Barlow Minister   Col. Anthony Walke } Church Wardens
                                   Col. Jacob Ellegood

Present { Capt. James Kempe   Mr. John Bonny   }
        { Mr. John Whitehurst   Mr. Job Gasking   } Vestry men
        { Capt. James Condon   }

The Parrish . . . . Dr:	li. Tobo:
To the Reverend Henry Barlow Convenient	16000
To Mr. Ezra Brooke Clerk of the Church	1000
To Capt. William Keeling clerk of the Eastern Shore Chappel	1000

VESTRY BOOK OF LYNNHAVEN PARISH

To Mr. Andrew Peacock clerk of the Uper Chappel	1000
To Lawrance Dawley for keeping John Bishop	700
To the Collector for Conveniency of the ministers Tobo:	4000
To Adam Tooly for keeping Dennis Cares Child	400
To John Redd for keeping another of Said Cares Children	300
To Eve Etheridge for keeping Horseys child	400
To Francis Moseley for Cleaning the Church &ca:	300
To Thomas Moore for keeping Edmond Ellegoods child	400
To Thomas Cartwright for keeping Franklins Child	300
To James Moore for keeping Anne Moore	200
To Eliza: Harman for keeping Baringtons Child	200
To Capt. William Keeling for cleaning Chappel	100
To Doctor William Happer per account	7104
To Michaell Fentriss for keeping Aron Sugg's Child	400
To William Oakham for keeping Eliza: Oakhams child	1000
To William Bodman for keeping Mary Buttery	800
To the Church wardens towards building a Chappel at Pungo	20000
To Edward Sharp for keeping & burying Thomas Moore	350
To Elizabeth Nicholson per Account	3075
To Arthur Sayer Clerk of the Vestry & by account	1030
To George Wishart for Insolvants	2095
To William Dale for making coffen &ca: for James Smith	60
To John Keeling for burying ditto &ca:	134
To Mary Morris towards her releif	250
To Thomas Hill Junior for Cleaning Spring Eastern Shore Chappel	50
To Batson Whitehurst for keeping & burying Thomas Gilbert	645
6 per Ct: for accounting & 4 per Ct: for cask on 63373	6337
	69710

Cr: By Francis Spratt & John Chapman	350	
By 1381 Tythables @ 35-3/4 per pole	49374-3/4	
By 1291 Ditto @ 15 per pole	19365	
Fraction carryed to the County leavy	624-1/4	69710

[37] appears beside "To William Oakham..."

Ordered that Maj. Nathaniel Newton Sherif receive from each Tythable person in this parrish 50-3/4 of tobo: (Except Blackwater who are to pay only 35-3/4) as above for the parrish Leavy this year & make payment thereof to each Claimer as above directed

Col. Anthony Walke haveing this day setled his account with this Parrish (the ballance of which due in his favour) is Sixteen pounds eight Shillings & Six pence therefore Ordered he be allowed the Same

[38]
Linhaven Parrish

At a Vestry held for laying the Leavy the 14th October 1742

Reverend Henry Barlow Minister   Col. Anthony Walke
                                      Col. Jacob Ellegood } Churchwardens

Present { Mr. Job Gasking   Mr. John Hunter
           Capt. James Nimmo   Capt. James Condon } Vestry men
           Mr. John Gornto

The Parrish is . . . . Dr:	li. Tobo:
To the reverend Mr. Henry Barlow minister Convenient	16000
To Mr. Thomas Grainger Clerk of the Church	1000
To Capt. William Keeling clerk of the Eastern Shore Chappell	1000
To Mr. Andrew Peacock clerk of the Uper Chappell	1000
To the Colector for conveniency of the ministers tobo:	4000
To Adam Tooly for keeping Dennis Cares Child	400
To Eve Etheridge for keeping Horseys child	400
To Francis Moseley for cleaning the Church	300
To Thomas Moore for keeping Edmond Ellegoods child	400
To Capt. Keeling for cleaning Eastern Shore Chappell	100
To Michael Fentriss for keeping Aron Sugg's child	500
To William Oakham for keeping Eliza. Oakhams child	500
To the Churchwardens towards building a Chapel at pungo	12000
To Arthur Sayer Clerk of the vestry & per account	480
To Mary Morris towards her releif	400
To Henry Lamount per account	180
To John Ashby for keeping his father & wifes mother	500
To Capt. James Condon for Insolvants	1144½
To Mr. George Wishart for Ditto	1049¾
To John Lamount for service done Richard Adams	265
To Anne Williams for keeping Anne Moore	150
To William Carrell for keeping James James	300
To Doctor Happer per account	490
To Doctor Robert Paterson per ditto	900
To Worsell Alderson for keeping Thomas Berry to this time	100
To Thomas Cartwright for Nursing Francis Cotton	500
To Eliza. Harmon for keeping Baringtons child	200
To John Harvey towards cure of his wife	800
6 per Ct. for accounting & 4 per Ct. for cask on 45059¼	4505
	49564¼

VESTRY BOOK OF LYNNHAVEN PARISH

Cr: By 1425 Tythables @ 26½ per pole	37762½	
By 1334 Ditto @ 8¾ per ditto	11672½	
fraction Carryed to the County Leavy	129¼	49564¼

Ordered that Capt. James Condon Sherif receive from each Tythable person thirty five & one quarter pounds of tobo: (Except black water who are to pay only 26½) as above for the parrish Leavy this Year & make payment thereof to Each Claimer as Above directed

[39] Agreed with ----- Pead widow to keep Anne Harvey Daughter of George Harvey Deceased the Ensuing Year for fifty Shillings to be paid out of the Said Harveys Estate if sufficient.

Agreed with William Pead to keep Elizabeth another of the sd Harveys Daughters the Ensuing year at forty shillings to be paid as above

Agreed with Mary Dudly to keep Mary another of the said George's Daughters the Ensuing Year for thirty shillings & to be paid as above

Test Arthur Sayer Clerk [of] Vestry

Linhaven Parrish } At a Vestry held for laying the leavy the 12th October 1743

Reverend Henry Barlow minister   Colo. Anthony Walke } Churchwardens
                                                   Colo. Jacob Ellegood }

Present { Mr. Job Gasking   Mr. John Hunter } Vestry Men
        { Major Nathaniel Newton   Mr. John Whitehurst }

The Parrish is . . . . Debtor	ll. Tobo:
To the Reverend Mr. Henry Barlow minister Convenient	16000
To Mr. Thomas Grainger Clerk of the Church	1000
To Capt. William Keeling Clerk Eastern Shore Chappel	1000
To Mr. Andrew Peacock Clerk of the Upper Chappel	1000
To the Collector for Conveniency of the Ministers tobo:	4000
To Francis Moseley for cleaning the Church &ca:	300
To Thomas Moore for keeping Edmond Ellegoods child	400
To Capt. William Keeling for keeping clean Eastern Shore Chappel	100
To Michaell Fentriss for keeping Aron Sugg's child	500
To William Oakham for keeping Eliza. Oakhams child	400
To Mary Morris towards her releife	400
To John Ashby for keeping his father & wifes mother	500
To John Lamount for Richard Adams	800
To Worsell Alderson & William Spann for keeping Thomas Berry	400
To Elizabeth Harman as per account	550
To William Dyer for cleaning uper chappel & boarding Wiggin	100
To Capt. Anthony Moseley as per account	250
To James Blair for cure of Abigall Cotton	800
To Francis Moseley for keeping & Burying Elizabeth Algrove [?]	364

To Major Nathaniel Newton as per account	180
To Capt. John Hutchings as per ditto	353
To John Holt for keeping his mother	200
To Eliza. Harman for care of Henry Chapman	100
To Sarah Whitehurst as per account	195
To Francis Ackiss for one leavy overcharged formerly	45
To John Fentriss for keeping & Burying Robert Peirt	300
To Edward Broughton for making coffen for Henry Chapman	25
To Peter & Solomon Malbone for cure of their brother Reod[orick?]	1000
To Elizabeth Nicholson as per account	400
To Thomas Cartwright for keeping Francis Cotton	250
To John Burfoot for additional work to upper Chappell	8000
To Capt. James Condon for Insolvents (from Mr. Wishart)	832
To ditto Insolvents, his own	2500
To Sarah Smyth for work done on the Gleeb house	150
To Doctor Paterson for salivating Eliza. Williams (& Sarah Dauley bal.)	992
To Barbara Keeling for Nursing Eliza. Williams	356
To Arthur Sayer Clerk of the Vestry & by account	896
To Thomas Grainger for making & fixing a [sun]Diall at the Church	400
To Col: Anthony Walke for ballance his account (remainder to be acctd)	2000
To John Key for keeping Eliza. Dauley	123
To the Church wardens to pay William Wiggin for painting Church &ca:	2173½
6 per Ct. for accounting & 4 per Ct. for cask on 50337½	5033
	55370½

Cr: By 1435 Tythables @ 38 per pole	53290	
fraction Carryed to the County Leavy	80½	55370½

[40] appears in left margin near "To Thomas Cartwright..."

Ordered that Capt. Thomas Walke Sherif receive from each Tythable person thirty eight pounds of tobo: as above for the parrish Leavy this Year and make payment thereof to Each claimer as above directed

Test Arthur Sayer Clerk [of] Vestry

Linhaven Parrish

At a Vestry held the 9th March 1743[/4]

Reverend Henry Barlow Minister

Colo. Anthony Walke } Churchwardens
Colo. Jacob Ellegood

Present:
- Capt. James Nimmo
- Mr. John Bonney
- Mr. John Gornto
- Mr. George Wishart
- Mr. Job Gasking
- Mr. John Whitehurst
- Major Nathaniel Newton

} Vestrymen

Pursuant to an Order of princess Anne County Court requiring us to cause a processioning of all land in our parrish according to the act of assembly. We do therefore order that the Severall persons hereafter named in their Severall presincts warn in the Inhabitants in their divisions to goe & procession all the lands therein taking care to Comply with the said act. Persons appointed to perform processioning are Nathaniel McClanahan & Tully Robinson on the north side of the Eastern branch, John Shipp & Tully Moseley the south side, Adam Thorowgood & Adam Lovett the lower part Western Shore, Arthur & Charles Whitehursts Upper part. James Ashley & Henry Jimason little creek. Henry Consolvo, John Lovett, Thomas Keeling & George Stiring the lower part of the Eastern Shore, John Russell, Henry Dauley, Henry Spratt, John James Upper part, Israel Kaller & John Simmons in black water to begin the 27th March and that they make return thereof According to Law.

[41] Mr. Dauly Latter having had a Tryall of his ability to perform the office of a Clerk is approved of, & now voted that he be admited clerk of the upper Chappel the Ensuing year &ca:

Thomas Walke, Anthony Moseley & John Whitehead being chosen as vestry men of this parrish & having taken the oaths Enjoyned and Subscribed the Test are Admited members of the said vestry

Arthur Sayer Clerk [of] Vestry

Linhaven Parish

At a Vestry held for Laying the leavy 24th October 1744

Mr. Henry Barlow Minister   Colo. Jacob Ellegood Churchwarden

Present
Mr. Edward Hack Moseley   Capt. Anthony Moseley
Mr. John Hunter   Mr. John Whitehurst   Vestry men
Mr. John Gornto   Mr. Job Gasking

The Parrish is . . . . Debtor	li. Tobo:
To the Reverend Mr. Henry Barlow minister	16000
To Mr. Thomas Grainger clerk of the Church	1000
To Capt. William Keeling clerk of the Eastern Shore Chappel	1000
To Mr. Dauley Latter clerk of the Upper Chappel	1000
To the Collector for the Conveniency of the ministers tobo:	4000
To Francis Moseley for Cleaning the Church &ca:	300
To Thomas Moore for keeping Edmond Ellegood child	400
To Capt. William Keeling for Cleaning the Eastern Shore Chappel	100
To Michael Fentriss for keeping Aron Sugg's child	400
To William Oakham for keeping Eliza. Oakhams child	400
To Mary Morris towards her releif	400
To John Ashby for keeping his wifes mother	500
To Paul Riggby for keeping Thomas Berry	450
To Elizabeth Harmon for keeping Knowland child	550
To William Dyer for cleaning Upper Chappel & Sinking a well	270
To John Holt for keeping his mother	500
To Thomas Cartwright for boarding Benjamin Burrowgh	500
To Edward Brown for keeping Axtead's [?] wife & 3 children	775
To Tully Robinson Smyth for one leavy overchargd last Year	61 3/4
To William Horsley for ditto	61 3/4

To Doctor Happer for Sallivating Katherine Cotton the 2nd time	510
To Arthur Sayer Clerk of the Vestry & per account	900
To the Churchwardens (for Oden Whitehurst & Henry Chapmans Estate)	1265
To ditto for repairs on the Gleeb houses	2000
To Cockroft Old for keeping another of Knowlands Children	500
To ditto for keeping James Barbers child about 3 months	125
To John Lamount for keeping Richard Adams	800
To Doctor Paterson for service done Edward Ward	100
To Barbara Keeling for nursing ditto	100
To Capt. James Condon for Insolvants	560
6 per Ct. for accounting & 4 per Ct. for cask on 35528½	3552
	39080½
Cr: By 1482 Tythables @ 26¼ per pole 38902½	
fraction carryed to the County leavy 178	39080½

[42] Ordered that Mr. Charles Smyth Sherif receive from Each Tythable person Twenty six & one quarter pounds of tobo. as Above for the parrish leavy this year, & make payment thereof to Each claimer as Above directed.

           Jacob Ellegood

In Obedience to An Order of Princess Ann County Court Bearing Date the 4th July 1744 We of the Jury have met upon the Land in Dispute Between Major Solomon Wilson & Capt. James Moore & having Weighed their papers & Evidence to us Produced & According to the Same have with the Surveyor of the said County Laid Out the said Land as Followeth towit Begining at a Markt Oak Near to Spratts Landing thence Runing along the Division Line that was Formerly made Between Francis & Thorowgood Spratt North East 60 degrees One Hundred & Sixty five pole to a red Oak Near the New Road Cleared by the said Major Solomon Wilson thence North West 15 degrees to the beaver Dams & adjoining to Henry Holmes Thence binding upon the said Holmes & Chapmans Creeks According to their Natural Bounds to the first Begining Oak Containing One Hundred Acres Being set apart by us for said Wilson & this our report Given Under our hands this 1st day of August 1744.

    William Hancock Senior & Seal James Carraway & Seal
    Edward Denby & Seal   Henry Holmes & Seal
    John Nicholas & Seal   William Dennie & Seal
    Nathaniel McClenahan & Seal Tully R. Smith & Seal
    John Harper & Seal   James Langley & Seal
    James Williamson & Seal   James Williams & Seal

        James Nimmo Surveyor & Seal

[43] Linhaven Parrish

At a Vestry held for laying the Leavy the 14th October 1745

Reverend Mr. Henry Barlow Minister Colo. Anthony Walke }
                 Colo. Jacob Ellegood } Churchwardens

Present {
Mr. Job Gasking   Mr. John Hunter
Mr. John Whitehurst Mr. John Gornto
Capt: George Wishart Capt. Anthony Moseley
Capt. James Nimmo
} Vestrymen

    The Parrish is . . . . Dr: [li. Tobo:]

To the Reverend Mr. Henry Barlow Convenient	16000
To Mr. Thomas Grainger clerk of the Church	1000

To Capt. William Keeling clerk [of the] Eastern Shore Chappel	1000
To Mr. Dauley Latter Clerk of the Upper Chappel	1000
To the Collector for Conveniency of the ministers tobo.	4000
To Francis Moseley for cleaning the Church &ca.	300
To Thomas Moore for keeping Edmond Ellegood's child	300
To Capt. William Keeling for cleaning Eastern Shore Chappel	100
To Michael Fentriss for keeping Aron Suggs child	400
To William Oakham for keeping Eliza. Oakhams child	250
To John Lamount for keeping Richard Adams	204
To William Dyer for cleaning the Upper Chappel well	200
To John Holt for keeping his mother	800
To Sarah Whitehurst for keeping Francis Cotton	800
To John Williams for keeping his Grandson	200
To William Crompton for making George Williams coffen	75
To Dauley Latter for Reading burial over Thomas Berry	50
To Henry Lamount & Nelly Jones for keeping Richard Adams 11 months	600
To John Casteel for keeping Francis Ellegoods child	400
To Horatio Woodhouse for tarring the Upper Chappel	100
To Edmond Absolum for keeping one of Katherine Knowlands children	200
To Thomas Cartwright for keeping & Burying Anne Douton	200
To Barbara Keeling for keeping Katherine Knowland child	400
To Doctor William Happer as per account	2990
To the Church wardens to be laid out in repairs on the Gleeb	10000
To Alexander Jameson towards his support	400
To John Ashby for keeping his father & wifes mother	500
To Cockroft Old for keeping another Knowlands children	500
To John Whitehead for keeping Thomas Berry about 6 months	500
To doctor James Blair for Sallivating Elizabeth Spann	500
To Henry Moore for boarding ditto	500
To Mr. Thomas Grainger for reading buriall Williams & Horsley	100
To William Martin for making coffen for said Williams	50
To Thomas Cartwright for nursing Robert Taylor	500
To Arthur Sayer Clerk of the Vestry & by account	360
6 per Ct. for accounting & 4 per Ct. for cask on 53479	5347
	58826
Cr: By 1491 Tythables @ 39-1/4 per pole 58521	
fraction carryed to the County leavy 305	58826

VESTRY BOOK OF LYNNHAVEN PARISH

[44] Ordered that Capt. William Cox Sherif receive from Each Tythable Thirty nine & one quarter pounds of Tobo. for the parrish leavy this Year & make payment thereof to Each claimer as Above directed

Linhaven Parrish

At a Vestry held for laying the Leavy the 9th day of October 1746

The Reverend Mr. Henry Barlow   Col. Anthony Walke & } Churchwardens
                                    Col. Jacob Ellegood

Present { Mr. Job Gasking   Capt. James Kempe
          Major Nathaniel Newton   Mr. John Gornto   } Vestry men
          Capt. Anthony Moseley   Mr. John Hunter

The Parrish is ....Dr.	[ll. Tobo.]
To the reverend Mr. Henry Barlow minister Convenient	16000
To Mr. Thomas Grainger Clerk of the Church	1000
To Capt. William Keeling clerk of the Eastern Shore Chappel	1000
To Mr. Doyley Latter clerk of the Upper Chappel	1000
To the Collector for Conveniency of the ministers tobo.	4000
To Robert Whitehurst for cleaning the Church	300
To Thomas Moore for keeping Edmond Ellegoods child	200
To Capt. William Keeling for cleaning Eastern Shore Chappel	100
To Michael Fentriss for keeping Aron Suggs child	200
To Mullatto Nell for keeping Richard Adams	800
To William Dyer for Cleaning Upper Chappel & well	200
To John Holt for keeping his mother	800
To John Ashby for keeping his wifes mother	500
To Edmond Absolum for keeping one of Katherine Knowlands Children	500
To Cockroft Old for keeping another K: Knowlands children	500
To Thomas Moore senior for Coffen & burying John Marsh	40
To widow Marsh for keeping John Marsh's child	250
To Mr. Barlow 1 leavy overchargd last year	67½
To Barbara Keeling for nursing Katherine Knowland	700
To Alexander Jimason towards his releif	300
To Arthur Sayer as by account	460
To Mr. Doyley Latter for reading burial Marsh & wife	60
6 per Ct. for Accounting & 4 per Ct. for cask on 28977½	2897
	31874½
Cr. By 1496 Tythables @ 21-1/4 per pole 31790	
Fraction Carryed to the County leavy 84½	31874½

[45] Resolv'd that a fram'd poarch of Eight foot long & six foot wide be built at the door of the dwelling house at the gleeb, & to be shingled, the work plain, & windoe shutters made for the windoes below & two flooers above to be made good.

Linhaven Parrish

At a Vestry held for laying the Leavy the 14th day of October 1747

Colo. Anthony Walke } Churchwardens
Colo. Jacob Ellegood

Present:
Capt. James Kempe
Mr. John Bonney
Mr. John Hunter
Capt. James Nimmo
Mr. John Gornto
} Vestry men

The Parrish [is] . . . . Dr: [li. Tobo.]

To the Reverend Mr. Henry Barlow Convenient	12000
To Mr. Thomas Grainger Clerk of the Church	1000
To Capt. William Keeling Clerk of the Eastern Shore Chappel	1000
To Mr. Doyley Latter Clerk of the Upper Chapel	340
To Mr. Cason Moore Clerk of the Upper Chapel 6 months	500
To the Collector for Collecting the ministers Tobo:	3000
To Robert Whitehurst for cleaning the Church	300
To Thomas Banks for keeping Benjamin Burrowgh	800
To Alec Marsh for keeping John Marsh an infant	400
To Thomas Moore for keeping Edmond Ellegoods child	200
To Capt. William Keeling for cleaning Eastern Shore Chappel	100
To John Lamount for keeping Richard Adams	800
To William Dyer for cleaning the Upper Chappel & well	200
To John Holt for keeping his mother	800
To John Ashby for keeping his wifes mother	500
To Edmond Absolum for keeping Katherine Knowlands Child	500
To Cockroft Old for keeping another Said Knowlands Child	400
To William Cason for keeping John Williams	200
To Barbara Keeling for keeping & Burying Katherine Knowland	840
To William Wiggin for painting & Glasing Gleeb &ca.	205
To Doctor Happer as by account	650
To Arthur Sayer Clerk of the vestry & by account	340
To the Churchwardens for books for chappels	1000
To the Reverend Mr. Robert Dickson Convenient	4000
To the Collector for Conveniency of ditto	1000
6 per Ct. for Accounting & 4 per Ct. for cask on 31075	3107
	34182
Cr: By 1543 Tythables @ 22 per pole 33946	
Fraction Carryed to the County Leavy 236	34182

Ordered that the Sherif receive from Each Tythable person in this parrish seventeen and a half [sic] pounds of neat Tobo. being the parrish leavy this year & make payment thereof to Each claimer as above directed

Pursuant to an Act of Assembly directing the processioning of Lands we do Order that the severall persons hereafter named, do warn in the Inhabitants in their Severall precincts to go & Procession all the Lands therein, taking care to Comply with the said act, & to continue from their begining untill they shall fully Compleat the Same. Persons appointed to perform the said processioning are William Robinson & John Ince[?] for the northside of the Eastern Branch, John Scott & William Martin the south side, John Moore & Adam Keeling for the lower precinct of the Eastern Shore, John Gornto junior, John Booth, Josias Morris junior & James Malbone for the Upper precinct of the Eastern Shore, Jonathan Saunders & James Ashley for Little Creek, Argall Thorowgood & John Harper junior, Arthur Whitehurst & Lemuel Fentriss son of John for the western Shore precinct, James Blair & John Simons for black water precinct

Anthony Walke

Linhaven Parrish

At a Vestry held the 13 day of July 1748

The Reverend Mr. Robert Dickson minister   Col. Anthony Walke Churchwarden

Present { Major Nathaniel Newton   Capt. James Kempe
          Mr. Job Gasking   Capt. James Nimmo } Vestrymen
          Major Thomas Walke   Mr. John Whitehurst

Resolved that the flooers of the old part of the Gleeb house above & below, be new laid, the uper flooers to be grovd, the under flooers only square joynt, new Sleepers, the roof to be new Shingled, & the dormands to be made Sash lights, new door case for the front doors & a poarch Eight by six foot well shingled to be built over the Same, the other outward doors to have Shells over them, & all the out doores to be made new, the wi[n]does to be mended & new Shetters made below, poarch over the seller door to be repair

Anthony Walke

[47]
Linhaven Parrish

At a Vestry held the 30th day of July 1748

The Reverend Mr. Robert Dickson minister   Col. Anthony Walke
                                            Col. Jacob Ellegood   Churchwardens

Present { Major Nathaniel Newton   Capt. James Kempe
          Mr. Edward Hack Moseley Mr. Job Gasking } Vestrymen
          Capt. George Wishart   Mr. John Gornto

This day Agreed with Samuel Hollowell to Shingle the roof of the old part of the Gleeb house, to make new flooers above & below the upper flooers to be grovd the under flooers to be Square joynt, dormands to have new frames & Sash lights , four doors above Stairs to be made new, & casings thereon, new Sleepers, four outside & three inside doors below the Stairs to be new done, a poarch over the Seller door to be repaird, one other poarch Eight by six foot over the front doore to be well framd, Shingled & finishd, three shells over the the other out doors, new door case to the front door & window Shetters to the Lower windoes, the said Hollowell to find himself & workmen dyet &ca. & to find all the plank, nails & whatever is wanting to Compleat to the above work, In Consideration of all which the Said Hollowell is to be paid by the parrish the sum of forty seven pounds Ten Shillings as full Satisfaction for the same, Thirty pound of which said sum is to be paid the Said Hollowell Immediately to Enable him to carry on the said work, & the remainder to be paid him when the work is fully Compleated in workmanlike manner

Anthony Walke

[48]
Linhaven Parrish

At a Vestry held for laying the leavy October 10th 1748

The Reverend Mr. Robert Dickson minister   Col. Anthony Walke } Churchwardens
                                            Col. Jacob Ellegood

Present { Capt. James Kempe   Major Nathaniel Newton
          Capt. James Nimmo   Mr. John Hunter
          Major Thomas Walke   Mr. John Whitehurst } Vestrymen
          Mr. John Gornto   Capt. George Wishart

VESTRY BOOK OF LYNNHAVEN PARISH

The Parrish [is] Dr:	[li. Tobo:]
To the Reverend Mr. Robert Dickson Minister Convenient	12000
To Mr. Thomas Grainger Clerk of the Church	1000
To Capt. William Keeling Clerk [of the] Eastern Shore Chappel	1000
To Mr. Cason Moore Clerk of the Upper Chappel	1000
To Mary Morris towards her releif	400
To the Collector for Conveniency of the ministers Tobo:	3000
To Robert Whitehurst for Cleaning the Church	300
To Alec Marsh for keeping John Marsh an Infant	400
To Thomas Moore for keeping Edmond Ellegoods child	200
To Capt. William Keeling for cleaning the Eastern Shore Chappel	100
To Cockroft Old for keeping & burying Richard Adams	950
To William Dyer for Cleaning the Upper Chappel & well	200
To John Holt for keeping his mother	800
To John Ashby for keeping his wifes mother	500
To Cockroft Old for keeping two of Katherine Knowlands children	800
To William Cason for keeping John Williams	300
To Thomas Cartwright for Nursing Eliza. Southern (to be paid Col. Walke)	1200
To Arthur Sayer Clerk of the vestry & by account	450
To the Churchwardens for repairs on the Gleeb	10000
To Robert Wood towards his releif	300
To John Sherwood for keeping his wifes mother	400
To Mary Whitehurst for keeping Mary McClary	400
To the Churchwardens for cure of Jobsons children	800
To Barbara Keeling for keeping William Sutton Whites child	400
To Doctor Happer for Sallivating Elizabeth Southern	1000
To William Dale for keeping Ruth McBrides child	400
To John Airs for keeping Robert Wood 4 months	200
6 per Ct. for accounting & 4 per Ct. for Cask on 38500	3850
	42350
Cr: By 1559 Tythables @ 27 per pole 42093	
Fraction Carryed to the County 257	42350

Ordered that the Sherif receive from Each Tythable person in this Parrish [twenty seven] pounds of Tobo: being the parrish leavy this year and make payment thereof to Each claimer as above directed

[49] Agreed by this vestry that James Kempe, Nathaniel Newton and John Hunter Gentlemen view & se[e] that the work now doing in & About the gleeb house be faithfully done & in workmanlike manner by Samuel Hollowell who is Imployd to do the Said work   Anthony Walke

VESTRY BOOK OF LYNNHAVEN PARISH 41

Lynhaven Parrish

At a Vestry held for laying the Leavy October 26th 1749

The Reverend Mr. Robert Dickson Minister   Col. Anthony Walke } Church Wardens
                                            Col. Jacob Ellegood

Present:
- Major Nathaniel Newton
- Mr. Job Gasking
- Mr. John Whitehurst
- Mr. John Gornto
- Capt. James Kempe
- Major Thomas Walke
- Mr. John Whitehead

Vestry men

The Parrish is . . . . . . Debtor   [ll. Tobo:]

To the Reverend Mr. Robert Dickson Minister Convenient	16000
To Mr. Thomas Grainger Clerk of the Church	1500
To Capt. William Keeling Clerk of the Eastern Shore Chappel	625
To Mr. Cason Moore Clerk of the Upper Chappel	1500
To Mary Morris towards her releif	400
To the Collector for Conveniency of the ministers Tobo:	4000
To Major Francis Moseley for Cleaning the Church	300
To Alec Marsh for keeping John Marsh an Infant	400
To Peter Ellet for keeping the Eastern Shore chappel	100
To William Dyer for cleaning the Upper Chappel & well	200
To John Holt for keeping his mother	800
To John Ashby for keeping his wifes mother	500
To Cockroft Old for keeping two of Katherine Knowlands children	700
To William Cason for keeping John Williams	300
To Arthur Sayer Clerk [of the] vestry & by account	615
To Charles Edwards (one leavy overchargd last year)	42
To Anne Land for ditto 42, & John Thorowgood Servant ditto 42	84
To John Sherwood for keeping his wifes mother	400
To John Airs for keeping Mary McClary	800
To Barbara Keeling for keeping one of Whites children	400
To William Dale for keeping Ruth McBrides child	400
To William Shurcraft for keeping Jones's child	400
To Robert Reed for keeping Elizabeth Southern 14 months	1160
To Adam Tooly for keeping ditto 2 months	160
To John Sullivant for repairing the Garden on the Gleeb Land	60
To Major Nathaniel Newton for negro & Cart carting pails [pales] for do:	20
To Andrew Brand towards his releif	500
To John Hunter towards building a house for Mary Broughton	1000
To the Reverend Mr. Robert Dickson for deficiency of his Gleeb	2200
To Alexander Legget for work done on the gleeb house by account	720

To John Absolum by ditto 480. To Mrs. Dudley for boarding ditto 500:	980
To Col. Jacob Ellegood for lime &ca: for the Gleeb house	820
To Mark Wood for boarding 2 Jobson's [children] &ca: by account	748
To Richard Bell towards his releif	200
To Elizabeth Omerry for keeping William Smiths child	460
To William Wiggins for painting the Gleeb &ca: by account	270
To the Churchwardens to pay Capt. Hutchings, Wm: Cartwright & Ackiss	3460
6 per Ct. for accounting & 4 per Ct. for cask on 43224	4322
	47546
Cr: By sundrys for Scalps wanting 1634	
By By 1629 Tythables @ 28 per pole 45612	
Fraction carryed to the County leavy 300	47546

[50]

Ordered that Mr. William Keeling Sherif receive from Each Tythable person Twenty two & a half [sic] pounds of Neat Tobo. for the parrish Leavy this year, & make payment thereof to Each claimer as above directed

Anthony Walke

Lynhaven Parrish

At a Vestry held for laying the leavy October 29th, 1750

The Revd. Mr. Robert Dickson minister   Major Jacob Ellegood } Churchward's
                                           Major Thomas Walke

Present { Mr. Edward Hack Moseley   Capt. James Kempe } Vestry men
        { Capt. Anthony Moseley   Mr. Adam Tooly   }

The Parrish is . . . . Dr: li. Tobo:

To the Reverend Mr. Robert Dickson minister convenient	16000
To Mr. Thomas Grainger Clerk of the Church	1500
To Capt. William Keeling Clerk [of the] Eastern Shore Chappel	1500
To Mr. Cason Moore Clerk of the Upper Chapel	1500
To Mary Morris towards her releif	600
To the Collector for Conveniency of the ministers tobo.	4000
To Major Francis Moseley for cleaning the Church	300
To Alec Marsh for keeping John Marsh an Infant	300
To Elizabeth Dyer for cleaning the Upper Chappel & well	200
To John Holt for keeping his mother	800
To John Ashby for keeping his wifes mother	500
To Cockroft Old for keeping one of Katherine Knowlands children	300
To ditto for keeping William Smiths child to this time	530
To Adam Robertson for keeping Mary McClary	800
To Barbary Keeling for keeping Whites child	350
To Thomas Elks for keeping Jones's child	300

	To Robert Reed for keeping Elizabeth Southern	800
	To Adam Tooly for keeping Corn for Andrew Brand	370
	To James Williamson toward his releif	800
	To Jane Boyds toward her releif	600
	To Andrew Brand toward his releif	600
	To Mary Williams widow	200
	To Capt. John Thorowgood paid doctor for Francis Spratt	500
	To Mr. John Thorowgood for keeping Fra. Spratt	600
	To George Jameson for work done for the Gleeb house as by account	320
	To Charles Gasking for building a Dairy at the Gleeb	800
	To Thomas Owens for keeping William Lawrances child	400
[51]	To Thomas Duffe toward his releif	400
	To Col. Anthony Walke Collector of Parish & county account	1450
	To James Buchanan for keeping Duncan Kings child 14 months	600
	To Edward Denby as by account for Owen Brosier	250
	To Robert Wood toward his releif } to be paid to Major Walke	300
	To Richard Bell toward his releif }	200
	To Robert Cartwright for building a Barn at the Gleeb	5200
	To Norfolk County for Nursing & Burying Jane Hutson &ca:	1250
	To Major Thomas Walke ballance his account	1548
	To John Montgomery 1 leavy over Charged last year	41
	To John Robertson for keeping Henry James's children	500
	To Edward Moseley for painting the Gleeb house	600
	To John Manen[?] towards his releif	1000
	To Richard Dudley for pulling up apple tree &ca: at the Gleeb	275
	To Arthur Sayer Clerk of the vestry & by account	635
	6 per Ct. for accounting & 4 per Ct. for cask on 49769	4976
		54745
	Cr. By sundrys for scalps wanting 2550	
	By 1640 Tythables @ 31-3/4 per pole 52070	
	Fraction carryed to the County leavy 125	54745

Lynhaven Parish } At a Vestry held for laying the Leavy October 10th 1751

Col. Jacob Ellegood } Churchwardens
Major Thomas Walke }

Present {
Col. Anthony Walke
Major Nathaniel Newton
Mr. Adam Tooly
Capt. James Kempe
Capt. George Wishart
} [Vestrymen]

The Parish . . . . Dr:	to Tob:
To the Reverend Robert Dickson minister Convenient	16000
To the Collector for Conveniency of the Ministers Tob:	4000
To Thomas Grainger Clerk [of the] Church	1500
To Capt. William Keeling Clerk [of the] Eastern Shore Chappel	1500
To Mr. Cason Moore Clerk [of the] upper Chappel	1500
To Mr. Patrick Brooks [for] keeping the Church	300
To Elizabeth Dyer for Cleaning the upper Chappel & Well	200
To Peter Ellit for Cleaning Eastern Shore Chappel	100
To Mary Morris towards her Releif	600
To John Holt for keeping his Mother	800
To John Ashby for keeping his Wife's Mother	500
To Cockroft Old for keeping one of Catherine Knowlands children	200
To Ditto for keeping William Smyths Child 1/4 year	150
To Adam Robinson for keeping Mary McClary	500
To Barbary Keeling for keeping Whites Child	400
To Thomas Elks for keeping Jones's Child	300
To James Williamson towards his Releif	200
To Thomas Owens for keeping William Lawrence's Child	500
To Richard Bell towards his Releife	200
To Jane Boyde towards her Releife	600
To John Davis for keeping Sarah Leefley	400
To Batson Whitehurst for Ditto	150
To Ditto for keeping Robert Baily 8 months	200
To William Shipp for Ditto	70
To Mr. Argyle Thorowgood for keeping Benjamin Burrows {to keep him till Jan. next	1000
To Joseph Hodges for keeping Thomas Garnor	350
To Robert Thorowgood for Ditto	260
To Benjamin Moseley for Ditto	200
To Mr. Adam Tooly for Andrew Brand	260
To Mrs. Anne Blair for keeping Ditto [&] finding Necessaries	528
To Richard Rogers for keeping & burying Southerns Child	250
To Mr. Joel Cornick [for] burying John Sweeny	200
To Col. Anthony Walke per account	100
To Thomas Banks per Ditto	592
To Mr. Charles Gasking for Garden at the Glebe	1470

[52]

VESTRY BOOK OF LYNNHAVEN PARISH   45

To Richard Dudley per account	1756
To Elizabeth Dial for keeping Ruth McBrides Child	250
To John Harper for keeping Buckhanans Children 43 days	150
To Dr. Christ Wright for Sundry Services	4390
To Major Thomas Walke per account	1178
To Richard Brown for keeping Williams Child	150
To Peter Ellit for Cleaning the Spring, omitted last year	45
To Major Thomas Walke per account	180
To the Church Wardens towards the Erecting New Chappel at Eastern Shore	12250
To Thomas Grainger Clerk [of the] Vestry	250
6 per Ct. for accounting & 4 per Ct. for Cask on 56679	5667
	62346
Cr: By 1648 Tithables @ 37-3/4 per pole 62212	
Fraction Carry'd to the County Levy 134	62346

Ordered that Mr. William Keeling Sherriff receive from each Tithable person 29½ Nett Tobo. for the parish Leavy this Year ensuing & make Payment thereof to Each Claimer as above directed

[53] Pursuant to an Act of Assembly directing the processioning of Lands, We do order that the Several persons hereafter named do warn in the Inhabitants in their Several precincts to go and procession all the Lands therein, taking Care to Comply with the said Act & to Continue from their Begining untill they shall fully Compleat the Same. Persons appointed to perform the said processioning are David McClenehan and Thomas Lawson for the North Side of the Eastern Branch, William Ackiss and Nath Nicholas the South Side, William Woodhouse junior & William Keeling junior & John Keeling Junior & John Munden junior the Lower precinct of the Eastern Shore, John Gornto, Dennis Dauley, Henry White & John Whitehead junior for the upper precinct of the Eastern Shore, Jacob Hunter & Thurmer Hogwood for Little Creek precinct, John Biddle & Edward Denby junior for the lower precinct of the Western Shore, Edmund Absolam & Richard Whitehurst junior for the upper precinct of the Western Shore, Henry Tripp and James Tooley junior for Black water precint

Lyn haven parish } At a Vestry held friday August 21, 1752

Present Col. Anthony Walke, Col. Jacob Ellegood & Maj. Thos. Walke, Ch: Ward:

      Major Nathaniel Newton   Capt James Kempe
      Capt. Anthony Moseley   Capt. George Wishart
      Mr. John Hunter

Ordered that the parson preach at each of the Chappels in equal turns with the Church, being every third Sunday

Ordered that there be a Church Yard Raild in with Cedar Rails & posts about 120 feet from East to West & about 140 ft. from North to South with two Gates &ca: And that Col. Anthony Walke, Col. Jacob Ellegood, Major Thomas Walke, Capt. James Kempe, Major Nathaniel Newton or any two of them to agree with Workmen to do the same.

[54] Lynhaven Parish } At a Vestry held fryday October 13th 1752   Col. Jacob Ellegood } Church wardens
                                                                                                                   Major Thomas Walke

Present Reverend Mr. Robert Dickson, Col. Anthony Walke, Capt. James Kempe, Capt. Arther Sayer, Capt. James Nimmo, Mr. Edward Hack Moseley, Capt. Anthony Moseley, Capt. George Wishart, Capt. John Whitehurst, John Bonney, senior

The Parish . . . . Dr:

To the Reverend Mr. Robert Dickson minister Convenient	16000
To 4 per Ct. Shrinkage on Ditto for 1751 & 1752	1280
To the Collector for Conveniency of the Ministers Tob.	4000
To Thomas Grainger Clerk of the Church	1500
To Capt. William Keeling Clerk of the Eastern Shore Chappel	1500
To Mr. Cason Moore Clerk of the upper Chappel	1500
To Mr. Anthony McKeel for keeping the Church	300
To Mrs. Margaret Ellit for Cleaning Chappel 1751 & 1752	200
To Ditto for Cleaning the Spring One Leavy	35
To Mrs. Elizabeth Dyer for Cleaning the Pungo Chappel and Well	200
To Mary Morris towards her Relief	600
To Mary Broughton	400
To John Holt [for] keeping his Mother	800
To John Ashby for keeping his Wife's Mother 6 months & Burying	300
To Ditto for keeping Sherwoods Child Six months	100
To Cockruft Olds for keeping Catherine Knowlands Child	200
To Adam Robinson for keeping Mary McClary 2 months	083
To Mary Otterson for Ditto 10 months	417
To Barbary Keeling for keeping Whites Child	200
To Ditto for keeping Sarah Leefly 1 Year	1200
To Thomas Ellis for keeping Jones' Child	
To James Williamson towards his Relief	200
To Thomas Owens for boarding attendance &c. Benj. Burrough 7 months ⎫	
To Ditto for Alexander Jameson 2 months 10 days ⎬	2000
To Ditto Robert Patteson a Boy for 1 month 10 days ⎭	
To John Snail for keeping Lawrences Child	400
To Richard Bell towards his Relief	200
To Jane Boyde towards her Relief	600
To Batson Whitehurst for keeping Robert Baily 3½ months	146
To Elizabeth Wilbur for Ditto	187
To Elizabeth Dial for keeping Ruth McBrides Child	200
To Sarah Dyer keeping James Sharwoods Child	400
To Ann Norris for keeping Duncan Kings Child	300
To William May for keeping Buchanans Child	600
To Mr. Matthew Pallet for keeping & Burying John Burfoot	400

[55]

To Alexander Leggit for keeping Sarah Albin 4 months	400
To John Murril for keeping Ditto 4 months	400
To Mr. Joel Simmons for keeping Love Stokes 4 weeks Small pox	700
To William Oakham for keeping his Daughters Child	200
To James Peetree for keeping Alexander Jameson 8½ months @ 10/	850
To Frances Petree for her Service in Attendance 8½ months @ 5/	425
To Mr. William Consaul for keeping Abegail Higgins 2 months & 9 days	250
To Ann Russel for Ditto finding Sugar & Wine 2 months & 2 days	310
To Dr. George Rovier for Sundry Services	4000
To Dr. Christopher Wright for Ditto	4000
To Mrs. Mary Dyson as Assignee of Francis Dyson for keeping Thomas Garnor 10 weeks	700
To Major Thomas Walke per account	1484
To Col. Anthony Walke per account	119
To Thomas Owens for keeping Alexander Jameson, Robert Patteson One Month, Making Clothes as per Account	400
To Thomas Cartwright for keeping Robert Patteson 5 months	500
To the Church Wardens for Errecting the Eastern Shore Chappel	12250
To Keeping & burying Mary Grines allow'd to Barbara Keeling	250
To Col. Ellegood for & in behalf of Benjamin Burrough	1000
To Dr. Arthur Campbel Medecines & Attendance for Thomas Gardner	430
To Thomas Grainger Clerk [of the] Vestry	1250
To Charges for Nursing Elizabeth Moore during Smallpox to the Church wardens of Elizabeth River parish	1200
To Major Nathaniel Newton Summoning Jury on a Drowned Man	180
To 6 per Ct. for accounting & 4 per Ct. for Cask on 66246	6624
	72870
Cr. By 1702 Tithables at 42-3/4 per pole 72760	
By Fraction Carried to County Leavy 110	72870

Ordered that the Sheriff or Church wardens Receive from each Tithable 33-1/4 Nett Tobaco for the Parish Leavy this Year Ensuing and make payment thereof to Each Claimer as above directed

        Anthony Walke

[56] At a Vestry held the 16th Day of May 1752

  Present Reverend Mr. Robert Dickson Major Thomas Walke a Church Warden

    Col. Anthony Walke, Major Nathaniel Newton, Capt. James Kempe, Capt. Anthony Moseley

Orderd and Appointed by this Vestry that Capt. William Keeling and Mr. Francis Thorowgood Land officiate as Vestry Men in the Parish of Lynhaven

Ordered by this Vestry That any One or Singular the above Members of this Vestry do purchase from the Estate of Mr. John Dudly deceas'd fifty Acres of Land, for the Use of the Glebe of the Parish of Lynhaven and the Purchaser is hereby by this Vestry impowerd to take Money upon Interest to defray the Charges of the Same

Lynhaven Parish

At a Vestry held the 1st of October 1753

Reverend Mr. Robert Dickson Minister   Capt. James Kempe } Church Wardens
                                        Capt. William Keeling }

Present   Col. Anthony Walke   Capt. Anthony Moseley   Major Thomas Walke
          Major Nathaniel Newton   Capt. George Wishart   Mr. Job Gasking
          Capt. John Whitehurst   Mr. Francis Land
          Mr. William Woodhouse

	lb. Tob.
The Parish . . . . is Dr:	
To the Reverend Mr. Robert Dickson minister Convenient	16000
To 4 per Ct. Shrinkage on Ditto	640
To the Collector for Collecting ministers Tobacco	4000
To Thomas Grainger Clerk [of the] Church	1500
To Mr. Charles Gasking Clerk [of the] Eastern Shore Chappel 6 months	750
To Mr. Cason Moore Clerk [of the] upper Chappel	1500
To Mr. Anthony McKeel for keeping the Church	300
To Ditto for keeping Abigail Mason 3 months	300
To Mary Ellit for keeping Clean the Chappel	100
To Mary Ellit for Cleaning the Spring	35
To Ditto [for] keeping Robert Baily 5 months 5 days	250
To Mrs. Elizabeth Dyer for Cleaning Pungo Chappel and Well	200
To Mary Morrise toward her Relief	600
To Mary Broughton	
To John Holt	
To Cockroft Old for keeping Catherine Knowlands Child	
To Mary Otterson for keeping Mary McClary 5½ months	230
To Mary Morriset for keeping Ditto 6 months	250
To Barbary Keeling keeping Whites Child	200
To Ditto keeping Sarah Leefly 10 months	1000
To Richard Bell towards his Relief	300
To Willoughby Ayres keeping James Sharwoods Child	400
To Ann Norris keeping Duncan Kings Child	300
To Cockroft Old keeping Buchannans Child	
To Mr. Robert Huggins for keeping Alexander Jameson 3½ months @ 10/ and Dressing his Leg	400
To Capt. William Keeling (deceased) his Estate 5 months attendance as Clerk	625

[57]

VESTRY BOOK OF LYNNHAVEN PARISH 49

To Mr. Charles Gasking per account	365
To the Church Wardens toward Erecting a Chappel at the Eastern Shore	25000
To Major Nathaniel Newton Railing the Church Yard post Gates &c. per account £10/15s/4d	2153
To Anthony McKeel per Account £2/5s	250
To Col. Anthony Walke & Son per Account	420
To Mrs. ---- Cone for keeping Boyds 2 Children 6 months	800
To John Keeling keeping Chambers 2 Children 3 months	240
To Ditto for keping Ben Burroughs Child 3 months @ 5/	150
To Capt. Lemuel Cornick for Insolvents Year 1752	1198
To Mr. Thurmur Hogwood [Hoggard] Coffin for Jane Boyd	53
To John Snail keeping William Lawrances Child	400
To the Church Wardens for maintainance of Boyds 2 Children ensuing year	1000
To Ditto to be Sold for Doctor Christopher Wrights Account of £42/5/6:	8455
To Robert Cartwright for making Coffin for Robert Patterson	50
To John Lamount for keeping and burying Sarah Albin	600
To Thomas Grainger Clerk [of the] Vestry	250
To 6 per Ct. for Accounting & 4 per Ct. for Cask on 71264	7126
	78390
To Capt. Lemuel Cornick allowance on 1198 Nett	299
To 10 per Ct. for Accounting & Cask	29
	78718
[Cr:] By 1263 Tithables at 48½ per pole 78715	

Orderd that the Sheriff or Church Wardens receive

[58]

Vestry Men Chosen — Capt. William Keeling, Mr. William Woodhouse, Mr. Francis Thorowgood Land, being Chosen Vestry Men of this Parish and having taken all the Oaths enjoind, and Subscribed the Test, are Admitted Members of the said Vestry

New Church Wardens — Agreed and Appointed by this Vestry that Capt. James Kempe & Capt. William Keeling Officiate as Church Wardens for the ensuing Year

Money at Interest — Resolved by this Vestry in Persuance to an Order passd the Last Vestry for taking up fifty pounds upon Interest for the purchasing an Addition to the Glebe Lands, that Maj. Thos.Walke having take[n] the above Sum of Fifty Pounds from Mr. Robert Dickson upon Interest That the said Thomas Walke pay the Lawful Interest of the Same unto the said Mr. Robert Dickson

Place New Chapple — Resolved by the Majority of three Voices of this Vestry That at or near Adjoining the place where the present Eastern Shore Chapple now Stands is a fit and Convenient Place to Erect a New Chapple & that the same be there Erected

Dimensions New Chapple — Resolved that the New Chapple at the Eastern Shore be built Fifty five foot Long, Twenty five feet wide in the Clear, with a Convenient Large Gallery not to be Less than Eighteen feet in Width at the West End, the Walls of the Said Chapple to be eighteen feet in Height, with three Windows on Each Side, two at the East End, and one in the Gallery. The Windows to be of the same Dimension with the Church Windows, The Communion to be Raild & Ballastered, The Walls of the said Church to be two Brick and half thick from the foundation to the Water Table and two brick thick upward, The Windows to be of good Crown Glass 8 by 10, In 6 lights by three beside the Arch. The Middle Isle to be five feet wide with four Wainscot pews two on the North and two on the South Side thereof, with a Decent Desk and pulpit the Whole Church to be Compleatly painted where tis requisite of a Sky Colour. The Covering [Roof] of the said Chappel to be of good heart Cypress Shingles and all the rest of the Work to be finish[ed] in a Workman-like manner after the Moddel of the Church

[59] At this Vestry the aforesaid Chappel being put up to the Lowest Bidder Mr. Joseph Mitchel of Norfolk having the Last Vote Voted to undertake and Compleat the aforesaid Chappel in a Workman-like manner by Christmas next Come Twelve months for Three Hundred and Twenty four Pounds Ten Shilling and he is According[ly] to Enter into Bond for the good performance of the Same

This Already Entered

Resolved by this Vestry in persuance to an Order passd the Last Vestry for taking up fifty pounds upon Interest for the purchasing an Addition to the Glebe Land that Major Thomas Walke having taken the above Sum of Mr. Robert Dickson that the said Thomas Walke pay the Lawful Interest thereof to the said Mr. Robert Dickson

Agreed that Anthony McKeel keep Abigail Mason the ensuing Year and that he be allowed for his trouble Twelve hundred lbs Tobacco

And that William Carrol, or any other person, keep Mary McClary the ensuing Year & that they be allowed Eight Hundred lbs Tobacco

Brought forward—

An Account of the whole Sum of Tobacco Levied for 1753	78718
To Mary Broughtons Relief	400
To 6 per Ct. for Accounting [&] 4 per Ct. for Cask on 400	40
To Col. Anthony Walke paid Thomas Williamson per Account for Benches at the Church	215
To plank for Ditto and Cartage for Ditto	125
To 6 per Ct. for Accounting [&] 4 per Ct. for Cask on 340	34

Orderd that the Sheriff or Church Warden receive from each Tithable 39-1/4 Nett Tobacco for the parish Levy this year Ensuing and make payment thereof to each Claimer as above directed

Anthony Walke

[60] At a Vestry held the 11th of October 1754

Present Revd. Mr. Robert Dickson minister Capt. James Kempe & Capt. William Keeling } Ch: Wardens

Vestry Men Col. Anthony Walke Col. Nathaniel Newton Major Thomas Walke
Mr. William Woodhouse Mr. John Whitehead Capt. George Wishart

The Parish is Dr:

To the Reverend Mr. Robert Dickson minister Convenient	16000
To 4 per Ct. Shrinkage on Ditto	640
To def[ic]iency Shrinkage Levied gross 1752 & 1753	258
To Thomas Grainger Clerk of the Church	1200
To Mr. Charles Gasking Clerk [of the] Eastern Shore Chappel	1200
To Mr. Cason Moore Clerk of Pungo Chappel	1200
To Hillery Pitt cleaning the Church	160
To Richard Davis keeping and Cleaning Eastern Shore Chappel	80
To Ditto Cleaning the Spring	28

	To Mrs. Elizabeth Dyer [for] cleaning pungo Chapel & Well	160
	To Mary Morris towards her Relief	480
	To Mary Broughton for Ditto	320
	To Cockroft Old [for] keeping Catherine Knowlands Child	160
	To William Carrol for keeping Mary McClary One year	640
	To Rob Dearmore [for] keeping Sarah Lufley 9 months 18 days	764
	To Richard Bew towards his Relief	160
	To Willoughby Aires [for] keeping James Sharwood Child	320
	To William Bonny to keeping Thomas Jones 20 days & Cartage	64
	To Anne Russel [for] keeping Thomas Jones 40 days	107
	To John Malbone [for] keeping Thomas Jones 3 months	200
	To Barbary Keeling [for] keeping Sarah Leefley 6 months 9 days	504
	To James Williamson [for] keeping & interring Abigail Mason	640
	To Reverend Mr. Dickson Interest on 50	400
	To Capt. Lemuel Cornick for Insolvants	171
	To Francis Harvey keeping the Church 4 months	80
	To Anne Norrice [for] keeping Duncan Kings Child	160
	To Mr. John Keeling [for] keeping Benjamin Burroughs	840
	To Doctor Christopher Wright per account £12.3.4	1948
	To Samuel Wilbur One Levy 6/9	55
[61]	To Anne Russel per account £3.4.6	516
	To William May [for] keeping Abigail Mason 5 months	400
	To ChurchWardens [for] maintaining Boyds 2 Children	800
	To Anthony McKeel besides paying the Doctor	400
	To Ditto omitted Last year in his account £2.5	160
	To Mary Brewer one Leavy 6/9	55
	To The Church Wardens Erecting Eastern Shore Chapel	14400
	To Doctor George Rouviere for curing Abigail Mason	800
	To William Batten [for] keeping Gibbs Children	560
	To Captain John Hutchings per account Abigail Mason	24
	To Elizabeth Oliver [for] keeping Mary Olivers Child	400
	To Col. Newton [for] Inquisition on John Guin	147
	To Cockroft Old [for] keeping Buchannans Child 2 years	480
	To Col. Anthony Walke per Account	174½
	To Thomas Grainger Clerk [of the] Vestry	200
	To 6 per Ct. for Accounting on 48455	2907
		51362

Cr: By 1721 Tithable at 29-3/4 is   51199

By Fraction Carryd to County Leavy   163   51362

Ordered that the Church Wardens or the Collector receive from each Tithable Twenty Nine Pounds and three quarters of a Pound of nett Tobacco for the Parish Leavy this year and make payment to each Claimer [as] above directed

January 2nd [1755]   Anthony Walke

Agreed in the above Vestry also that William May keep Buchanans Child for 100 pounds of Tobacco

Likewise that Capt. Kempe pay out of the Parish Money Six pounds to Mary Cartwright for keeping Alexander Jameson

Likewise agreed with Sarah Oakham to keep her Daughters Child the ensuing year and that she have 250 pounds Tobacco.

[62] Memorandum of Repairs to be made at the Chapple at Pungo agreed with Thomas Williamson to Compleat November 2nd 1754 Viz: To put in all New Sils & Sleepers of Good Oak, and Lay the floor all new with good seasoned plank 1⅛" All the Pews and Seats &c to be taken down and Carefully put up again also the Galery Seats repaired: to put in what Shingles is wanting in the Cover [roof] and find Tarr & put on the Same. And Paint the Windows. The whole to be Compleatly repaired in a good & Workman-Like manner for which and on Compleating the Same The Vestry have agreed to give and allow him the said Thomas Williamson £20 to be Levied next October

At a Vestry held this Twelfth day of March 1754 [/55]

Present Revd. Robert Dickson Minister   Capt. James Kempe } Church Wardens
                                             Capt. William Keeling}

    Col. Anthony Walke   Col. Nathaniel Newton   Major Thomas Walke
    Capt. George Wishart   Mr. John Bonney   Mr. William Woodhouse
    & Mr. Francis Thorowgood Land   Vestrymen

This Day Received from Mr. Joseph Mitchel the New Eastern Shore Chappel and do discharge him from his obligation of Building and finishing the Same the above Vestry being Satisfied with his performance thereof

                                                       Anthony Walke

Editor's Note: Since this entry, dated 12th March, 1754, comes between the minutes for 11th October, 1754, and those for 15th August, 1755, it was manifestly misdated in accordance with the old style calendar, which had been abandoned in 1752, and under which the year 1755 did not begin until March 25, instead of on January 1, as required by the Calendar Act, which made the change. The existing third Eastern Shore Chapel was therefore completed in 1755, instead of 1754, as inscribed over its west doorway.

At a Vestry held the 15th day of August 1755

Present Capt. William Keeling   Church Warden

Vestry Men   Col. Anthony Walke   Col. Nathaniel Newton   Major Thomas Walke
            Mr. William Woodhouse   Capt. George Wishart   Mr. Francis Thorowgood Land

[63] Pursuant to an Act of Assembly for preventing Controversies Concerning the bounds of Land, That once in every four Years the Bounds of every Persons Land shall be processioned & gone round, and the Land marks renewed, and for dividing this parish into Convenient precincts, and for appointing intelligent freeholders for the performing such processioning, at Such a time as Shall to the said Vestry seem Convenient, and to see that such processionings be duely performed between the Last day of September and the Last day of March next Ensuing, and for receiving an Account in return of every person's Land so processioned as also their failure herein, and their particular reasons for so failing, and also for keeping and providing of a Register, for

the Recording of Such Proceedings in processioning, as also for the preventing Mistakes, in the said Register, as in the said Act is directed. Pursuant to the Directions in the said Act it is ordered that the Church Wardens, at least three Sundays before Such persons Shall proceed in Such processioning, shall give publick Notice thereof at the Church

Persons appointed to perform the said processioning are John Chapman and James Moore for the North Side of the Eastern Branch, Benjamin Dingly Gray and William Ackiss for the South Side thereof. William Woodhouse jr., William Keeling jr., John Keeling jr., and John Munden jr. for the Lower precinct of the Eastern Shore, John Whitehurst Son of James, Jonathan James Son of John, Jonathan Jackson & William Whitehead for the upper precinct of the Eastern Shore. James Nimmo & William Hunter for Little Creek precinct, John Biddle and Edward Denby jr. for the Lower precinct of the Western Shore, Francis Clark, Samuel Wilbur and Lemuel Fentriss son of John for the upper precinct of the Western Shore, Henry Tripp and James Tooly for Black Water precinct

Anthony Walke

[64] At a Vestry held the 30th Day of September 1755

Present Mr. Robert Dickson minister

Capt. James Kempe & } Church Wardens
Capt. William Keeling

Col. Anthony Walke Major Thomas Walke Mr. John Whitehead Capt. George Wishart Mr. Francis Thorowgood Land and Mr. William Woodhouse Vestry Men

The Parish is Dr:	Nett Tobo:
To Reverend Mr. Robert Dickson minister Convenient	16000
To 4 per Ct. Shrinkage on Ditto	640
To Cask omitted Last year	640
To another omission in Netting	62
To 4 per Ct. for Cask [on] minister's Tobo.	640
To Thomas Grainger Clerk of the Church	1200
To Mr. Charles Gasking Clerk of the Eastern Shore Chapel	1200
To Mr. Cason Moore Clerk of Pungo Chapel	1200
To Col. Anthony Walke [for] his overseer's Cleaning Church	240
To Richard Davis [for] keeping and Cleaning Eastern Shore Chapel	200
To Ditto [for] Cleaning the Spring	30
To Mrs. Elizabeth Dyer [for] Cleaning pungo Chapel and Well	160
To Mary Morris towards her Relief	480
To Mary Broughton for Ditto	300
To Richard Bell towards his Relief	160
To Willoughby Aires for keeping James Sharwood's Child	320
To Barbary Keeling [for] keeping Roger Hattens Child 4 months	320
To Ditto [for] keeping Sarah Easeley 7 months	560
To John Keeling Sr. [for] keeping Ben Burroughs	1120
To Anne Russel for keeping Sarah Jones, the Ballance of her Account is	120

	To Ditto [for] keeping Abby Cotton 1 month	200
	To Patrick Flanakin [for] keeping Ruth Smyth	200
	To Mrs. Mary Cartwright for keeping Alexander Jameson	960
	To Mr. Joseph Mitchel as an Addition to his price for building [the] Eastern Shore Chapel	4000
	To Mr. Benjamin Dingley Grey for keeping & interring Edmond Joynes	200
	To Mr. Job Gasking one Levy	29-1/4
	To William Oakham [for] keeping [his] Sister's Child	200
	To Col. Anthony Walke & Son per Account £2.14.10	522
	To William Flanakin [for] keeping Ruth Smyth 6 months	400
	To John Keeling to keeping James Kays Child £3.10	666
[65]	To John Snail for keeping William Lawrance's Child	400
	To Mr. John Bonney to keeping Thomas Jones 9 months @ 700	525
	To William May [for] keeping Buckhannan's Child	80
	To Doctor Christopher Wright per Account £4	761
	To Mr. James Dunn per Account £4.17.6 at 10/6	928
	To Mr. Rob Cartwright per Account 17.6	166
	To the Church Wardens to pay Mr. Dickson's Interest, Mr. Henley's Account & other Charges	10000
	To Thomas Williamson for repairing Pungo Chapple	4000
	To William Carrol keeping Mary McClary	700
	To the Church Wardens [for] maintaining Boyd Child	500
	To Josiah Morrice [for] keeping Burk's Widdow	320
	To Edward Green Sr. 1 Levy for the year 1753	40
	To John Brown Son of Edward 1 Levy for year 1754	30
	To Thomas Grainger Clerk of the Vestry	200
	To 6 per Ct. for Accounting on 51619	3097
		54716
	Cr: By 1740 Tithables at 31-1/4 is 54375	
	By Fraction Carried to the County Levy 341	54716

Ordered that the Church Wardens or the Collector receive from each Tithable Thirty one pounds and one half of Nett Tobacco—for the parish Levy this year and make payment to each Claimer as above directed

November 17th 1755 Memorandum of Agreement made with Thomas Williamson— To paint the Chappel at pungo that is all the pews that are not already painted, also the Breasting of the Gallery the Communion Table & Ballesters and the Outside of both the Doors he finding paint Oyl and to finish and Compleat the same in a workmanlike manner on Consideration whereof the Vestry agrees to give and allow him three pounds Current money to be Levyd next October in Tobo.

[65½]   Agreed in this Vestry that Mr. Joseph White succeed Mr. John Keeling (lately deceased) as a processioner for the Lower precinct of the Eastern Shore

Likewise Mr. Adam Thorowgood is appointed as processioner with Mr. John Biddle in the Lower precinct of the Western Shore in the Room of Edward Denby jr., whom they think fit to discharge.

Agreed & appointed by this Vestry that Major Thomas Walke & Collo. Nathaniel Newton Officiate as Church Wardens the ensuing Year

Memorandum that Mrs. — Carrol is to have 800 lbs. Nett Tobacco on keeping Mary McClary the Ensuing Year

Agreed with Josiah Morrice on his keeping Burk's Widdow the ensuing year, that he be allowed for the Same fifty Shillings

             Anthony Walke

[Sketch: Branch or Cove, Big pine, W by N 46 po, w. Oak]

In Obedience to an Order of the Worshipful the Justices of Princess Anne County Court made at a Court held for the said County the Twenty first day of October One thousand seven hundred and fifty five and the Same renewed at a Court held for the same County in the Month of November now last past & then next ensuing made and renewed for the Surveying processioning and laying out the Bounds on Line in Dispute Between Doctor Christopher Wright and Mr. William Robinson We Gershom Nimmo Surveyor of the Said County, And Adam Lovet, George Jameson, Charles Smallwood, James Carroway Senior, George Weblin, Charles Gasking, John Biddle, Robert Cartwright, Job Gasking, Enoch Whitehurst, Robert Huggins and Lewis Price, Jurors duly summoned, Impanneld, Elected, Tried and Sworn for that purpose (being Summoned by the Sheriff of the said County & Sworn by David McClenehan Gentleman one of his Majesties Justices of the Peace for said County in the Presence of both the said parties) did accordingly meet together and go on the Land in Difference and there having a due regard to all patents papers and Writings produced to us, (as also to the Evidence & Allegations of each of the said parties in relation thereto did duly Consult and Consider thereof and having thereon unanimously agreed did Order and direct the said Gershom Nimmo as Surveyor aforesaid to Survey, Procession and lay out the Line or Bounds in dispute between the said parties as above (that is to say) Beginning at a Pine directly opposite to the head of a Branch or Cove which makes up near to the new Road or path that now leads to the said Robinson's dwelling house and from thence by a W by N Course according to a Line of Marked trees markd by us in that Course up to a Corner white Oak standing in a Line of markd trees between the said Parties, It appearing to us that that place and Course is the true place where and Course by which the Line in dispute ought to run and be Established the Same appearing to us to have been the bound or Line of that part of the Land formerly belonging to Mark powel the Elder deceas'd and now held by the said Doctor Christopher Wright by Virtue of a Purchase by him thereof made of the Reverend Mr. Henry Barlow adjoining to that part of the Land formerly belonging to John Thorowgood deceas'd now held and Claimed by the said William Robinson by Virtue of a Purchase by him thereof made from William Keeling of the said County Gentleman as is the place where and Course by which the said William Robinson Insisted the same ought to run and be Established which is a good distance without the Place where the said Christopher Wright contended the Same ought to be, he having contended the same ought to be and run by a Ditch which appeared to us to be on said Robinsons Land that during the whole time of Settling and running the Line or Bound in dispute aforesaid the Sherriff of the County Attended us to have removed force if any should have been offerred Agreeable to said Order & this is our Report Given under our hands and Seals the 5th day of December 1755.

             Gershom Nimmo Surveyor & Seal

Lewis Price	& Seal	Adam Lovett	& Seal
James Carroway	Seal	Robert Cartwright	Seal
Enoch Whitehurst	Seal	Job Gasking	Seal
Charles Gasking	Seal	Robert Huggins	Seal
John Biddle	Seal	George Weblin	Seal
George Jameson	Seal	Charles Smallwood	Seal

[67]

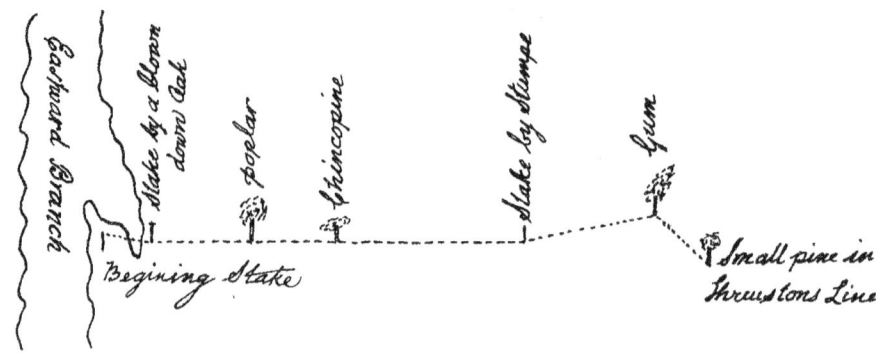

In Obedience to an Order of the Worshipful the Justices of Princess Anne County Court made at a Court held for said County the seventeenth day of February in the year of Our Lord one thousand seven hundred and fifty six and the same renewed at a Court held for the said County in June following for the Surveying processioning and Laying out the Bounds or Line in dispute between Thomas Fazakerly and George Sparrow, We Gershom Nimmo Surveyor of said County & Arthur Sayer, Anthony Moseley, James Kempe, Nathaniel McClenehan, David McClenehan, John Hopkins, Nathaniel Nicholas, Tully Moseley, Alexander Poole, Richard Whitehurst, James Williamson, and Richard Berry, Jurors duely summoned impanelled and Sworn for that purpose, being summoned by the Sheriff of said County and sworn by Gershom Nimmo Gentleman one of his Majesties Justices of the peace for said County in the presence of both the said parties and accordingly meet together and go upon the Land in difference and there having a due regard to all patents papers and Writings produced to us as also to the Evidence and Allegations of each of the said parties in relation thereto did duely Consult and Consider thereof and having thereon unanimously agreed did order and direct the said Gershom Nimmo as Surveyor aforesaid to Survey procession and lay out the Lands or bounds in dispute between the said Parties as above (that is to say) Beginning at a Stake on the South Side of the Eastward Branch of Elizabeth River thence running South 26 degrees West 13½ poles to a Stake by a blown down Oak then S 14 degrees West 27 poles to a poplar thence S 16 degrees West 23 poles to a Chincopine still the same Course which is S 16 degrees West: 54½ poles to a Stake by a pine Stump thence S 6 degrees West 36½ poles to a Gum a Corner leading to Threustons Line thence S 56 degrees West 20 poles to a small pine in the said Threustons Line it appearing to us that the aBove Courses is the True place where the Line in dispute ought to run and be Established, the Same appearing to us to be the line that Eve Etheridge made to divide the said Land between her two Sons David and Anthony Etheridge who sold the same to Thomas Fazakerly and George Sparrow and is the same Place where and Course by which the said Thomas Fazakerly insisted the same ought to run and be established which is a good Distance on the said George Sparrows Land from the place where the said George Sparrow insisted the said Line ought to be, he having Contended the same ought to be & run a South Course which appears to us to take the said Thomas Fazakerlys Land that during the Whole time of Settling & running the said Line or Bounds in dispute as aforesaid the Sherrif of the County attended us to have removed force if any should have been Offered agreeable to said Order and this is our Report Given under our hand and Seals this 22nd day of June 1756

[68]

Arthur Sayer	& Seal	Nathaniel Nicholas	& Seal
Anthony Moseley	& Seal	Tully Moseley	& Seal
James Kempe	& Seal	Richard R Whitehurst	& Seal
Nathaniel McClenehan	& Seal	Alexander Poole	& Seal
David McClenehan	& Seal	James Williamson	& Seal
John I Hopkins	& Seal	Richard R Berry	& Seal

Gershom Nimmo Surveyor & Seal

Tully Robinson Sheriff & Seal

[69] At a Vestry held the 23rd Day of October 1756

Present The Reverend Robert Dickson minister

Col. Nathaniel Newton } Church Wardens
Major Thomas Walke

Vestry Men
Col. Anthony Walke   Capt. James Kempe   Capt. Anthony Moseley
Mr. Adam Tooley   Capt. John Whitehurst   Mr. John Whitehead
Capt. George Wishart Mr. Francis Thorow^d Land Mr. William Woodhouse

The Parish of Lynhaven is Dr:	Nett Tobo:
To the Reverend Mr. Robert Dickson Minister Convenient	16000
To 4 per Ct. Shrinkage on Ditto	640
To 4 per Ct. for Cask for Ditto	640
To Thomas Grainger Clerk of the Church	1200
To Mr. Charles Gasking Clerk of the Eastern Shore Chapel	1200
To Mr. Cason Moore Clerk of Pungo Chapel	1200
To Col. Anthony Walke [for] his overseer cleaning the Church	240
To Richard Davis [for] keeping clean Eastern Shore Chapel and Spring	160
To Mrs. Elizabeth Dyer [for] cleaning Pungo Chapel & Well	160
To Mary Morris toward her Relief	480
To Mary Broughton toward her Relief	300
To Willoughby Aires for keeping James Sherwoods Child	300
To Barbary Keeling [for] keeping Roger Hattons Child	960
To Ditto keeping Sarah Easeley - 2 months	160
To John Keeling keeping B. Burroughs 1440 & Keys Child Ditto 160	1600
To Elizabeth Oliver keeping Mary Olivers Child the year 1755 omitted	400
Ditto 1756	400
To Josiah Morris keeping widdow Burk one year	400
To William Oakham keeping Sisters Child 1 year	150
To William Flanakyn keeping Ruth Smyth 12 months @ £5 paid in the Last levy 400 lbs. Tob: @ 10/6 remainder due £2.18 is	464
To Richard Williamson keeping and intering William Smith	200
To Robert Deermore keeping Sarah Easeley 6½ months	520
To William Davis keeping Ruth Smith 4 months	267
To William Leversage Credit for 1 Levy	40½
To Thomas Williamson painting Chapel at pungo £3	480
To Mr. John Bonney diging Well [and] fixing frame at pungo Chapel	100
To Col. Nathaniel Newton Summoning 2 Juries Inquisition on 2 drown men	293
To Credit Mary Sharwood one Levy	40½
To James Williamson toward his Relief	200

VESTRY BOOK OF LYNNHAVEN PARISH

[70]

To Anne Russel nursing Mary Malbone	200
To William Carrol keeping Mary McClary	800
To Col. Anthony Walke & Son per Account £1.15.11½	288
To Major Thomas Walke per Ditto £7.9.8	1197
To Reverend Mr. Robert Dickson per Ditto £3.13.7½	589
To Mrs. Amy Keeling keeping Sarah Easeley 3½ months @ 10/	280
To Mr. James Dunn per Account	40
To Mr. Edward Moseley per Account £3.2.9-3/4	502
To George Ball for one levy overcharged last Year	40½
To the Churchwardens for discharging Ministers debt	8000
To Mrs. Mary Cartwright keeping Alexander Jameson	960
To Robert Davis keeping Michael Sherwoods Child	160
To Thomas Grainger Clerk of the Vestry	200
To Ditto keeping and clearing the Parish of one of Boyds Children	120
To 6 per Ct. for Accounting on 42331 -	2539
	44870
Cr: By 1802 Tithables at 24-3/4	44599
By George Ackiss	160
By Mr. John Haynes	80
By Fraction carried to the County Levy	31
	44870

Ordered That the Church Wardens or Collector receive from each Tithable Twenty four pounds and three quarters of a pound of Nett Tobacco for the Parish Levy this year and make payment to each Claimer as above directed

Agreed with Michael Eaton, James Eaton & James Cason to keep Elizabeth Eaton their Mother among them and that they be allowed five Pounds among them to be levied next parish Levy

Agreed with Anne Russel to keep Christian King at fifteen shillings a month

[71]

Agreed to allow Mrs Burkett or any other person for the keeping of Milburn Bryan a Child the ensuing Year 400 Wt. of Nett Tobacco

Agreed likewise to allow John Milleson 300 Wt. of nett Tobacco for keeping his mother in Law the Ensuing Year

At a Vestry held the 15th October 1757

Present the Reverend Robert Dixon Minister

    Colo. Nathaniel Newton } Church Wardens
    Major Thomas Walke

Colo. Anthony Walke   Capt. James Kempe   Mr. John Bonney
Mr. William Woodhouse   Capt. Anthony Moseley   Capt. George Wishart

The Parish of Lynhaven is Dr.   Nett Tobo:

To the Reverend Mr. Robert Dixon Minister Convenient	16000

To 4 per Ct Shrinkage on Ditto	640
To 4 per Ct. for Cask on Ditto	640
To Joseph Collinson Clerk of the Church from February 5th	833½
To Ditto Clerk of Vestry from Ditto	133½
To Mr. Charles Gasking Clerk[of] Eastern Shore Chappel	1200
To Mr. Cason Moor Clerk of Pungo Chappel	1200
To Colo. Anthony Walke's Overseer cleaning the Church	240
To Mrs. Elizabeth Dyer cleaning Pungo Chapel & Well	160
To Richard Norman for keeping Eastern Shore Chappel	160
To Edward Moseley Junior for a Chest for the Church's use	112
To Mary Morris towards her Relief	480
To Mary Broughton Ditto	300
To Barbary Keeling for keeping Hattons 2 Children	960
To Mrs. Amy Keeling for keeping Sarah Leasley 3 Months	250
To Andrew Small for keeping Ditto 6½ Months	541
To Church Wardens for paying John Fentress for keeping Alex^r Jamison	~~1600~~
To Josiah Morris for keeping Widow Burk 1 Year	400
To John Millison for Ditto Sarah Briggs Ditto	300
To William Carrol Ditto Mary McClary Ditto	800
To Anthony Barnes Ditto Frances Barnes ½ Year	200
To Anne Berry for keeping her 2 Children to this time	400
To Anne Russel for keeping Christian King 5 Months	600
To Ditto William Harvey 4 Months	480
To John Keeling for keeping Christian King 3 Months	360
To Thomas Rascow for Ditto 3 Weeks	60
To Mary Lester for keeping & burying Ditto	280
To William Turton towards his Relief	300
To William Davis for keeping Ruth Smith & Child 1 Year	800
To Batson Whitehurst for keeping 2 of Elizabeth Burges's Children	500
To Dr. Christopher Wright for Medicine &ca.	2898
To Mrs. Elizabeth Burket for keeping Milburn Brian & Child 1 year	400
To Messrs. Calvert & Keeling for the use of Hatton's 2 Children	166
To Colo. Anthony Walke as per Account	700
To Elizabeth Oliver for keeping Eleanor Oliver 1 Year	400
To Dinah Gold towards her Relief	300
To Francis Harvey for keeping William Harvey about 3 Months	100

[72]

To a Levy towards building a poor house to be lay'd in the Hands of the Overseers	10000
To Church Wardens towards getting a Silver Flagon, Cup, 2 hard Metal Plates & Bason, a Table Cloth & 2 Napkins	4000
To 6 per Ct. accompting on 48294	2897½
	51191½
To Fraction carried to the County Levy	80½
	51272
Cr: By 1768 Tythables at 29 51272	

Order'd that the Collector receive from each Tythable 29 lbs. Nett Tobacco for the Parish Levy this Year & make payment to each Claimer as above directed

Agreed to give John Millison for keeping Sarah Brigs 1 year 800 lbs. Nett Tob.

Agreed to give Anne Berry for keeping her 2 Children the ensuing Year Four Pounds.

Agreed to give Courtney Fentress for keeping her 3 Children the ensuing Year 800 lbs. Nett Tobacco

[73] Agreed to give Batson Whitehurst for keeping 2 of Elizabeth Burges's Children the ensuing year to commence the 27th October 800 lbs. Nett Tobacco

Agreed to give William Flanigin for keeping Ruth Smith & Child the ensuing year 800 lbs. Nett Tobacco

Agreed to give Mrs. Burket for keeping Milburn Brian & Child the ensuing Year 400 lbs. Nett Tobacco

Agreed to employ Dr. Price to serve the Parish the ensuing year

Agreed to give William Cason for keeping Elizabeth Eaton the ensuing year 960 lbs. Nett Tobacco

Agreed to give Sarah Wood for keeping her Daughter the ensuing year 800 lbs. Nett Tobacco

Agreed that Major Thomas Walke & Mr. Francis Thorowgood Land officiate as Church Wardens the ensuing year

At a Vestry held the 8th Day of June 1758

Present the Reverend Robert Dickson Minister

Major Thomas Walke
Mr. F. Tho^d Land   } Church Wardens

Col. Anthony Walke   Col. Edward Hack Moseley   Capt. George Wishart, & Mr. William Woodhouse

Agreable to Act of Assembly made in the year 1757, 'Tis hereby order'd that a certain Tract or Parcel of Land left to the Parish by James Jouslin be sold at Public Vendue by the Church Wardens: one half to be paid at acknowledging the Deeds, & the rest at 12 Months

Orderd that in Case the Church Wardens have Opportunity of purchasing a convenient Parcel of Land for the use of the Parish on reasonable Terms, it be accordingly done.

[74] At a Vestry held the 21st October 1758

Present the Reverend Mr. Robert Dickson Minister

Major Thomas Walke
Mr. Francis Thorowgood Land } Church Wardens

Col. Anthony Walke   Capt. James Kempe   Capt. George Wishart
Mr. William Keeling & Mr. William Woodhouse

The Parish of Lynhaven Dr.	Nett Tobo:
To the Reverend Mr. Robert Dickson Minister convenient	16000
To 4 per Ct. Shrinkage on Ditto	640
To 4 per Ct. for Cask on Ditto	640
To Joseph Collinson Clerk of Church & vestry	1400
To Mr. Charles Gasking Ditto Eastern Shore Chapel	1200
To Mr. Cason Moore Ditto Pungo Chapel	1200
To Mrs. Elizabeth Dyer [for] cleaning Ditto & Well	120
To Richard Norman for keeping Eastern Shore Chapel	120
To Anthony McKeel Ditto Church	150
To Mary Morrice towards her Relief	360
To Barbary Keeling for keeping Roger Hattons Children 7 Months	420
To Mrs. Mary Broughton towards her Relief	225
To Andrew Small for keeping Sarah Leesley 12 Months	750
To Dinah Ship Ditto Eleanor Burk Ditto	225
To John Millison Ditto Sarah Briggs Ditto	600
To Darcus Carol Ditto Mary McClary	600
To Moses McClallan Ditto Frances Barnes Ditto	240
To Anne Berry Ditto her 2 Children Ditto	480
To William Flanegin Ditto Ruth Smith Ditto	600
To Batson Whitehurst Ditto 2 Elizabeth Burges's Children Ditto	600
To Dr. Price per Account £15	1800
To Elizabeth Burkit for keeping Milburn Brian & Child	300
To Elizabeth Oliver Ditto Eleanor Oliver	225
To William Cason Ditto Elizabeth Eaton £6	720
To Mary Malbone Ditto her Sister's Child	300
To Elizabeth Woodhouse Ditto Florence Griskil's Child	180
To Dinah Ward for Relief to Aby Vial	180
To Ditto Ditto Bridget Martin	60
To Thomas Easter Ditto Henry Holmes' Children	360
To Robert Burfoot for keeping Elizabeth Oast 4 Months £1.5	150

[75]

To Sarah Wood for keeping her Daughter 12 Months		600
To Dinah Gold towards her Relief		225
To Richard Ball for keeping Sarah Davis' Child 7 Months 7/6		105
To Mr. George Logan per Account 20/		120
To Anne Russel for keeping Florence Griskel's Child		270
To Col. Walke & Son as per Acount £1: 9:		174
To The Reverend Robert Dickson Ditto £2: 2: 6:		255
To Francis Harvy for keeping Alexander Jameson & Benjamin Burroughs 1 Year £10		1200
To Ditto as per Account for burying Benjamin Burroughs 11/3		67½
To Robert Cartwright as per Account 12/6		75
To Major Thomas Walke as per Account £2: 12: 1:		312½
To 6 per Ct. Accompting on 34249		2055
		36304
To Fraction carried to County Levy		296
Cr: By 1830 Tythables at 20 lbs.		36600

Order'd that the Collector receive from each Tythable 20lbs. Nett Tobacco for the Parish Levy this year & make Payment to each Claimer as above directed

Agreed to give Mary Lester £4 for keeping Alexander Jameson the ensuing Year

Agreed to give Robert Burfoot £5 for keeping Elizabeth Oast the ensuing Year

Agreed to give Dr. Price to attend the Sick belonging the Parish the ensuing Year £20

Agreed to give Richard Ball to keep Sarah Davis' Child this ensuing Year £1:10

Agreed to give John Millison £6 for keeping Sarah Brigs the ensuing Year

Agreed with William Ward to keep Mary McClary the ensuing Year for £6

Agreed to give John Bonney Junior £6 for keeping Eliz. Eaton the ensuing Year

Anthony Walke

[76] At a Vestry held the 18th of September 1759

Major Thomas Walke & Mr. Francis Thorowgood Land Churchwardens

Present
Col. Anthony Walke   Col. Nathaniel Newton   Capt. James Kempe
Capt. Anthony Moseley   Capt. John Whitehurst   Capt. William Keeling } Vestrymen
Capt. George Wishart

Order'd that Mr. James Moon & Mr. John Hancock Procession the lines of the North side of the Eastern Branch Precinct, John Matthias and Jonathan Hopkins for the south side of the Eastern Branch Precinct, Thomas Haynes & James Griffen for Little Creek Precinct, Robert Huggins & William Moseley for the Lower Part of the western Shore Precinct, Frederick Boush & Willoughby West for the upper Part of the western shore Precinct, Smith Shepard, John Pallett, William Cox & Henry Harrison, for the Lower part of the Eastern Shore Precinct, Charles Handly, Henry Woodhouse, Jonathan Bonney, & Jonathan Jackson for the upper part of the Eastern shore Precinct, John Simmons junior & James Smith for Black water Precinct And that they make Return of the same According to Law

Pursuant to an Act of Assembly for preventing Controversies Conserning the bounds of Lands, that once in Every four years the Bounds of Every persons Land shall be processioned, and gone Round, and The Land Marks Renewed, and for Deviding this parish into Convenient precincts, we have appointed the Above Named persons for The performing such processioning at such time as shall to the said Vestry seem Convenient, & to see that such processioning be Duely performed Between the Last Day of September & the Last Day of March Next Ensuing, and for Receiving an Account in Return of Every person's Land so processioned as Also their failures herein, & there particular Reason for so failing, and also for keeping & providing a Register for the Recording of such processioning, as also for the preventing Mistakes in the said Register, as in the said Act is Derected, pursuant to the Derections in the said Act, it is Order'd that the Church wardens at Least three sundays before such persons shall proceed in such processioning, shall give publick Notice at the Church

Test Charles Gasking Clerk [of the] Vestry

[77] At a Vestry held the 28th of September 1759

Present the Reverend Mr. Robert Dickson Minister

Major Thomas Walke & Mr. Francis Thorowgood Land } Church wardens

Mr. John Bonney   Capt. James Kempe   Capt. John Whitehurst } Vestrymen
Capt. William Keeling Capt. Anthony Moseley   Capt. George Wishart

The Parish of Lynhaven [is] Dr:	Nett Tobo:
To the Reverend Mr. Robert Dickson Minister Convenient	16000
To 4 per Ct. for shrinkage on Ditto	640
To 4 per Ct. for Cask on Ditto	640
To Mr. Joseph Collinson Clerk of Brick Church	1272
To Charles Gasking Clerk of Eastern Shore Chapel	1200
To Mr. Cason Moore Clerk of Pungo Chapel	1200
To Mrs. Elizabeth Dyer for Cleaning pungo Chapel & well	160
To Mr. Richard Norman for Cleaning Eastern Shore Chapel	160
To Mr. James Garton for Cleaning of Brick Church	200
To Mary Morriss towards her Relief	400
To Mary Broughton towards her Relief	260
To Mrs. Barbourer Keeling for mistake in keeping Roger Hatton's Children Last year	400
To Mrs. Elizabeth woodhouse for keeping Roger Hatton's Children	960
To Andrew Small for keeping Sarah Leasly & bur[y]ing &ca.	550
To Dinah Ship for keeping Elanor Buck	300
To John Millenson for keeping Sarah Brigs &ca.	200
To William Ward for keeping Mary McCleary	680
To John Barnes Eastate for keeping frances Barnes 4 months	100
To Ann Berry for keeping her 2 Children	500
To William James for keeping Ruth Smith	600
To Elizabeth Burkitt for keeping Milburn Brion's Child	400

To Elizabeth Oliver for keeping Elanor Oliver	300
To Thomas Ward Sr. for keeping William Turton one year & half	600
To John Bonney for keeping Elizabeth Eaton	960
To Abigal Cotton for keeping her Child	400
[78] To Dinah Gold toward her Relief	300
To Robert Burfoot for keeping Elizabeth Oast 6 months	400
To Alexander Harvey for keeping of Ditto	400
To Mary Lester for keeping Alexander Jamison	640
To Richard Bald for keeping Sarah Davis Child	240
To Doctor Lewis Price for attending the parishoners	3200
To James Dunn per Account - £4: 15: 0:	280
To William Garton per Account - £5: 15: 0:	920
To William Biddle for 2 Levies he being Constable this 2 years past & Not allow'd for the same	80
To Batson Whitehurst for keeping Elizabeth Burgess' Children	500
To Mr. Thomas Rey[nolds?] Walker per Account £1: 19	312
To Mr. Moses Roberts for keeping frances Barnes 1½ years	360
To the Church wardens to be apply'd for the Support of William Pasleys Children	1200
To Major Thomas Walke per Account £7: 13: 2:	1226
To Ann Williamson toward her Relief	400
To Doctor Lewis Price per Account £4: 10: 0:	720
To Doctor Christopher Wright for Salivating Anthony McKeal per Account - £5: 0:	800
To Ditto for attendance & Medicine for Vesty Jacob per Account £3:10:	560
To Doctor George Roveire for Cureing Mary Cuttance	3200
To Thomas Easter for keeping Henry Holmes Child	400
To the Churchwardens to pay to Mr. William Bornden Marchant in London for Ballance of Church Ornaments shipt by him for the Middle Chapple the sum of £16: 11: 8:	2651½
To 6 per Ct. for Accounting on 4787½	2872
	50743½
Cr: By 1935 Tythables at 26 per pole 50310½	
By Fraction Carried to County Levy 433	
	50743½

Ordered that the Churchwardens or Collector Receive from Each Tithable Twenty Six pounds of Neet Tobacco for the parish Levy this year & make payment To Each Claimer as above Derected

              Anthony Walke

Agreed with Elizabeth woodhouse to keep Roger Hattons Children the Ensuing year for six pounds

Ordered that there be a Well Dug at the Eastern Shore Chapple & that the Churchwardens agree with any person for that purpose & that the same be Brickt & a pump fixt in it &ca.

Ordred that Mr. Richard Collinson Offishuate as Clerk for the Brick Church

[79] Agreed with Doctor Lewis Price to attend the sick belonging to the parish the Ensuing year for Twenty pounds

Agreed with Thomas Ward Sr. to keep William Turton the Ensuing year for Three pounds two shillings & six pence

Agreed & Resolved by this Vestry that Major Thomas Walke & capt. William Keeling Serve as Church wardens the Ensuing year

Agreed & Resolved by this Vestry that Mr. John Wilkins Succeed Mr. John Simmons lately Deceased as processioner for Blackwater precinct

At a Vestry Held the 29th of September 1760

Present the Reverend Mr. Robert Dickson Minister

Major Thomas Walke & Capt. William Keeling } Churchwardens

Present Colo. Anthony Walke   Capt. James Kempe   Capt. George Wishart
         Capt. John Whitehurst   Mr. William Woodhouse   Mr. John Whitehead
                                                         Vestry men

	Neet Tobo:
The Parish of Lynhaven [is] Dr:	
To the Reverend Mr. Robert Dickson Minister Convenient	16000
To 4 per Ct. for shrinkage in Ditto	640
To 4 per Ct for Cask on Ditto	640
To Mr. Richard Collinson Clerk of Brick Church	1200
To Charles Gasking Clerk of Eastern Shore Chapple	1200
To Ditto Clerk of Vestry	200
To Ditto for book to Record the processions in	39
To Mr. Cason Moore Clerk of upper Chapple	1200
To James Garton for Cleaning the Brick Church	180
To Samuel Mosses for Cleaning Eastern Shore Ditto	120
To William Dyer for Cleaning pungo Do.	120
To Mary Broughton Towards her Relief	195
To Elizabeth Woodhouse for keeping Roger Hattons Children	720
To Dinah Shipp for keeping Elanor Burk	225
To Ann Berry for keeping her Two Children	375
To William James for short payment last year	150
To Tully Williamson for keeping Ruth Smith	600
[80] To James Cason for keeping Elizabeth Eaton	720
To Abigal Cotton for keeping her Child	300

To Sarah Edmonds towards her Relief	300
To Mary Lester for keeping Alexander Jamison	480
To Ann Williamson Towards her Relief	200
To Margret Whitehurst for keeping Elizabeth Burgesses Child	187½
To Ann Olds for keeping her Child in the year 1758	225
To Doctor Lewis Price for Attending the Parishoners	2400
To Ditto per Account	480
To the Churchwardens to be Applied for the support & Clothing William Pasley's Children	1050
To William Garton per Account	1320
To Edward Capps for keeping Milburn Brions Child	300
To Maximilian Bush [Boush] for 2 levies he being Constable 2 years & not allowed	110
To Thomas Easter for keeping Henry Holme's Child	240
To Col. Anthony Walke per Account	131
To Major Thomas Walke per Account	2942
To Solomon Wilkins per Account	633
To William Cox per Account	322
To Doctor Christopher Wright per Account	867
To Elizabeth Olderson towards her Relief	180
To Henry Johnson for making Coffen for William Absalom	30
To Mr. John Ackiss for Sundrys for Elizabeth Brand	150
To Elizabeth Oliver for keeping Elanor Oliver	---
To 6 per Ct. for Accounting on 37371½	2242
	39613½
Cr: By 1919 Tythables 20½ per pole 39339½	
To a fraction Carried to County Levy 274	39613½

Orderd that Capt. William Keeling Sherif Receive from Each Tythable person twenty pounds & a half of Neet Tobaco for the parish Levey this year and make payment to Each Clamer as above.   Anthony Walke
                                Test Charles Gasking Clerk [of] Vestry

Agreed with Mrs. Mary Lester to Keep Alexander Jamison the Ensuing year for £5: 0: 0:

Agreed with William Dyer to Keep Elizabeth Eaton the Ensuing year for £6:0:0:

Agreed with James Cason to Keep William Tirton the Ensuing Year for £4: 0: 0;

Agreed with William Garton to keep Elizabeth Oast the Ensuing Year £6:-0: 0:

Agreed with Doctor Lewis price to attend the sick belonging to the Parish The Ensuing year for £20: 0: 0:

Agreed that Capt. James Kempe & Capt. William Keeling Serve as Church wardens the Ensuing year

Agreed that the Church wardens have 80 lbs. of Neet Tobacco for Every time They find the Ellements

Memorandum: that on the 20th Day of October 1760 That Mr. Adam Tooley Resigned Serving any Longer as a vestry man, & Mr. Thomas Olds was Chosen in his Room, therefore orderd that he be Summond to Serve Accordingly, Also Capt. Anthony Moseley Resigned Serving any longer as a vestry man, and that Capt. Jonathan Saunders was Chosen in his Room therefore Orderd that he be summoned to Serve Accordingly, also Mr. John Bonney Resigned Serving any Longer as A Vestry man, and Mr. Dennis Dauley was Chosen in his Room therefore Orderd that he be Summond to Serve Accordingly

Princess Anne County

April the 25th Day 1761 This Day Came Capt. Jonathan Saunders, Mr. Thomas Olds & Mr. Denis Dauley & took the oaths of Allegiance To Serve as Vestry men for the said County & Parish of Lynhaven

        Jonathan Saunders
        Thomas Old
        Dennis Dawley

October 13th, 1762

The following Person hath taken the oaths of a vestry Man and Subscribed to be Conformable to the Doctrine & Discipline of the Church of England as Required by Act of Parliament

        Thomas Rey[nold]s Walker

[82]

At A vestry Held the 26th Day of October 1761

Present The Riverend Mr. Robert Dickson Minister

    Capt. James Kempe
    Capt. William Keeling   Church wardens

Present

Col: Anthony Walke,   Col. Nathaniel Newton,   Capt. John Whitehurst,
Mr. John Whitehead,   Mr. William Woodhouse,   Capt. Jonathan Saunders,
Mr. Dennis Dawley &   Mr. Thomas Old   Vestry Men

The Parish of Lynhaven [is] Dr:	Neet Tobo:
To the Reverend Mr. Robert Dickson Minister Convenant	16000
To 4 per Ct: for Shrinkage on Ditto	640
To 4 per Ct. for Cask on Ditto	640
To Mr. Richard Collinson Clerk of the Brick Church	1200
To Charles Gasking Clerk [of] Eastern Shore Chapple	1200
To Mr. Cason Moore Clerk [of] upper Chapple	1200
To James Garton for Cleaning brick Church & making up the graves	240
To Capt. William Keeling for Cleaning Eastern shore Chappel	180
To William Dyer for Cleaning upper Chapple	120
To Mary Broughton Towards her Relief	195
To Tully Williamson for keeping Ruth Smith	600
To Ann Williamson Towards her Relief	200
To Alexander Keeling for keeping William Hatton son [of] Roger	375
To Andrew Small for keeping John Hatton son [of] Roger	375
To Sarah Edmonds Towards her Relief	300
To John Mearanor[?] for keeping Alexander Jamison	555
To Edward Caps for Keeping Milbur[n] Brions Child	200
To Thomas Easter for keeping Henry Holme's Child	180

To Elizabeth Olderson towards her Relief	180
To Josiah Dough for keeping Elizabeth Brand 5 months	420
To William Fentress for k[eep]ing of Ditto 1 month @ 15/	90
To Samuel Boush for keeping Francis Spratt	240
To Anthony McKeel per Account 5/6	33
To Col. Anthony Walke per Account £9: 5: 3½	1112
To William Moseley per Account 11/	66
To Robert Huggins per Account £2: 6: 9:	280½
To William Garton per Account £13: 8: 6:	1611
To William Godfry per Account £1: 0: 0:	120
To Josiah Morris Sr. for keeping Eloner Burk 6 months	112½
To William Fentress [of] Blackwarter for keeping Eloner Burk 6 months	112½
To Elizabeth Harvey widow of Francis Towards her Relief	300
To George Oldner, he being Constable last year & not allow'd for it 8/1½	48-3/4
To Doctor Lewis Price for tending the Parishoners	2400
To the Eastate of Major Thomas Walke	143
To Sarah Cason widow of James for keeping William Turton	480
To William Dyer for keeping Elizabeth Eaton	720
To Anthony Williamson for Making Cloaths for Joshua Pasley	18
To Capt. James Kempe for finding the Ellements at Brick Church	240
To Capt. William Keeling for Ditto [at] Eastern Shore Chapple	240
To Mr. John Bonney for Ditto [at] upper Chapple	240
To Charles Gasking Clerk [of] Vestry [for] Recording Processions and Copying Acts of Assemblys	860
To the Church wardens for the Support of the parishoners the Ensuing year	10000
To Col. Nathaniel Newton per Account	585
To 6 per Ct. for Accounting on 45052-1/4	2703
	47755-1/4
Cr: By 1973 Tithables at 24 per pole is 47352-1/4	
Fraction Carried to County Levey 403	47755-1/4

[page marker 83 appears beside "To William Fentress [of] Blackwarter" line]

Orderd that the Church wardens or Collector Receive from Each Tithable Tweenty four pounds of Neet Tobaco for the parish Levy this year and Make payment to Each Claimer [as] above Derected

         Anthony Walke

          Test Charles Gasking Clerk [of] Vestry

Agreed with Doctor Lewis Price to attend the parishoners the Ensuing year for £20

Ordered that the Church wardens Sell that Tract of Land that Major Thomas Walke give to the parish in his last Will & Testament And the Money Arising therby to be laid out in young Slaves for the support of the said parish

Ordered that the Church wardens Agree with any Person to Repair the Parish houses & find such Meterials as is wonting for them.

[84] On the Motion of Mr. Jonathan Porter it is agreed that he Build A Gallery in the North side of the Easternshore Chapple, from the gallery to the Eastermost End of said Chapple, and that Col. Nathaniel Newton, Capt. William Keeling & Mr. William Woodhouse or any two of them do Vew & Derect him in the Same

Agreed with George Trouton & his wife to look after and Take Care of the Parishoners the Ensuing year for £12:0.0. The said Trouton & wife to have their Dyit found them

Test Charles Gasking Clerk Vestry

At a Vestry Held the 13th of October 1762

Present the Reverend Mr. Robert Dickson Minister

Capt. James Kempe
Mr. Thomas Renolds Walker } Church Wardens

Colo. Anthony Walke   Colo. Nathaniel Newton   Capt. John Whitehurst
Mr. William Woodhouse Mr. John Whitehead   Capt. Jonathan Saunders
Mr. Dennes Dawley   & Mr. Thomas Old, Vestery Men

The Parish of Linhaven	Dr.	lbs. tobo:
To the Reverend Mr. Robert Dickson		16000
To Ditto for Shrinkage & Cask		1280
To Mr. Richard Colerson Clerk of the Brick Church		1200
To Mr. Cason Moore Clerk of the Upper Chappel		1200
To Charles Gasking Clerk of the Eastern Shore Chappel		1200
To Ditto per Account & Clerk of the Vestery		310
To Anthony McKeel for Cleaning Brick Church &ca:		240
To Mr. Thomas Renolds Walker for Cleaning the Eastern Shore Chappel		180
To Ditto For Account		452
To Mrs William Dyer for Cleaning the upper Chappel		120
To Mary Brawton [Broughton] towards her Relief		195
To Sarah Edmonds Towards her Relief		300
To Elizabeth Alanson Towards her Relief		180
To Sarah Green towards Her Relief for Children		500
To Robert Ward for Keeping Mary Ward		300
To Nowdinna Henley For 1 Leavy over Charged Last year		60
To Ann Denby For 3 Leaveys over Charged Last year		180
To John Fentress son of Michal per Account		90
To Adam Thorowgood per Account		519
To John Biddle per Account		432
To William Garton per Saddle For the Parish		60

[85] appears next to "To Sarah Edmonds Towards her Relief"

To George Cox per Account	690
To Doctor Lewis Price For Attending the Parishoners	2400
To Robert Huggins per Account	68
To Colo. Anthony Walke & son per Account	4504
To Robert Cartwright for Keeping Harpers Child	406
TO 6 per Ct. On Accounting on 33066	1983
	35049

Cr: By 2021 Tithables @ 17 [lbs.] per Pole is 34357		
Fraction Carried to County Leavy	692	35049

Ordered that the Church Wardens or Collectors Receive From Each Tithable Seventeen Pounds of Neet Tobacco For this year and Make Payment to Each Claimer [as] Above Directed

           Anthony Walke

Ordered that Major Anthony Walke send For stuff to make Two Gounds [gowns] For the Minister &ca:

[86] Agreed With George Trouton & Wife to Look after the Parishoners And Take Care of them the Ensuing year For £12:0.0. The said Trouton & Wife to have their dyit Found Them

Orderd that the Church Wardens Pay Capt. William Keeling £11:3:11½: Also Pay Capt. James Kempe   £4:1:11:

Likewise that they Tar Paint&Whitewash the Brick Church, Tar & Whitewash the Easternshore Chappel & other Nesesarys that shall be wanting & be paid out of the money Levyed Last year In the hands of the Church wardens Likewise that Capt. Dennes Dawley Agree with Any Person to Repair the upper Chappel And Bring his Account to the Next Leavy Laying & He shall Be Paid &ca.

         Test Charles Gasking Clerk [of] Vestry

Princess Anne County At a Vestry Held the 8th day of October 1763

  The Reverend Mr. Robert Dickson Minister

  Capt. James Kempe and
  Mr. Thomas Reynolds Walker } Churchwardens

Present Colo. Anthony Walke Colo. Nathaniel Newton Capt. John Whitehurst
Mr. William Woodhouse Capt. William Keeling & Capt. Jonathan Saunders
Gentlemen:

The Parish of Lynhaven [is] Dr:	Neet Tobo:
To the Reverend Mr. Robert Dickson Minister Convenlant	16000
To Ditto for shrinkage & Cask	1280
To Cason Moore Clerk of Pungo Chapple	1200
To Charles Gasking Clerk of Eastern Shore Chapple	1200
To Ditto Clerk of the Vestry	250
To Anthony McKeel for Cleaning the Church & yard	270
To Mr. Thomas Reynolds Walker for Cleaning Eastern Shore Chappel	180
To ditto per Account . . £10:12:4½	1274-1/4

	To ditto for finding the Elements [at] Eastern Shore Chappel ₵ 80 lbs. Each Time	240
	To William Dyer for Cleaning Pungo Chappel	180
[37]	To Mary Broughton Towards her Relief	195
	To Sarah Edmonds Towards her Relief	300
	To William Moseley Senior per Account £2:18:	848
	To Mary Barnes for Keeping her son Jonathan	500
	To Anthony McKeel Towards his Relief	300
	To Elizabeth Harvey Towards her Relief	300
	To Duncan McCaull for Reading at Brick Church 3 months	300
	To John Bulman for Reading at ditto 9 months	900
	To William Maye for his wife's attending the Parishoners one year	740
	To James Carraway per Account . . . £1:0:11:	125½
	To Robert Huggins per Account . . . £0:10:8:	64
	To Colo: Nathaniel Newton for summonding Jury & Taking Inquisition on a Negro Girl of John Lovett's, & William & John Purdys ditto	294
	To Colo. Anthony Walke & son per Account . . . £6:15:8:	814
	To Capt. James Kempe per Account . . . £24:14:11:	2969½
	To ditto for finding the Elements for the Brick Church 80 lbs. Each Time	240
	To William Nimmo Senior for making Coffens for Thomas Green & hatton	120
	To Jonathan Porter per Account . . . £10:16:	1296
	To Robert Cartwright for Keeping Harper's Children	719½
	To Mr. John Bonney for finding Elements for Pungo Chappel 80 lbs. Each time	240
	To Pheby Dyer for Keeping her Children	500
	To John Norris for his wife's Boarding & Cureing Joshua Pasley's scald head	540
	To the Churchwardens for the use of George Trouton	1440
	To the dittos for the Repairing of the Brick Church & Chappels	10000
	To 6 per Ct. for Accounting on 45320	2719
		48039

Cr: By 2110 Tithables at 22-3/4 lbs per pole is   48003

      fraction carried to the County leavy   36   48039

Ordered that the Churchwardens or Collectors Receive from Each Tithable Tweenty Two pounds & 3/4 of Neet Tobacco for this year and make payment to Each Claimer as above Directed

                          Anthony Walke

Agreed with John Cox & his wife to take Care and Look after the Parishoners the Ensuing year for £12:0:0: the said Cox & wife to have their Dyet found them, & that they Indeavour to make Corn pease purtatus &ca: also to Rase fowls &ca for the support of said Parishoners

[88]

Mr. John Bullman Having had a Tryall of his ability to perform The office of a Clerk is approvd of and now Voated that he be admitted Clerk of the Brick Church the Ensuing year &ca.

Agreed with Doctor Lewis Price to take Care and Look after the Parishoners the Ensuing year and to apply such Means as is Necessary for them, & that the said Price gives Good attendance unless hendred By sickness, then the Churchwardens send for any other Doctor and he be paid out of the said prices Salary, and in consideration of the above The said price is to have £20:0 per year

Memorandum: that James Powers is agreed   pay forty shillings toward the Cure of John Curtis

Princess anne

Pursuant to an order of Princess anne County Court Requiring us to Cause a processioning of all Lands in our Parish According To the Act of Assembly, we do therefore order that the Severall persons Hereafter named in their Several precincts warn in the Inhabitants In their Divisions to goe & procession all the Lands therein, taking Care to Comply with the said Act, persons appointed to perform Processioning are, George Jamison & william Dudley for the north side of the Easton Branch precinct, Samuel Tenant & Charles Williamson for the south side of the Easton Branch precinct: William Nimmo and Thomas Hunter son of Thomas for the Little Creek precinct: Robert Thorowgood and Robert Cartwright for the Lower part of the western shore precinct: Hillery Snale & John Lovett son of Thomas for the upper part of the western shore precinct: Erasmus Haynes, Henry Keeling, William Brock Junior & Henry Cornick for the Lower part of the Easternshore precinct: Anthony Barnes Junior, Anthony Leggitt, John Whitehead Junior and Charles James for the upper part of the Easternshore precinct: Gidion White & William Simmons for Black warter precinct And that they make Return According to Law

Test Charles Gasking Clerk [of] Vestry

[89]
Princess ann County

At a Vestry Held the 6th Day of October 1764

The Reverend Robert Dickson Minister

Capt. James Kempe and
Mr. Thomas Reynolds Walker } Churchwardens

Present

Colo. Anthony Walke   Capt. John Whitehurst   Mr. John Whitehead
Mr. William Woodhouse   Capt. William Keeling   Capt. Jonathan Saunders
Mr. Thomas Olds   &   Mr. Dennis Dawley   Vestry men

The Parish of Linhaven [is] Dr:	Neet Tobo:
To the Reverend Mr. Robert Dickson minister Conveniant	16000
To ditto for shrinkage & Cask	1280
To Mr. John Bulman Clerk of Brick Church	1200
To Mr. Cason Moore Clerk of Pungo Chaple	1200
To Charles Gasking Clerk of Easternshore Chaple	1200
To Anthony McKeel for Cleaning Brick Church & Yard	270
To ditto Towards his Relief	300
To Mr. Thomas Reynolds Walker for Cleaning Easternshore Chaple	270
To ditto for finding the Ellements for the Easternshore Chaple	240
To William Dyer for Cleaning pungo Chaple 6 months	90
To Charles Cason for Cleaning ditto 6 months	90
To Mary Broughton Towards her Relief	250

To Sarah Edmonds Towards her Relief	400
To Mary Barnes for keeping her son Jonathan	500
To Elizabeth Harvey Towards her Relief	180
To Henry Kinzee for a levy over Charg'd last year	50
To John Wickins per Account 16/	96
To Mr. Thomas Olds per Account £7:4:2:	865
To Pheby Dyer Towards her Relief & Children	500
To Capt. James Kempe for finding the Ellements at Brick Church	240
To ditto per John Cox per Account 16/	96
To Mr. John Bonney for finding the Ellements at pungo	240
To Henry Dawley for a levy Over Charg'd last year	50
To Colo. Anthony Walke & son per Account £12:3:6-1/4	1461-1/4
To William Nimmo Sr. per Account 20/	120
To Doctor Lewis Price for Attending the parishoners	2400
To John Bishop for keeping George Green	360
To Samuel Rea Towards his Relief	720
To Tully Williamson for Cureing Francis Barnes of a scald head	180
To Abia Consaulvo Towards her Relief & four Children	600
To Charles Gasking Clerk of Vestry & for Recording the processions	800
To The Churchwardens Towards Building Mary Broughton a house	510
To 6 per Ct. for Accounting on 32758-1/4	1965
	34723-1/4

[90]

Cr: By 2121 Tithables @ 16-1/4 lbs. per pole is 34442

    Fraction Carried to the County Levy   281   34723-1/4

Ordered that Capt. Jonathan Saunders Receive from Each Tithable 16-1/4 lbs. of Neet Tobacco for this year and Make payment to Each Claimer as above Directed

Agreed with John Bishop & wife to take Care & Look after the parishoners the Ensuing year for £12:0:0: The said Bishop & wife to have Their Diet found them, & the said Bishop is to Endeavour to make Corn Pease portators on the said parish [land?] & also to have fouls Raised for the Support of the said parishoners

Agreed with Richard Murray to keep Anguss McCaul's 2 Children the Ensuing year for £6

Ordered that the Churchwardens find junk for the parishoners To pick the Ensuing year

Ordered that Mr. Andrew Stewart pay John Cox Twelve pounds out of the parish Money in his hands

Ordered that the said Stewart pay Anthony Williamson Seven Shillings out of the same

VESTRY BOOK OF LYNNHAVEN PARISH

Ordered that Capt. James Kempe be paid £26:1:11: out of the Money in his hands that was Due from Mrs. Noro Parsons

Ordered that the Churchwardens or Mr. Stewart pay Thomas Williamson Teen pounds

The churchwardens to vew the upper chapl — Ordered that the Churchwardens Capt. William Woodhouse and Capt. Dennis Dawley Vew & look over the Repair that the said Thomas Williamson is to make in pungo Chaple & see that he put no Bad Stuff in the said Chapple

Anthony Walke

October 12th day 1765

[91] **Vestry man** — Major Anthony Walke Being Chosen a Vestry man of this Parish & having taken All the Oaths enjoining & subscribed The Test are Admitted a member of the said Vestry

Anthony Walke Junior

Princess Anne County

At A vestry Held the 12th Day of October 1765

The Reverend Mr. Robert Dickson Minister

Capt. James Kempe & Mr. Thomas Rey[nolds] Walker Church wardens

Present — Colo. Anthony Walke, Capt. John Whitehurst, Capt. William Keeling, Capt. William Woodhouse, Capt. Dennis Dawley, & Mr. Thomas Olds, Vestry men

The Parish of Lynhaven [is] . . . . Dr:	Neet Tobo:
To the Reverend Mr. Robert Dickson Minister Conveniant	16000
To ditto for Shrinkage & Cask	1280
To Mr. John Bulman Clerk of the Brick Church	1200
To Mr. Cason Moore Clerk of Pungo Chapple	1200
To Charles Gasking Clerk of Eastern shore Chapple	1200
To ditto Clerk of Vestry	250
To Anthony McKeel for Cleaning Brick Church & yard	270
To ditto Towards his Relief	300
To Mr. Thomas Rey[nolds] Walker for Cleaning Eastern shore Chapple	240
To ditto per Account £5:15:3:	692
To ditto for finding the Ellements Eastern shore Chapple	240
To Mr. Tully Williamson for Cleaning pungo Chapple	180
To Mary Broughton Towards her Relief	250
To Sarah Edmonds Towards her Relief	400
To Mary Barns for Keeping her son Jonathan	500
To Elizabeth Harvey Towards her Relief	180
To Colo. Nathaniel Newton for Inquisition on Drown'd persons	549
To Pheby Dyer Towards her Relief & Children	400
To William Biddle per Account 3/9	22½
[92] To Capt. William Woodhouse Senior per Account £2:0:0:	240
To Mr. Thomas Olds per Account £7:15:7:	933½
To Mr. George Corprew per Account £2:19:0:	354

To Mr. James Williamson Newton per Account £1:3:	168
To Mr. John Bonney Senior [for] finding the Ellements: upper Chapple	240
To Capt. James Kempe for finding Ellements for Brick Church	240
To Samuel Rea Towards his Relief	720
To Colo. Anthony Walke & son per Account £46:12:1-3/4	5593
To ditto as Assignees of Doctor Lewis Price	1200
To ditto as assignees of William Nimmo Senior £7:11:9:	910
To John Malbone 2 levies over charged in 1762: & 63:	104
To Richard Murry for keeping Angus McCauls 2 Children	840
To Abia Consaulvo Towards her Relief & 4 Children	600
To John Michal Kenline for making ministers gounds	90
To John Biddle per Account £3:3:9:	383
To Ruth Smith Towards her Relief	200
To Harison Banks for Rent of house for Samuel Rea	150
To the Churchwardens Towards the Support of the parishoners	4400
To 6 per Ct. for Accounting on . . . 42719	2563
	45282

Cr: By 2203 Tithables @ 20½ lbs. per pole is   45100

Fraction Carried to the County Levy   182   45282

Ordered that Mr. John Ackiss Sherif Receive from Each Tithable 20½ lbs of Neat Tobaco for this year & make payment to Each Claimer as above Directed

            Anthony Walke
            Charles Gasking Clerk of Vestry

[93]
Stewart to pay

Ordered that Mr. Andrew Stewart pay Capt. James Kempe Churchwarden The sum of Twenty pounds Nineteen Shillings & one penny it Being the Ballance Due from him to the parish.

Capt. Kempe to pay

Ordered that Capt. James Kempe pay to Colo. Anthony Walke & son Assignees of John Bishop the Sum of Six pound Eleven Shillings out of the money in his hands Which is the sum of £19:15:2:

Capt. Kempe to pay

Ordered that Capt. James Kempe pay Thomas Williamson the sum of Twenty one pounds Eighteen Shillings & Eightpence out of the money he is to Receive from Mr. Stewart

Agreed with Richard Murry to Keep Anguss McCauls 2 Children The Ensuing year for £6:0:0:

Agreed with Thomas Gorden to Keep Thomas Oldners Child The Ensuing year for £4:0:0:

Agreed with Tully Williamson to find Bricks @ 25/ per Thousand for the upper Chapple

Capt. Kempe's Motion for Gallery

On the Motion of Capt. James Kempe it's unanimisly Agreed & Liberty given him to Erect a hanging pew on the North side of the Brick Church

Mr. Edwd Moseley's Motion for Gallery

On the Motion of Mr. Edward Moseley Junior for a Gallery in the Brick Church on the South side, it's therefore Granted him, so that the same do not Effect the pulpitt

Capt. Keeling's Motion for Gallery

On the Motion of Capt. William Keeling, it's unanimisly Agreed & liberty given him, to Erect a hanging pew on the South side of the Eastern shore Chapple, adjoining the other gallery at His own Cost, the Stairs to Run up in the S.W. Corner.

Agreed with Capt. William Woodhouse Senior to Keep Anne Colly's Child the Ensuing year for £5

Agreed with John Bishop to take Care & Look after the parishoners the Ensuing year for £12:0:0: per year & they to have their Dyet found them, & he the said Bishop is to Endeavour to make a Crop of Corn pease &ca.

           Charles Gasking Clerk of Vestry

[94] Princes Anne County

At a Vestry Held the 13th Day October 1766

Present   The Reverend Mr. Robert Dickson Minister

   Capt. James Kempe [&] Mr. Thomas Reynolds Walker   Church Wardens

Colo. Anthony Walke   Colo. Edward Hack Moseley   Colo. Nathaniel Newton
Capt. John Whitehurst   Capt. William Keeling   Capt. William Woodhouse
Capt. Dennis Dawley &   Mr. Thomas Olds   Vestry men

The Parish of Lynhaven [is] Dr.	Neat Tobaco
To the Reverend Mr. Robert Dickson Minister Convenient	16000
To ditto for Shrinkage & Cask	1280
To Mr. John Bulman Clerk of Brick Church	1200
To Mr. Cason Moore Clerk of upper Chappel	1200
To Charles Gasking Clerk of Eastern shore Chappel	1200
To ditto per Account & Clerk of Vestry	490
To Anthony McKeel for Cleaning Brick Church	270
To ditto Towards his Relief	300
To Mr. Thomas Rey[nolds] Walker for Cleaning Eastern shore Cappel	270
To ditto for finding the Ellements for Eastern shore Chappel	240
To ditto per Account £1:13:	198
To Mr. Tully Williamson for Cleaning upper Chappel	180
To Mary Broughton Towards her Relief	150
To Sarah Edmonds Towards her Relief	400
To Elizabeth Harvey Towards her Relief	300
To Thomas Lewis per Account £1:5:	150
To Abia Consaulvo towards her Relief & 3 Children	400
To Mr. Thomas Olds per Account £3:12:8:	436
To Mr. John Bonney for finding the Ellements [for] upper Chappel	240
To Capt. James Kempe [for] finding Ellements [for] Brick Church	240
To ditto per Account £10:10:7:	1263-1/4
To ditto Assignee of John Bishop	1440
To Thomas Gorden for Keeping Thomas Oldner's Child	480

	To Capt. William Woodhouse for keeping Ann Colleys Child	600
	To ditto per Account 15/	90
	To Richard Murry for keeping Angus McCaul's 2 Children	720
	To Thomas Scophus 1 levy overcharged last year	50½
[95]	To William Nimmo for making Jonathan Harper's Coffen	45
	To Colo. Anthony Walke 1 levey Overcharged last year	50½
	To ditto per Account £47:5:1-3/4:	5670½
	To Capt. William Keeling per Account £2:8:4:	290
	To Mary Barns for keeping her son Jonathan	500
	To Elizabeth Fountain for keeping Margaret Fountain	600
	To William Biddle per Account £3:18:6:	471
	To Col. Nathaniel Newton per Account	503
	To John Denny for making William Willett['s] Coffen	45
	To Thomas Williamson per Account £13:2:5:	1575
	To Mary Moroner per Account £1:11:3:	187½
	To the Church wardens, toward the Repair of the Brick Church and Support of the parishoners the Ensuing year	5500
	To 6 per Ct. for Accounting on . . 45225-1/4	2713
		47938-1/4
	Cr: By 2272 Tithables @ 21 lbs per pole is 47712	
	By fraction Carried to County levey 226	47938

Ordered that Capt. Frederick Boush Sherif Receive From Each Tithable 21 lbs. of Neat Tobaco for this year & make Payment to Each Claimer as above Derected

                    Anthony Walke

Agreed with Thomas Gorden & wife to keep Thomas Oldner's Child the Ensuing year for £3:0:

Agreed with Richard Murry & wife to keep Angus McCaul's 2 Children the Ensuing year for £6:0:

Agreed with Mary Cear to keep her 2 Children the Ensuing year for £3:6:8:

[96] Agreed with Doctor Robert Paterson to take Care & look after The parishoners the Ensuing year & that he Bring his Account in at the laying of the Next parish levey.

Agreed with Ann Fleer to keep her 3 Children the Ensuing year for £5:0:0:

Agreed with John Bishop & wife to take Care & look after The parishoners the Ensuing year for the Sum of £12:0: per year

Agreed with Thomas Turner to keep Bridgett Colley the Ensuing year for £2:10:

Agreed with Capt. William Woodhouse to keep Margrett Colley the Ensuing year for £5:0:

Agreed with Mr. Edward Moseley to Repair the Brick Church the Ensuing year & that the Church wardens pay Him for the Same.

On the Motion of Charles Gasking for a Greater allowance as Clerk of the Eastern shore Chappel & Clerk of the Vestry that he The said Gasking have for the said Services 2000 lbs. of Neat Tobaco per year, & that Mr. John Bulman & Mr. Cason Moore Clerks of The Brick Church & pungo Chappel have 1650 lbs. of Neat Tobaco Each per year for their said Services &ca.

Charles Gasking Clerk of Vestry

[97]
Princess Anne County

At a vestry held the 14th of October 1767

[Present] The Reverend Mr. Robert Dickson Minister

Capt. James Kempe & Mr. Thomas Rey[nolds] Walker } Church wardens

Present

Colo. Anthony Walke   Colo. Edward Hack Moseley   Capt. John Whitehurst
Capt. William Keeling   Capt. Dennis Dawley   &   Capt. William Woodhouse

The Parish of Lynhaven [is] . . . Debtor	Neet Tobaco
To the Reverend Robert Dickson Minister Conveniant	16000
To ditto for shrinkage & Cask	1280
To Mr. John Bulman Clerk of Brick Church	1650
To ditto for Burying Anne Rice	30
To Mr. Cason Moore Clerk of the upper Chapple	1650
To Charles Gasking Clerk [of] Eastern shore Chapple & Vestry	2000
To Anthony McKeel for Cleaning the Brick Church	270
To ditto towards his Relief	360
To Mr. Thomas Rey[nolds] Walker for Cleaning Eastern shore Chapple	270
To ditto for finding the Ellements [for] Eastern shore Chapple	240
To Mr. Tully Williamson for Cleaning upper Chapple	180
To ditto per Account £1:5:0:	150
To Mary Broughton Towards her Relief	150
To Sarah Edmonds towards her Relief	400
To Elizabeth Harvey towards her Relief	300
To Abia Consolvo towards her Relief & 3 Children	400
To Mr. John Bonney Deceased for finding the Ellements: upper Chapple	240
To Capt. James Kempe for finding Ellements for Brick Church	240
To Thomas Gorden for keeping Thomas Oldner's Child	420
To Willis Linten for 1 levey Over Charged last year	60½
To Richard Murry for keeping Angus McCaul's Children	720
To Elizabeth Fountain towards her Relief	600
To Anne Fleer for keeping her Children	600
To Thomas Turner for keeping Bridgett Colley	300
To Mr. William Woodhouse (son of Capt.) for keeping Margrett Colley	600
[98] To Colo. Anthony Walke & son Assignees of John Bishop	1440
To ditto Assignees of Mary Kear	400

VESTRY BOOK OF LYNNHAVEN PARISH 79

To ditto per Account £43:17:2:	5263
To ditto for 1 levy Over Charges last year	50½
To Ruth Smith towards her Relief	300
To Argan Grimstead towards her Relief & 3 Children	400
To Thomas Ward Senior for maintaining William Turton some time since	800
To John Dolby per Account £0:13:	78
To Anthony Williamson for keeping George Price	336
To Charles Broughton for keeping Thomas Broughton's Child	420
To Hillery Brinson for 1 levy Overcharged last year	60½
To Winney Oharrow [O'Hara?] towards her Relief & 2 Children	300
To William Biddle 1 levy overcharged & making a Coffen	105
To Doctor Robert Paterson per Account £9:0:6:	1083
To Jonathan Porter per Account 7/6	45
To Thomas Scophus 1 levy overcharged	60½
To Mary Barnes for keeping her son Jonathan	500
To Thomas Olds per Account £3:3:10	383
To Capt. Frederick Boush per Account £0:17:6:	105
To ditto for Insolvants	2678½
To Daniel Dudly per Account £2:0:0:	240
To Mr. Edward Moseley (son of Francis)	36
To the Churchwardens Towards the Support of the Parishoners the Ensuing year	2000
	46194½
To 6 per Ct. for Accounting on	2771
	48965½

Cr: By 2296 Tithables @ 21-1/4 per pole is 48790

By Fraction Carried to County levy   175   48965

Ordered that Capt. Frederick Boush Sherif Receive from Each Tithable 21-1/4 lbs. of Neat Tobaco for this year and make payment to Each Claimer as above

Anthony Walke

[99]

Vestry Man chosen

Mr. Anthony Lawson being this day Appointed Vestryman and Desired that he take the Oaths Accordingly

Order to sell Negro wench Rachal

Agreed & Resolved by this vestry that the Church wardens sell the Negro wench Rachal belonging to the Parish & that the Money Ariseing thereby be applyed towards buying another Negro

Agreed with Richard Murry to keep Angus McCaull's Child the Ensuing year for £3:0:0:

Agreed with Mary Kerr to keep her 2 Children the Ensuing year for £2:10:

Agreed with Anne Fleer to keep her 3 Children the Ensuing year for £3:6:3:

Agreed with Charles Broughton to keep Thomas Oldner's Child the Ensuing year for £3:0:0:

Agreed with Thomas Simmons to keep Bridgett Colly the Ensuing year for £1:15:

Agreed with Mr. William Woodhouse (son of Capt.) to keep Margrett Colley the Ensuing year for £5:0:

Agreed with John Dolby to take Care & to look after the Parishoners the Ensuing year, he to build a hen house Crib & Repair the Garden & all Other Necessarys in the Carpenters way &ca. for £12: per year

On the Motion of Colo. Edward Hack Moseley to Build a pew in the Brick Church behind the front door so as Not to Discommode the Communion it is therefore granted him, and to Move the front Door Close to the Justices wife's pew.

Ordered that the Church wardens In case of John Dolby's Misbehaviour to Remove him, & Place who they think Proper to take Care & look after the parishoners.

[100]   At a vestry Held the 14th of October 1767

Ordered that Mr. Thumar [Thurmer] Hoggard & Mr. Perrain Smith Procession all the land on the North side of the Eastern Branch Precinct and make Return According to Law.

Thomas Wiles & John Mathias Procession the South side of The Eastern Branch and make Return According to Law.

William Wishart & Francis Moore Procession Little Creek Precinct and make Return According to Law.

Mr. Andrew Stewart & Mr. James Carraway Procession the lower Precinct of the western shore & make Return according to law.

Mr. James Whitehurst (son of Capt.) and Mr. Joshua Mathias Procession The upper precinct of the western shore.

Mr. John Keeling Senior & Mr. Peter Nolly Ellegood, Joel Cornick Senior, & Mr. John Haynes Procession the Lower Precinct of the Eastern shore.

Mr. Jonathan Jackson, Thomas Williamson, James Hendley, Jonathan Whitehead & John James, Procession the upper Precinct of the Eastern shore.

Mr. James Tooly & Willoughby olds Procession Black warter Precinct.

Anthony Walke

Test Charles Gasking Clerk of Vestry

At A vestry held the 7th of July 1768

Present   Capt. James Kempe, Colo. Edward Hack Moseley, Mr. Thomas Rey[nolds] Walker, Capt. Dennis Dawley & Mr. Thomas Olds

Francis Moore being Appointed one of the Procession Masters for little Creek Precinct last vestry & is since Dead ordered that John Collins son of George & William Wishart Procession all the land in little Creek Precinct & make Return of the same According to Law.

James Kempe

[101]
Princess Anne County   At a vestry held the 24th of October 1768

The Reverend Mr. Robert Dickson Minister

Capt. James Kempe & Mr. Thomas Rey[nolds] Walker } Church wardens

Present   Colo. Edward Hack Moseley   Capt. John Whitehurst   Capt. William Woodhouse
Mr. Thomas Olds   Capt. Dennis Dawley   & Maj. Anthony Walke
Vestry men

The Parish of Lynhaven [is] . . . . . Dr.	Neat Tobaco
To the Reverend Mr. Robert Dickson Minister conveniant	16000
To Ditto: for shrinkage and Cask	1280
To Mr. John Bulman Clerk of the Brick Church	1650
To Mr. Cason Moore Clerk of the upper Chaple	1650
To Charles Gasking Clerk of Eastern shore Chaple & Vestry	2000
To Ditto Assignee of Jonathan Porter	45
To Anthony McKeel for Cleaning Brick Church	270
To Ditto towards his Relief	360
To Mr. Thomas Rey[nolds] Walker for Cleaning Eastern shore Chaple	270
To Ditto for finding the Ellements [for] Eastern shore Chaple	240
To Ditto per Account £6:2:0:	732
To Tully Williamson for Cleaning upper Chaple	180
To Mary Broughton towards her Relief	150
To Sarah Edmonds towards her Relief	400
To Elizabeth Harvey (widow of Francis) towards her Relief	300
To Abia Consolvo towards her Children's Relief	400
To Jonathan Bonney [for] finding Ellements [for] upper Chaple	240
To Capt. James Kempe [for] finding Ellements [for] Brick Church	240
To Ditto per Account £10:18:4:	1310
To Charles Broughton for keeping Thomas Oldner's Child	360
To Richard Murrey for keeping Angus McCaules Child	360
To Elizabeth Fountain towards her Relief	600
To Anne Fleer for keeping her 3 Children	400
To Thomas Simmons for keeping Bridgett Colly	210
To William Woodhouse for keeping Margrett Colly	600
To Colo. Anthony Walke & son Assignees of Mary Kear	300
To Ditto Assignees of Ditto for keeping Abigal Frost's Child	60
To Ditto per Account £23:15:5-3/4:	2853
To Ditto Assignees of John Dolby	468
To Mary Barnes for keeping her son Jonathan	500
To James Braithwaite & Company 8/6	51
To John Gisbon per Account £8:18:	1068
To Dinah Mason for the Support of her Children	200
To Darcass Franklin for keeping Henry Kinsey's Child	240
To John Jamieson for one levy Over Charged last year	29
To Blazan Vangover for keeping Francis welding	480

[102]

To George Trouton for looking after the Parishoners 8 months	960
To William Fentress for one levy Over Charg'd Some time past	61
To Ditto for keeping Lidia Fentresses Child 12 months	360
To Richard Douge per Account £2:10:	300
To John Cox Ditcher towards his Relief	100
To Mr. John Ackiss per Account £7:13:	918
To James Williamson (Warehouse) per Account £3:0:0:	360
To Mark Tune per Account £1:13:4:	200
To Doctor John Bowser per Account £11:15:6:	1413
To Richard Williamson per Account £5:5:	630
To Elizabeth Omeary per Acount 15/	90
To James Garton towards his Relief	300
To Colo. Lemuel Cornick per Account £3:7:6:	405
Argan Grimstead towards her 2 Children's Relief	400
To the Church wardens towards the Support of the Parishoners the Ensuing year	3000
	46569
To Commition on 46569 lbs. @ 6 per Ct. is	2794
	49363

Cr: By 2302 Tithables @ 21-1/4 per pole is 48918

By Fraction 445

49363

Ordered that the Churchwardens Receive from Each Tithable 21-1/4 lbs. of Neat Tobaco for this year and make payment to Each Claimer as above.

James Kempe

Charles Gasking Clerk of the Vestry

[103]
Agreements

Agreed with Anne Fleer to keep her 3 Children the Ensuing year for £4:3:4:

Agreed with Richard Murrey to keep Angus McCauls Child the Ensuing year for £3:0:0:

Agreed with Mary Kear to keep her 2 Children the Ensuing year for £2:10:

Agreed with Charles James to keep Ruth Smith the Ensuing year for £3:6:8:

Agreed with Thomas Harvey to keep George price the Ensuing year for £3:0:0:

Agreed with Charles Broughton to keep Thomas Oldners Child the Ensuing year for £3:0:0

Agreed with Elizabeth Harvey (widow [of] Thomas) to keep her 3 Children the Ensuing year for £4:3:4:

Agreed with Lemuel Wakefield to keep Lemuel Gasking's Child the Ensuing year for £3:0:0:

Agreed with Elizabeth Omeary to keep her 4 Grandchildren the Ensuing year for £5:0:0:

Agreed with William Woodhouse to keep Margrett Colly the Ensuing year for £4:

Agreed with George Trouton & wife to take Care & look after the Parishoners the Ensuing year for £12:0:0: per year.

Capt. James Kempe and Mr. Thomas Rey[nolds] Walker being Continued Churchwardens for the Ensuing year its therefore ordered that they Execute their office accordingly.

            Charles Gasking Clerk of Vestry

At a vestry Held the 14th of November 1769

Present Capt. James Kempe [&] Mr. Thomas Rey[nolds] Walker Churchwardens

Colo. Edward Hack Moseley Capt. John Whitehurst Mr. William Woodhouse
Capt. Dennis Dawley Vestry Men

Lawson a vestry man

Mr. Anthony Lawson being Chosen a vestry man of this parish and he having taken the Oaths Enjoin'd & Subscribed the Test is admitted member of the same.

            Anthony Lawson

[104] Robinson a vestry man

Capt. Tully Robinson, Being Chosen a vestryman of this Parish & he having taken the Oaths Enjoin'd & Subscribed the Test is Admitted a member of this vestry

            Tully Robinson

Princess Anne

At a vestry Held the 9th Day of October 1769

The Reverend Mr. Robert Dickson Minister

   James Kempe   } Gentlemen Church wardens
   Thomas Rey[nolds] Walker }

Present

Edward Hack Moseley John Whitehurst William Woodhouse
Dennis Dawley Anthony Walke and Tully Robinson Gentlemen Vestry

The Parish of Lynhaven [is] Dr:	Neat Tobaco
To the Reverend Mr. Robert Dickson Minister Convenient	16000
To Ditto for Shrinkage & Cask	1280
To Mr. John Bulman Clerk of Brick Church	1650
To Mr. Cason Moore Clerk upper Chapple	1650
To Charles Gasking Clerk Eastern shore Chapple & Vestry	2000
To James Williamson per Account £2:0:0:	240
To Anthony McKeel for Cleaning Brick Church	270
To Ditto Towards his Relief	360
To Mr. Thomas Rey[nolds] Walker for Cleaning Eastern shore Chapple	270
To Ditto for finding the Ellements [for] Eastern shore Chapple	240
To Major Anthony Walke Assignee of Mary Kear	300
To Ditto Assignee of Lemuel Wakefield	360
To Ditto Assignee of Elizabeth Harvey (widow of Thomas)	500
To Ditto per Account £20:15:9½	2494-3/4
To Mr. Thomas Old per Account £5:17:6:	705
To Jonathan Bonny for finding Ellements [for] upper Chapple	240
To Richard Williamson for keeping Murphy's Child	90

VESTRY BOOK OF LYNNHAVEN PARISH

To Argan Grimstead for keeping her 2 Children	400
To Mary Marrener for keeping Abigal frosts Child	360
To Charles Broughton for keeping Thomas Oldners Child	360
To Elizabeth Omery for keeping her 4 Grand Children	600
To Blazan Vangover for keeping Francis Welden	480
To Thomas Willis for one levy over Charged last year	35-1/4
To Patiance Edgar per Account £2:10:	300
To Sarah Edmonds towards her Relief	400
To Mary Broughton towards her Relief	150
To John Cox Ditcher towards his Relief	100
To Elizabeth Harvey towards her Relief	500
To William Woodhouse (son of Capt.) for keeping Margrett Colly	480
To Lucy May per Account £0:10:	60
To Mary Barns for keeping her son Jonathan	500
To Charles James for keeping of Ruth Smith	400
To Ann Fleer for keeping her 3 Children	500
To Capt. Edward Cannon per Account £	366
To Doctor John Bowser per Account £12:0:0:	1440
To Sarah Cason for keeping her 3 Children	600
To Ruth Smith towards her Relief	400
To Mary Kear for keeping her 2 Children	300
To Richard Murry for keeping Angus McCauls Child	360
To Major Anthony Walke Assignee of thomas Harvey	360
To James Braithwait & Company	70
To George Troughton for looking after the parishoners	1440
To Elizabeth Omery for keeping John Davis' young Child	400
To Joel Cornick Collector for fraction last year	150
To Tully Williamson for Cleaning upper Chapple	180
To the Church wardens towards the Support of the parishoners the Ensuing year	3000
	43341
To 6 per Ct: on 43341 is	2600
	45941
Cr: By 2297 Tithables at 20 lbs is 45940	
fraction 1	

[105]

Ordered that Mr. Joel Cornick Junior Receive from Each tithable 20 lbs of Neat Tobaco the Ensuing year and make payment to Each Claimer as above

James Kempe
Charles Gasking Clerk of the vestry

[106] October the 9th 1769

Agreements

Agreed with Richard Williamson to keep Patrick Murphys Child the Ensuing year for £ 3:0:0:

Agreed with Mary Marrener to keep Abigal frost Child the Ensuing year for £3:

Agreed with Elizabeth Peetree to keep her 2 Children the Ensuing year for £3:6:8:

Agreed with Ann Fleer to keep her 3 Children the Ensuing year for £3:6:8:

Agreed with Charles Broughton for to keep Thomas oldners Child the Ensuing year for £3:0:0:

Agreed with John Trowers & his wife to take Care and look after the parishoners the Ensuing year and the said Trowers is to Endeavour to make Corn Peas purtators &ca for the sum of £11:0:0: per year

On the Motion of Capt. James Kempe to Cut a window on the North side of the Brick Church opposet to his hanging Pew liberty is therefore granted him

Colo. Edward Hack Moseley Junior Being Chosen A vestry man of this Parish, it's therefore ordered that he take the Oaths Enjoined thereto &ca

Agreed and Resolved by this vestry that Capt. James Kempe & Mr. Thomas Rey-[nolds] Walker Continue Churchwardens the Ensuing year

Ordered that Mr. Joel Cornick Junior Collect the Parish Levies the Ensuing year, he giving bond & Security to the Church wardens for the performance of the same

On the Motion of Mr. James Williamson in Behalf of Mr. Walter Lyon & Mr. Thumar [Thurmer] Hoggard to Cut a window on the South side of the Brick Church opposet to their hanging Pews, liberty is therefore granted him &ca

Mr. Anthony Lawson & Capt. Tully Robinson being Chosen vestry men of this Parish, & they having taken the oaths Enjoined and Subscribed the Test is Admitted members of the said vestry

James Kempe

Charles Gasking Clerk of vestry

[107] At a vestry Held the 10th of October 1770

Colo: Edward Hack Moseley Junior being Chosen a vestry man of this Parish and he having taken the Oaths Enjoined and Subscribed the Test is admitted a member of the Same— and also Subscribed to be Conformable to the Doctrine and Disapline of the Church of England

Edward Hack Moseley Junior

At A vestry Held the 10th Day of October 1770

The Rev. Robert Dickson Minister

James Kempe and Thomas Rey. Walker } Church wardens

John Whitehurst   William Woodhouse   Dennis Dawley
Anthony Walke   Tully Robinson   Edward Hack Moseley } Vestry men

Dr: The Parish of Lynhaven	Neat Tobaco
To the Rev. Mr. Robert Dickson minister Conveniant	16000
To Ditto for shrinkage & Cask	1280
To John Bulman Clerk [of the] Brick Church	1650
To Cason Moore Clerk [of the] upper Chapple	1650

To Charles Gasking Clerk [of the] Eastern shore Chapple & Vestry	2000
To Ditto assignee of Doctor John Bowser	69
To Anthony McKeel for Cleaning Brick Church	270
To Ditto Towards his Relief	360
To Capt. James Kempe [for] finding Ellements [for] Brick Church	240
To Ditto Omitted last year for Ditto	240
To Ditto per Account £7:2:7:	855½
To Mr. Thomas Rey[nolds] Walker for Cleaning Eastern shore Chapple	270
To Ditto [for] finding Ellements [for] Eastern shore Chapple	240
To Ditto per Account 7/11	48
To Ditto Assignee of Richard Williamson	366
To Tully Williamson for Cleaning upper Chapple	180
To Mr. Thomas Olds for keeping John Hails orphan	420
To George Durant Corprew for keeping Jonathan Hailes	240
To Major Anthony Walke per Account £29:6:7-3/4	3520
To James Braithwaight & Company	94
To Anne Whitehurst per Account £1:7:0:	162
To Jonathan Bonney [for] finding Ellements [for] upper Chapple	240
To Sarah Edmunds Towards her Relief	400
To Mary Broughton towards her Relief	150
To Mary Marroner for keeping Abigal Frosts Child	360
To Elizabeth Peetree for keeping her 2 Children	400
To Anne Fleer for keeping her 3 Children	400
To Charles Broughton for keeping Thomas Oldner's Child	360
To Martha Fentress towards her Relief	600
To Sarah Harvey for keeping her 2 Children	200
To Rachal Nokes for keeping her 2 Children	400
To Blazan Vangover for keeping Francis Welden	480
To Capt. John Whitehurst towards the Support of two orphans of Thomas Cason	500
To James Williamson per Account £1:0:0:	120
To Andrew Small for keeping Mary Laurance's Child	100
To Smith Shipherd per Account £1:15:4:	212
To Mr. John Ackiss per Account £3:7:1:	403
To Mr. John Keeling per Account £0:17:6:	105
To Capt. James Kempe for 114 lbs of Beef @ 12/6	86
To William Woodhouse (son of Capt.) for keeping Margrett Colley	480
To Joel Cornick for Insolvants for year 1768 & 69:	1114
To Ruth Smith Towards her Relief	500

[108]

VESTRY BOOK OF LYNNHAVEN PARISH

To Capt. Frederick Boush for Insolvants year 1767	508
To Jane Jones towards the Support of her 3 Children	600
To Susannah Nichols towards the support of her 2 Children	480
To John Moore for keeping Solomon Heaths Child	240
To Mary Barnes for keeping her son Jonathan	500
To Doctor John Bowser per Account £7:0:9½:	844-3/4
To the Churchwardens towards Building the upper Chapple	10000
To Ditto towards the Support of the parishoners the Ensuing year	2000
	52951-3/4

[109] To 6 per cent on 52951-3/4 . is   3177

                                                                                                  56128-3/4

Cr: By 2350 Tithables @ 23-3/4 . . is   55813-3/4
       By Fraction   315
                                    56128

Ordered that Mr. Jonathan Hopkins Receive from Each Tithable 23-3/4 lbs. of Neat Tobaco the Ensuing year & make payment to Each Claimer as above.

                                       James Kempe

Agreed with Mary Marrener to keep Abigal Frosts Child the Ensuing year for £3:10:

Agreed with Elizabeth Harvey to keep her 2 Children the Ensuing year for £2:10

Agreed with Elizabeth Peetree to keep her Child the Ensuing year for £2:10:

Agreed with Anne Fleer to keep her Children the Ensuing year for £2:10:

Agreed with George Troughton and wife to take Care & look after the parishoners the Ensuing year for £12:0:0:

James Kempe & Thomas R. Walker Gentlemen is this day Chosen Church wardens for the Ensuing year

Agreed with Elizabeth Omeary to keep her 2 Grand Children the Ensuing year for £1:13:4:

Agreed with Tully Williamson to keep his Brother Anthony Williamson the Ensuing year for £4:0:0: as per Note

Agreed with William Dawley to keep Ruth James the Ensuing year for £4:3:4:

John Trowers & wife having misbehaved at the poor house and not Complyed with their Agreement, It's Resolved by this Vestry that they have nothing for their Services

Order'd that the vestry be ajourned till vestry in Course   James Kempe

[110] At A vestry Held the 22nd Day of October 1771

The Reverend Mr. Robert Dickson Minister

James Kempe & Thomas Rey[nolds] Walker   Churchwardens

Present   Edward Hack Moseley Senior   John Whitehurst   William Woodhouse
           Anthony Walke & Tully Robinson   Gentlemen [of the Vestry]

Pursuant to an Act of Assembly for preventing Controversies Concerning the bounds of Lands, that once in every four years The bounds of every persons Lands shall be Processioned and Gone Round and the Land markes Renewed and for Dividing this parish into Convenient precincts and for appointing Intelligent freeholders for the performing such processioning at such a time as shall be to the said vestry Seem Conveniant and to see that Such processionings be duly performed between the Last day of September and the Last day of March next Ensuing and for Receiving an Account in Return of every persons Land so processioned as also their Failures herein and their perticular Reasons for so failing, and also for keeping & providing of a Register for the Recording of such proceedings in processioning as also for preventing Mistakes in the said Register as in the said Act is directed. Pursuant to the Directions in the said Act, it is ordered that the Churchwardens at Least Three Sundays before such persons shall proceed in Such processioning shall Give publick notis thereof at the Church.

Persons Appointed to perform the said processionings are, James Moore & Charles Williamson in the north side of the Eastern branch precinct, Charles Mathias, John persons, and Christopher Whitehurst in the south side Eastern branch precinct, Christopher Wright & Thomas Ewel for Little Creek precinct, Lemuel Thorowgood & Hillary Whitehurst for the Lower precinct Western shore, Erasmus Haynes, James Lovett Junior & John Stone for the upper precinct western shore, Jacob Ellegood Gentleman, John Lovett Junior, John Cornick & Joel Cornick Junior for the Lower precinct Eastern shore, William Shipherd, James Cason (son of John), William Woodhouse, Nathan Bonney, James Moore & Nathan Cornick for the upper precinct of Eastern shore, George Durant Corprew & John Woodard for black warter.

[111] At A vestry Held the 22nd Day of October 1771

The Reverend Robert Dickson Minister

James Kempe & Thomas Rey. Walker } Churchwardens

Edward Hack Moseley Senior   John Whitehurst   William Woodhouse
Anthony Walke & Tully Robinson   Gentlemen of the Vestry

Dr. The Parish of Lynhaven	Neat Tobaco
To the Reverend Mr. Robert Dickson Minister Conveniant	16000
To Ditto for shrinkage & Cask	1280
To John Bulman Clerk [of the] Brick Church	1650
To Cason Moore Clerk [of the] upper Chapple	1650
To Charles Gasking Clerk [of the] Eastern shore Chapple & vestry	2000
To Capt. James Kempe [for] finding the Ellements [for] Brick Church	240
To Ditto per Account £0:13:4:	110
To Mr. Thomas Rey[nolds] Walker for Cleaning Eastern shore Chapple	270
To Ditto per Account £0:3:10:	53
To Ditto [for] finding Ellements [for] Eastern shore Chapple	240
To Anthony McKeel for Cleaning Brick Church	270
To Ditto Towards his Relief	360
To Tully Williamson for Cleaning upper Chapple	180
To Ditto for keeping his Brother Anthony 9 months	320
To Mary Marrener for keeping Abigal frosts Child	150
To Thomas Harvey for keeping Anthony Williamson 3 months	160

	To George Troughton for Looking after the parishoners	1440
	To William Dawley for keeping Ruth James	500
	To Major Anthony Walke per Account £21:9:1:	2574½
	To Ditto Assignee of Elizabeth Harvey	309
	To Ditto Assignee of John Trowers	300
	To Ditto for 13 Barrels Corn & 1 Bushel @ 10/0 paid John Trowers 18d for trays 18d	801
	To Sarah Edmonds towards her Relief	400
	To Doctor Chraigdillia per Account £16:14:7:	2007½
	To Elizabeth Peetree for keeping her Child	300
	To Anne Fleer for keeping her Child	300
	To Rebecca Salmons for keeping Betty plats Child	200
[112]	To Joshua Hopkins for one levy over Charg'd last year	31
	To Mary Whitehurst towards the Support of her 3 Children	600
	To Richard Murry for keeping Angus McCauls Child	360
	To Elizabeth Omeary for keeping her 2 Grand Children	200
	To Ditto per Account 11/1	66
	To John Dyer for keeping Ruth Aires	500
	To Henry Caps for keeping Sally Caps	420
	To Patt Murphy for keeping Mary Laurance's Child	421
	To Susannah Nickcols towards the support of her 2 Children	480
	To Elizabeth Consaulvo towards the Support of her 4 Children	800
	To Rachal Nokes towards the Support of her 2 Children	400
	To Blazan Vangover for keeping Francis Welden	480
	To Anne Godfry for keeping Bartholomew Scots Child	200
	To James Williamson per Account 10/	60
	To Sarah Harvey for keeping her Child	200
	To Martha Fentress towards her Relief	600
	To John Moore for keeping James Heath	200
Nov. 26, 1771	To Capt. John Whitehurst towards the Support of Thomas Casons Children	530
	To Colo. E. Hack Moseley for Coppying of Presentments of Grand Jurys	84
	To Mr. John Ackiss per Account £7:12:6:	915
	To Capt. Erasmus Haynes per Account 12/6	75
	To James powers for keeping James Lesters Child	360
	To alse Marsh towards her Relief	400
	To Frances Sullivant for keeping her 2 Children	600
	To Marke Moore for one levy Over Charged Last year	31

To Mary Barnes for keeping her son Jonathan	500
To Ruth Smith towards her Relief	500
To jean Jones towards the Support of her Children	600
To the Churchwardens towards building upper Chapple	15000
To Ditto towards the Support of the parishoners the Ensuing year	2000
	61669
To 6 per Ct. on 61669 .. is	3700
	65369

[113]

Cr: By 2416 Tithables @ 27 lbs. per pole is	65232
fraction of	137
	65369

Ordered that Mr. Jonathan Hopkins Sheriff Receive from Each Tithable 27 lbs. of nett Tobaco the Ensuing year and make payment to Each Claimer as before mentioned.

           James Kempe

Agreed with Elizabeth Omeary to keep her Grand Child the Ensuing year for £1:13:4:

Agreed with Anne Godfry to keep Bartholomew Scott's Child the Ensuing year for £3:0:0:

Agreed with George Troughton to keep James Murphy's Child the Ensuing year for £2:0:0:

Agreed & Resolved by the vestry that James Garton take Care and Look after the parishoners the Ensuing year, and if he the said Garton should Misbehave the Churchwardens to turn him out and place some Other person in his place

Agreed with John May to keep Mary Willit the Ensuing year for £2:0:0:

Agreed with Lydda Willyroye to keep Mary Fentress the Ensuing year for £1:13:4:

Agreed with Thomas Olds Junior to keep John Hailes the Ensuing year for £3:0:

Ordered that the Churchwardens purchase four Linnen Wheals for the parishoners to work with

Major Anthony Walke & Mr. William Woodhouse Senior is this day Chosen Church wardens for the Ensuing year

Agreed by the Majority of this Vestry that Mr. John Bulman be Continued as Clark of the Brick Church Dureing Pleasure

           Charles Gasking Clerk of Vestry

Lyn-haven Parish

[114]

Princess Anne County

At a Vestry held the 17th day of June 1772

    Present

   The Reverend Robert Dickson Minister

Anthony Walke Senior Gent. William Woodhouse Senior Gent. Church-Wardens

James Kempe Gent., John Whitehurst Gent.,
Thomas Old Gent., Dennis Dawley, Gent.,
Thos. Rey. Walker Gent., Anthony Lawson Gent., } Vestry-men
John Ackiss Gent., Tully Robinson Gent.,
and Edward Hack Moseley Gent.

It having been represented to this Vestry, and they well knowing that the present Chapel at Pungo is at this Time in a very Ruinous state and condition, and therefore vastly dangerous to Assemble and meet therein to offer up Prayers &c. to Almighty God, for which the said Chapel was erected and built.

It is therefore Ordered and directed by the above Vestry That James Kempe Gent., Edward Hack Moseley Senior, Gent., and Dennis Dawley Gent., or any three of them, be and are, appointed Commissioners for the Letting out, contracting and Agreeing with some sufficient able, and proper Workman, for the building of a new Chapel at or near the said Place of the following Dimensions, the Workman with whom the abovesaid Commissioners or any three of them shall (after Advertiseing Publickly) contract and Agree with, entering into Bond with sufficient security for the true Performance of such clauses as shall be in such Bond inserted for the finishing thereof agreeable to the said Commissioners, or any three, their approbation.—

Vizt. Seventy five Feet in Length } from outside to outside
Thirty Feet in width

The Walls to be Twenty Feet to the square, and from the Foundation to the Water Table to be three bricks thick and from thence upward to be two bricks thick.

Two Doors one on the South side near the East end and the other in the West End, each Door to be Arched and eight Feet to the Arch and 4 Feet in Width.

Five Windows on the North side   Arched and Glazed with best
Four Ditto on the South side   crown Glass 9 in. by 11 in.
Three Ditto in the East end . . . . of same dimensions

The above Windows to contain six Lights in height and four Lights in breadth, each, exclusive of the Arches.

Two Arched Windows into a Gallery at the West End, to contain each twelve Lights of the same Dimensions, to wit 9 inches by 11 inches, exclusive of the Arches.

A Gallery at the West End to be twenty five Feet deep.

To be Plaistered and Painted were necessary and finished to the approbation of [the] Commissioners.

James Kempe

Lynhaven Parish } County of Princess Anne

At a vestry held the twenty first day of October one Thousand seven hundred and seventy two.

Present: The Reverend Robert Dickson Minister

  Capt. William Woodhouse Sen'r & Major Anthony Walke Church-Wardens

  Capt. James Kempe, Col. Edward Hack Moseley, Sen'r, Capt. Dennis Dawley, Mr. Thomas Reynolds Walker, Mr. Anthony Lawson, Mr. John Ackiss, Capt. Tully Robinson & Col. Edward Hack Moseley Junior, Vestry-men

Major Anthony Walke presented his Account of Dr: & Cr: on Account of Communion money which having been read the same is allowed.

On the Petition of Frances Smyth, Ordered that 40/. be levied for her towards her maintaining her child.

Agreed with William Capps to keep Mary Lester Orphan of James Lester and a Negro of her's the ensuing Year for the sum of £4.

Agreed with Anne Godfrey widow of Smyth Godfrey deceased to keep her three Children the ensuing Year for 600 lbs. Tobo.

Agreed with Mary Whitehurst Widow of Samuel Whitehurst to keep her three children the ensuing Year for 600 lbs. Tobo.

Agreed with John Wells to keep Lidia Land, Orphan of Francis Land, the ensuing Year for £3.

Agreed with William Gilbert Gray to keep [Judah] Land Orphan of Francis Land, the ensuing Year for £3.

Agreed with William Land to keep Elizabeth Land Orphan of Francis Land the ensuing Year for 200 lbs. of Tobo.

Agreed with John Chapple to maintain his daughter Betty the ensuing year for 300 lbs. of Tobacco

Agreed with Betty Broughton to maintain her four children the ensuing Year for 800 lbs. of Tobo.

Agreed with Charles Broughton to maintain John Easter son of Mary Easter the ensuing Year for 200 lbs. of Tobacco.

[116] Lynhaven

1772 21st October	The Parish of Lynhaven Dr:		
	To the Reverend Robert Dickson Minister	16000	
	To Ditto for Shrinkage and Cask	1280	
	To Ditto by Account	80	17360
	To John Bulman Clerk of Brick Church	1650	
	Ditto per Account	90	
November 26th	Ditto per Account	30	1770
October 21st	Cason Moore Clerk of Pungo Chapel		1650
	Capt. Charles Gasking Estate late Clerk of Eastern shore Chapel		1178-1/4
	Thomas Abbott present Clerk of Eastern shore Chapel per Account		1188
	Mr. Thomas Rey^s Walker for cleaning Eastern shore Chapel	270	
	and finding Elements there	240	510
	John Cumberfoot Assignee of Mary Hewit	366½	
November 26th	Ditto	60	426½
October 21st	John Kenline by Account		39
	George Chapel for keeping Jonathan Barnes		210
	Frances Smyth by Petition		240
	Anthony McKeel for cleaning Brick Church	270	
	Ditto . . . for support	500	770
	Mr Walke for finding Elements at Brick Church	240	
	ditto by Account	1734	
	ditto on Account of Judah Land for John Wells and William Gilbert Gray	147-3/4	2121-3/4
	William Sorey for keeping a stranger		336
	Martha Nimmo by Account		469½
	Susannah Nichols for maintaining two children		480
	Mr Peter Singleton by Account	102-1/4	
November 26th	. . . ditto . . . by ditto	60	162-1/4
October 21st	James Williamson by ditto	180	
November 26th	. . . ditto . . . by ditto	60	240
October 21st	Blazen Vangover for keeping Frances Welden		480

William Dawley for keeping Ruth James	500
Rachel Nokes for support of her two children	400
William Salmons for maintaining Betty Platt's Child	360
Elizabeth Consaulvo for maintaining her Children	800
Mary Leversage for maintaining two Children	400
Charles Broughton for maintaining John Easter	125
George Troughton for maintaining James Murphey Orphan of Patrick Murphey	240
Elizabeth Petree for maintaining her child	300
Sarah Edmonds for her support	400
Elizabeth Harvey widow of Thomas	300
Martha Fentress towards her support	600
Frances Sullivan for maintaining her 2 Children	500
Mark Toone for maintaining his three Children	600
[117] To Adam Robinson by Account	195
Mary Randolph by Account	564
Capt. James Kempe by Ditto	174
Col. Lemuel Cornick by Ditto	63
Capt. John Whitehurst by Ditto	60
Jane Jones	500
Alice Marsh	600
Jonathan Bonney for finding the Elements at Pungo Chapel for the Years 1771 & 1772	480
Thomas Olds Junior	720
Sarah Sharwood widow of James for maintaining her Children	600
Anthony Williamson for his support	480
The Commissioners towards building Pungo Chapel	23000
Mr John Ackiss by Account	240
Doctor Hugh Craigdellie by Account	2631
William Moseley for attending Parish House	822
Elizabeth Omerry for maintaining her Grandchildren	600
John Maye for Molly Willet	240
Mary Whitehurst for her support	500
Anne Godfrey for Bartholomew Scott's Child	300
The Church Wardens for support of Parish-house & Poor	3000
	70925-1/4
To 6 per Cent. on collecting	4255
	75180-1/4

1772   Cr: By 2448 Tithables @ 30-3/4 lbs. per pole is 75076 lbs. Tobo.

By a Fraction due from Sheriff   [104]

November 26th Ordered that Mr. John Hancock Sheriff Receive from each Tithable 30-3/4 lbs. of Neat Tobacco for this Year and make paiment to each Claimer as above

Teste Thomas Abbott Clerk of Vestry   James Kempe

Parish of Lynhaven } County of Princess Anne

At a Vestry the twenty sixth day of November, one thousand seven Hundred and seventy two.

Present: The Reverend Robert Dickson Minister

     Capt. William Woodhouse . . Church Warden

     Capt. James Kempe, Capt. John Whitehurst
     Mr. Thomas Old, Capt. Dennis Dawley,
     Mr. Thomas Reynolds Walker and
     Mr. Edward Hack Moseley, Junior,   Vestry-men

Agreed with John Nicholas to keep Elizabeth Southern's child the ensuing year by Order for 50/-

[118] Ordered that the minister and readers of this Parish do on every Sunday throughout the Year begin the Divine service at the Hour of eleven o'Clock in the 'forenoon and further Ordered that the Church Wardens do send for three Dials for the Latitude 37°, one of each to be fix'd at the Church, one at the Eastern shore Chapel and one at Pungo Chapel.

Capt. William Woodhouse senior and Mr. Anthony Lawson This day were elected Church-Wardens for the ensuing Year.

Mr. William Moseley is continued overlooker of the Poor and Parish-House the ensuing Year, he having agreed upon the usual Terms.

Ordered that the money heretofore levied (and collected by the Sheriff of this County and now in his hands) for the purpose of erecting a New Chapel at Pungo be paid by the said Sheriff into the Hands of the Commissioners appointed by a former Vestry and that they apply the same to and for the use the same was Levied.

Ordered that Mr John Hancock present Sheriff collect and receive the Tobacco by this Vestry Levied, and make paiment according to the several Claims, and that he be allowed 6 per Cent. for collecting the same

Thomas Abbott was this day elected Clerk of the Vestry of this Parish.

Ordered that Vestry be adjourned 'till legal Notice given.

     Teste   James Kempe
Thomas Abbott, Clerk of Vestry

[119]   Parish of Lynhaven }
     County of Princess Anne

     At a Vestry held the 8th day of September 1773

         Present

     The Reverend Robert Dickson Minister

     Capt. John Whitehurst, Major Anthony Walke,
     Mr. Thomas Reynolds Walker, Capt. Dennis Dawley, } Vestry-men
     Mr. John Ackiss & Capt. Edward H. Moseley Junior

It having been represented to this Vestry that by the former Order made relative to the Walls of the New Chapel now erecting and building at Pungo the said Walls from the Water Table upwards will be to slender and weak for a

Building of such Dimensions, which being taken into consideration by this present Vestry the said representation is approved off, and thereupon Agreed with Hardress Waller the Undertaker to carry up the Walls of the said Chapel from the Water table to the heighth of the thickness of two Bricks and a half in thickness, which the said Hardress Waller at this Vestry agreed to do for the additional sum of seventy five Pounds, The same being Levied for him at the Laying of the next Parish Levy.

The said Hardress Waller also undertakes for a further Sum of Five Pounds to place in each Gavel [gable] End one Circular Window of at Least four feet Diameter, as the same will be as well useful as Ornamental to the said Chapel which is Ordered accordingly.

Ordered that Vestry be adjourned 'till legal notice given.

Teste Thomas Abbott Clerk Vestry   John Whitehurst

[120]   Parish of Lynhaven
       County of Princess Anne

At a Vestry held the 18th day of October 1773

Present

The Reverend Robert Dickson Minister
Mr. Anthony Lawson Church-Warden
Capt. James Kempe, Col: Edward Hack Moseley, Senior,
Capt. Dennis Dawley, Mr. Thomas Reynolds Walker
and Col. Edward Hack Moseley, Junior

Vestry-men

The Parish of Lynhaven	Dr. Lbs. Tobo.
To the Reverend Robert Dickson for Salary	16000
for Shrinkage and Cask	1280
John Bullman Clerk of Brick Church for Salary	1650
Thomas Abbott Clerk of Eastern Shore Chapel and Vestry	2000
Cason Moore Clerk of Pungo Chapel for Salary	1650
Mr. Anthony Lawson for finding Elements at Brick Church	240
Mr. Thomas Reynolds Walker for finding Elements at East^n shore Chap^l	240
Mr. Jonathan Bonney for finding Elements at Pungo Chapel	240
Anthony McKoil for cleaning Brick Church	270
Mr Thomas Reynolds Walker for cleaning Eastern shore Chapel	270
Mr. Tully Williamson for cleaning Pungo Chapel 1772 & 1773	540
William Capps for keeping Mary Lester Orphan of James Lester and her Negro one Year past	480
John Chapel for keeping his Daughter one Year past	300
Betty Broughton for keeping her four Children one Year past	800
Charles Broughton for keeping John Easter son of Mary Easter one Year past	200
John Nicholas for keeping Eliz. Southern's Children one Year past	300
Thomas Olds Senr for keeping Elizabeth Heath's Child 8 Months	320
Thomas Olds Senr for keeping said Child 4 months coming	160
Alice Marsh for her Support	600
John Nicholas for support of Eliz. Southern's Child one Year coming	300

To John Chapel for support of his Daughter one Year coming	300
Anthony McKeil for his support	500
Elizabeth Gorden Widow of John Gorden deceased for support of two children	600
Capt. Dennis Dawley for support of Sarah Sharwood's Children	600
John Bonney Senior for looking after Pembrook Brown	180
Anthony Fentress for one Acre of Ground whereon to erect the New Chaple at Pungo and breaking his other Land	600
[121] John Dyer for keeping Ruth Airs 1772 & 1773	1000
William Dawley, son of John, for support of Ruth James	500
Elizabeth Consaulvo for support of her 3 Children	800
Catharine Wood for support of her 3 Children	1000
Tully Barns for support of Mary Lester Orphan	360
Anne Godfrey Widow of Smyth for support of 3 Children	900
Mary Whitehurst Widow of Samuel for support of 3 Children	900
Elizabeth Toone for support of her 3 Children	900
Jonathan Hopkins by Account	282
Rachel Nokes for support of her 2 Children	600
Anthony Williams for his support, to be paid Mr. Walke for his Use	480
Elizabeth Cooper for support of 2 Orphans of Thomas Weddell	600
Mary Leversage for support of her 2 Children	600
Blazen Vangover for support of Frances Weldon	480
Frances Sullivan for support of her 2 Children	500
James Brewer for keeping John Norris's Child from 11th Feby last till this Time 200	
James Brewer for keeping John Norris Child this Year 300	500
Elizabeth Omerry for support of her 3 Grand-children	900
William Salmons for keeping Betty Platt's Child	480
George Troughton for keeping Pat Murphey's son	240
Hardress Waller by Account for temporary repairs at the Old Chapel at Pungo	1444
James Lamb by Account	1244
Mary Willing for support of her Daughter Mary	600
Capt. Dawley for support of Ruth Smith	600
	45230

David McClenahan Gent. was this day unanimously elected a Vestry-man in the place and stead of Capt. Tully Robinson deceased.
Ordered that this Vestry be adjourned until Tuesday the 16th of November next

Teste Thomas Abbott Clerk Vestry   James Kempe

VESTRY BOOK OF LYNNHAVEN PARISH 97

[122]] Parish of Lynhaven
County of Princess Anne

At a Vestry held the 14th December 1773.

Present

The Reverend Robert Dickson Minister
Capt. William Woodhouse Senior, Church-Warden
Capt. James Kempe   Col. Edward Hack Moseley Sr.
Capt. Dennis Dawley Mr. Thomas Reynolds Walker }Vestry-men
Mr. Anthony Lawson & Col. Edward Hack Moseley Jr.

The Parish of Lynhaven	Dr. Lbs. Tobo.
To Lemuel Newton by Account	630
The Commissioners of Pungo [Chapel] for defraying the Expence of Building and finishing thereof	42000
Mr. Anthony Walke by Account	439-3/4
Thomas Langley by Ditto	480
The Estate of Capt. John Whitehurst by Account	240
Mr. Hardress Waller by Account	24
Doctor Hugh Craigdellie by Account	3441
William Berry for keeping Dinah Creed six months	600
Sarah Edmonds for her relief	400
John Wells for keeping Lidia Land the last year	360
William Gilbert Gray for keeping William Land last year	360
Susannah Nicholas for support of two children	480
Mr. John Bullman by Account	120
Mr. Daniel Dudley by Ditto	60
Mr. James Lamb by Ditto	18
Mr. William Land for keeping Elizabeth Land orphan of Francis Land	200
Frances Jobson for keeping her two children	600
Charity McCaull for her support	240
Elizabeth Petree for her supporting a Child	300
Hannah Fallen for support of her three Children	900
The Church-Wardens for supporting two Children Orphans of Thomas Harvey deceased	600
Peter Norley Ellegood by Account	26-1/4
Sarah Axtead for her support	300
James Williamson by Account	240
Betty Broughton by Agreement last Year	800
William Salmons by Account	360
James Smith for keeping Thomas Lester	480
Jane Jones for support of two Children	540

VESTRY BOOK OF LYNNHAVEN PARISH

[123]

To John Maye for keeping Mary Willett	240
Messrs. William White & Co. Ballance of their Account	468-1/4
William Moseley by Account	1524
George Troughton for taking care of (and Living at the Parish house) the Poor, He finding himself and his own family with Provisions the ensuing Year by Agreement.	1920
Henry Smawn for keeping an Orphan Child of the late Charles Norris deceased from September 4th to this time and for the ensuing Year	327
Charles Broughton for keeping John Easter	420
Mary Whitehurst Widow of Samuel per Agreement	600
Ann Godfrey Widow of Smith Godfrey per Agreement	600
Mary Whitehurst for her support	500
Martha Fentress for her support	600
Thomas Abbott for sundry Services	240
Amount Carried over	62648-1/4

Capt. Jacob Ellegood and Capt. William Nimmo were this day elected Vestry-men in the room of Capt. Tully Robinson and Capt. John Whitehurst deceased.

Capt. William Woodhouse is by his consent continued Church-Warden and Mr. John Ackiss is elected another Church-Warden in the Room and stead of Mr. Anthony Lawson.

John Hancock Gent. is elected and appointed Collector of the Levies for the above Tobacco he having given Bond and security according to Law.

Ordered that Vestry be adjourned until legally called.

James Kempe

[124]

Princess Anne County
Parish of Lynhaven

At a Vestry held the 14th January 1774

Present

The Reverend Robert Dickson Minister
Mr. John Ackiss Church-Warden
Capt. James Kempe   Col. Edward Hack Moseley Sr.
Mr. Thomas Old   Mr. Thomas Reynolds Walker   Vestry-men
Mr. Anthony Lawson   Col. Edward Hack Moseley Jr.
     & Capt. Jacob Ellegood

The Parish of Lynhaven	Dr. Lbs. Tobo.
To the Church Wardens for support of Parish-house and Parishoners the Present Year	3000
Messrs. White & Co. for 3 sets of Bishop Secker's Works	1128
Capt. Jacob Ellegood this day qualified according to Law as a Vestry-man and took his Seat accordingly	.
Amount of Tobacco Levied 18th October Last	45230½
Levied 14th December Last	62648-1/4
Sheriff's Commission at 6 per Ct. for Collecting	6720-1/4
	118727

The Parish of Lynhaven   Cr:

By 2505 Tithables at 47½ lbs. Tobo. per Poll is 118987½
    The Tobacco in the Sheriff's hand to be ⎫
    Collected & accounted for Next Year   ⎭

Ordered that Mr. John Hancock Gent. receive from each Tithable Person 47½ lbs.
of Nett Tobacco the ensuing year and make paiment to each Claimer as above.

                                           James Kempe

[125] Princess Anne County ⎫ At a Vestry held the 25th October 1774
       Parish of Lynhaven   ⎭

                        Present

        The Reverend Robert Dickson Minister
        Capt. John Ackiss Church-Warden
        Capt. James Kempe   Mr. Thomas Old, Sr.   ⎫
        Capt. Dennis Dawley   Mr. Thomas Reynolds Walker   ⎬ Vestry-men
        Mr. Anthony Lawson   Col. Edward Hack Moseley, Jr. ⎪
               and Col. Jacob Ellegood   ⎭

To the Reverend Robert Dickson Minister his Salary	16000	
for Shrinkage and Cask	1280	
by Account	390	17670
Mr. John Bullman his Salary, as Clerk of Brick Church		1650
Mr. Cason Moore his Salary as Clerk of Pungo Chapel		1650
Thomas Abbott his Salary as Clerk of Eastern shore Chapel & Vestry		2000
Capt. James Kempe for finding Elements at Brick Church		240
Mr. Thomas Reynolds Walker for Ditto at Eastern shore Chapel		240
Mr. Jonathan Bonney Sr. for ditto at Pungo Chapel		240
Franky McKeil for Cleaning the Brick-Church		270
Mr. Thomas Reynolds Walker . Ditto . Eastern shore Chapel		270
Mr. Tully Williamson Sr. Ditto Pungo Chapel		270
Mr. Jonathan Bonney Sr. for a Coffin for Amy Cowper a poor woman		60
Burrough Moseley by Account		419
Elizabeth Gordon Widow of John Gordon deceased		600
Elizabeth Price Widow of Adam Price deceased		500
Charity McCaull for her support		270
Alexander Keeling by Account		57
Willoughby Berry for keeping an Orphan by Account		180
William Gilbert Gray, for maintaining William Land, Orphan of Francis Land deceased		360
John Wells for maintaining Lidia Land Orphan of Francis Land dec[d]		360
James Brewer for maintaining John Norris's Orphan		300
Mary Whitehurst Widow of Samuel for support of 2 Children		600
Blazon Vangover for support of Frances Weldon		480
John Cornick by Account		84
Sarah Edmonds for her relief		400

To Mr. Anthony Walke by Account	2439-1/4
The Church Wardens of St. Brides, Norfolk County	408
Elizabeth Consaulvo for support of 3 Children	800
Elizabeth Omerry for support of 1 infirm Child	500
Charles Broughton for support of 1 Orphan	420

Anthony Fentress is appointed Sexton of Pungo Chapel in the room of Tully Williamson Sr. late Sexton

Amount Tobacco Carried forward 33737-1/4

[126] Doctor John Hodgson is appointed Surgeon and Apothecary at the Parish-House, in the Room of the late Doctor Hugh Craigdallie deceased, during the Pleasure of the Vestry.

Ordered and appointed that Capt. John Ackiss, Col. Edward Hack Moseley, Jr., and Col. Jacob Ellegood do meet upon the Glebe Lands and view the same together with the Buildings thereon, and make their report of the state and condition thereof to the next Vestry.

Ordered that Vestry be adjourned untill Thursday the 24th of November next.

James Kempe

[127] Princess Anne County / Parish of Lynhaven } At a Vestry held the 24th November 1774

Present

The Reverend Robert Dickson Minister
Capt. John Ackiss, Church-Warden,
Capt. James Kempe   Capt. Dennis Dawley
Mr. Thos Reys Walker Maj. Anthony Walke } Vestry-Men
and Col. Jacob Ellegood

The Parish of Lynhaven	Dr.	Lbs. Tobo.
To Messrs. William White & Co. by Account		456
Capt. James Kempe by Account		150
Mr. Thomas Reynolds Walker by Account		241
Mr. Edward Moseley by Account		36
Adam Robinson for support of Ruth James		600
Capt. Dawley for support of Ruth Smith		600
" " for support of Sarah Sharwood		400
Susannah Nichols for support of 2 Children		480
Frances Sullivan for support of 2 Children		400
Jane Jones for support of 2 Children		400
Elizabeth Broughton for support of 4 Children		800
Mary Whitehurst for support		500
Martha Fentress for support		600
Peter Singleton by Account		174
Thomas Old Jr. by Account		315

VESTRY BOOK OF LYNNHAVEN PARISH   101

George Cox by Account	205½
James Smith by Account	36
The Church-Wardens for support of Sarah Axtead	300
" " " for support of Charles Norris's Orphan	300
Whiddon Milleson for support of Abigail Milleson	480
Frankey McKeil for support of her two Children	480
Tully Barnes for support of Mary Lester	360
Hannah Fallen for support of 3 Children	800
Capt. John Ackiss the Ballance of his Account	450½
Amount Tobacco carried forward	9564-3/4

Doctors Ramsay and Taylor are appointed Surgeons and Apothecaries at the Parish-House of this County, in the place and stead of Doctor Hodgson, who was elected the last Vestry to serve in those Stations, during pleasure.

Ordered that Maj. Anthony Walke pay into the Hands of the Church-Wardens the Tobacco levied in Vestry the 26th day of November 1771, and that the same be Applied by the said Church-Wardens towards the support of the Parishoners and Parish-House.

Capt. John Ackiss is continued Church-Warden the ensuing Year, and Col. Jacob Ellegood is elected the other Church-Warden in conjunction with Capt. John Ackiss in the room of Capt. Woodhouse deceased.

[128] This day Mr. Anthony Walke Junior, Gent., was elected a Vestry-man in the Room of Capt. William Woodhouse, Sr., deceased.

Frankey McKeil is appointed to take care of the Church, the Ensuing Year as Sexton.

Ordered that Vestry be adjourned untill the 13th day of December next.

James Kempe

Princess Anne County } At a Vestry held the 13th day of December 1774
Parish of Lynnhaven }

Present

The Reverend Robert Dickson Minister
Capt. James Kempe,   Thomas Reynolds Walker
Maj. Anthony Walke   Col. Edward Hack Moseley, Jr. } Vestry
Col. Jacob Ellegood   Capt. John Ackiss   } men
    and Capt. William Nimmo

Ordered that 1440 lbs. of Tobacco be Levied [for] George Troughton for attending the Parishoners and Parish-house till this Time 12 Months, and that he be allowed his Provision during that Time at the said Parish-House.

Thomas Reynolds Walker Gent. having entered into Bond, with approved Security, for collecting the Levies for this present Year, and paying thereof to the several claimants according to Law; it is Ordered that he enter into his Office accordingly.

The Gentlemen appointed by a former Vestry This day made their Report of the state of the Houses and Buildings at the Glebe of this Parish that the same require sundry necessary repairs; therefore Ordered that Thomas Reynolds Walker and Col. Jacob Ellegood Use their best endeavors to employ a workman capable of repairing the same; the expences of which repairs are to be levied at the laying of the next levy.

Ordered that the Parish have Credit for 480 lbs. of Tobacco which was levied last Year for the support of Anthony Williams[on] deceased and which Tobacco is in the hands of the late Collector and be by him paid to the present Collector of the Levies for this Year.

[129]

The Parish of Lynhaven	Dr.	Lbs. Tobo.
To George Troughton Overseer of the Poor		1440
The Church Wardens for support of Anne Harvey		600
" " " for support [of] Anne Godfrey's 2 Children		600
" " " for support of Frankey Jobson's 2 Children		600
Mary Leversage for support of 2 Children		600
Capt. James Kempe by Account		30
Frances Holmes by Account		360
John Maye for keeping Molly Willett ensuing Year		300
Amount of Tobacco Levied 25th October last		33737-1/4
Amount of Tobacco Levied 24th November last		9564-3/4
6 per Ct. to Collector on the above Tobacco		2870
Total Amount Levied is		50702

The Parish of Lyn-haven	Cr.	
By 2514 Tithables at 20 lb Tobacco per poll is	50280 lb	
Tobacco Levied for Anthony Williamson now in the hands of the late Collector	480	
	50760	

Ordered that Thomas Reynolds Walker Gent. collect and receive from each Tithable person twenty pounds of Nett Tobacco and pay the same as above directed.

Ordered that Vestry be adjourned until legally called.

Teste Thomas Abbott   Clerk of   James Kempe
                      the Vestry

[130]   Princess Anne County } At a Vestry held 26th of October 1775
        Parish of Lyn-haven }

Present

Capt. James Kempe   Capt. Dennis Dawley
Thomas Rey^s Walker   Anthony Walke, Sr.
Edward Hack Moseley, Jr.   Jacob Ellegood
    and William Nimmo, Vestry men

Parish of Lynhaven is	Dr.	Lbs. Tobo.
To the Reverend Robert Dickson for Salary		16000.
------------------------------ for Cask & Shrinkage		1280
John Bullman's Estate for 4 Months Salary at Church		530
Cason Moore Clerk of Pungo [Chapel] for Salary		1650
Thomas Abbott Clerk of Eastern shore [Chapel] & Vestry for salary		2000

VESTRY BOOK OF LYNNHAVEN PARISH

To Capt. James Kempe for finding Elements at Church	240	
----------------- by Account for a Barrel of Pork	330	570
Thomas Reynolds Walker for finding Elements at East^n shore	240	
---------------------- for cleaning Eastern shore Chapel	270	
---------------------- Assignee of Josiah Dauge	357	867
Jonathan Bonney Sr. for finding Elements at Pungo [Chapel]		240
Anthony Fentress for cleaning Pungo Chapel		270
Frankey McKeil for cleaning Brick Church	270	750
--------------- for support of 2 Children	480	
Blazen Vangover for support of Frances Weldon		480
James Brewer for maintaining John Norris's Child		300
Catharine Wood for support of her Children		600
The Church-Wardens for support of Anne Harvey's Child		600
Hannah Fallen for support of her family		800
Anne Godfrey for support of her family		600
Elizabeth Consaulvo for support of her family		800
Doctor Charles Earl by Account		108
Charity McCaull for support of her family		270
James Lamb by Account		45
William Keeling Sr. by Account		225
Martha Fentress for support		600
Col. Edward Hack Moseley Jr. by Accompt		400
Rachel Nokes for support of herself and Children		600
Mary Leversage for support of herself and Children		600
Ruth Smith to be paid Capt. Dawley		600
Ruth James to be paid William Dawley Sr.		600
Taylor, Widow, for her support		360
Anne Mills for support of her Children		360
John Campbell by Account		175
Anthony Walke Esq. by Account		1482½

Doctor John Reid is appointed Physician & Surgeon to the Parish during pleasure

Agreed with George Troughton to attend the Parish house the ensuing Year on the same terms and Conditions as he attended the same last Year   1440

Amount of Neat Tobacco brought forward   36202½

[131] This day Thomas Reynolds Walker Esq. entered into Bond with security for collecting and paying the Parish Levy.

Vestry is adjourned until the 23rd day of November next.

Teste Thomas Abbott Clerk of Vestry   James Kempe.

Princess Anne County
Parish of Lyn-haven } At a Vestry held the 23rd day of February 1776

Present

The Reverend Robert Dickson Minister
Capt. John Ackiss Church Warden
Mr. Thomas Old,   Capt. Dennis Dawley,
Col. Thomas Rey^s Walker Major Anthony Walke, } Gentlemen of the Vestry
and Col. Edward Hack Moseley Junior

The Parish of Lynhaven	Dr.	Lbs. Tobo.
To Amount of Tobacco levied October 26, 1775		36202½
Doctors Ramsay and Taylor & Co. by Account		3808½
Doctor Reade by Accompt		1650
Capt. John Ackiss by Accompt		146-1/4
Capt. Peter Singleton by Account		294½
William Oakem [Oakham] by Account		199
Mr. Thomas Old by Accompt		1200
James Seneca by Accompt		420
Mary Whitehurst by Petition		500
John Woodland for keeping Ann Moore an Orphan		540
Matthew Godfrey for keeping William Etheredge		180
Jeremiah Plummer for keeping Robert Reade		300
Priscilla Wells, in behalf of John Wells her husband, to be paid Mr. Walke		360
William Gilbert Gray for keeping William Land Orphan of Francis L.		360
Elizabeth Price for support		500
Whiddon Millerson for support of Abigail Millerson		480
Henry Smawn for support of Charles Norris's Orphan Child		300
Mr. Edward Moseley for his services as Clerk of Brick Church		412
Tully Barnes for maintaining Mary Lester		300
George Broughton by Account		360
Capt. John Cornick by Accompt		756
The Church Wardens for support of Parish-house		2000
		51268-3/4
To Six per Cent. to Collector on said Tobacco		3076
	Lbs. of Tobo:	54344-3/4

The Parish of Lynhaven

By 2510 Tithables, at 21-3/4 lbs. per Poll   54592½

Ballance due the County in the Hands of the Collector to be Subtracted } 247-3/4   54344-3/4

Ordered that Thomas Reynolds Walker Esq. do collect and receive for every Tithable in this Parish. Twenty one Pounds and three quarters of a Pound of of Neat Tobacco and pay the same to each Claimant as above directed.

Mr. Edward Moseley was this day appointed Clerk of the Brick Church in the place and Stead of Mr. John Bullman deceased.

Mr. Thomas Old desiring to resign his seat in Vestry, Mr. George Durant Corprew is elected a Vestryman in his place and Stead.

Capt. John Ackiss and Col. Jacob Ellegood are continued Church-Wardens.

Ordered Vestry be adjourned.   Thomas Old.

[132] Princess Anne County } At a Vestry held the 26th of November 1776.
Parish of Lynhaven

Present

Capt. James Kempe   Capt. Dennis Dawley
Col. Thomas Rey^S Walker   Mr. Anthony Walke, Sr.
Col. Edward Hack Moseley, Jr.   Mr. Anthony Walke, Jr.
     and Capt. George Durant Corprew

The Parish of Lynhaven	Dr.	Lbs. Tobo:
To Mr. Edward Moseley Clerk of Brick Church for Salary	1650	
for ensuing Year's Salary	1650	3300
Mr. Cason Moore Clerk of Pungo Chapel for Salary	1650	
for ensuing Year's Salary	1650	3300
Thomas Abbott Clerk of Eastern shore Chapel for Salary	2000	
for ensuing Year & Vestry	1650	3650
Col. Thomas Rey^S Walker for Elements at Eastern shore Chapel	240	
for cleaning the same	270	510
Mr. Jonathan Bonney Sr. for Elements at Pungo Chapel	240	
by Account	300	540
Widow Franky McKeil for cleaning Brick Church	270	
for support of two children	480	750
Mr. Anthony Walke Sr. by Account		969½
Capt. William Keeling Sr. by Account		232½
Capt. John Cornick by Account		720
Mr. Charles Broughton by Account		840
Mr. Adam Keeling by Account		1236
Doctor John Reid by Account		218
Mr. William Heath by Account		300
Tully Barnes for support of Mary Lester		250
John Woodland for keeping Anne Moore		540
James Brewer for keeping John Norris's Child		300

To Charity McCaull for support	270
Thomas Smith for keeping Anne Knight to this Time	600
The Church Wardens for support of Anne Knight ensuing Year	1080
Mary Leversage for support	600
Frances Harrison for support of an Infirm child	500
Elizabeth Consaulvo for support of two Children	360
Anne Godfrey for support of two Children	360
Martha Fentress for her support	600
Rachel Nokes for support of her Children	600
Mary Whitehurst for her support	500
Jonathan Whitehurst for support of Ruth Smith	600
Anthony Fentress for cleaning Pungo Chapel	270
Lbs Tobacco @ 2^d per [lb.]	24046
6 per Cent. on Collecting 24046 lbs. of Tobacco	1442-3/4
	25488-3/4

Ordered that the Register of this Parish be lodged with Mr. Edward Moseley Clerk of the Brick Church and that he Register all Births in the Parish until further Orders.

Ordered that Capt. Edward Cannon be appointed Collector of the Parish Levy, He giving Bond and Security to the Church-Wardens.

Col. Edward Hack Moseley Sr. and Captain Dennis Dawley are elected Church-Wardens for the Year ensuing.

Ordered that Vestry be adjourned until Notice given.

James Kempe.

[133] Princess Anne County, Parish of Lynhaven } At a Vestry held the 18th of February 1777

Present

Capt. James Kempe, Colonel Edward Hack Moseley, Senior, Captain Dennis Dawley, Colonel Thomas Reynolds Walker, Colonel Edward Hack Moseley, Junior, Captain William Nimmo, Mr. Anthony Walke, Junior, & Captain George Durant Corprew.

The Parish of Lynhaven	Dr. Lbs. N^t Tobo:
To amount of Tobacco Levied November 26th, 1776	24046
The Church Wardens for support of the Poor &c.	4500
Capt. Dawley for support of William Cox's 4 Orphans	1000
William Heath by Account	120
The Estate of Capt. William Woodhouse deceased by Account	360
Jonathan Whitehurst for supporting Mary Smith 6 months past	300
Thomas Willoughby by Account	330
Jonathan Whitehurst for supporting Mark Toone's 2 Orphans	360

VESTRY BOOK OF LYNNHAVEN PARISH

To Whiddon Millerson for support of Abigail Millerson	480
6 per Cent. on collecting 31496 lbs of Tobacco	1890
	33386

The Parish of Lynhaven   Cr: lbs

By 1854 Tithables at 18 lbs of Tobacco per Poll is   33372

Ordered that Captain Edward Cannon do collect and receive for each Tithable person in this Parish, eighteen Pounds of Neat Tobacco, and pay the same to each Claimant the respective Quantities of Tobacco to their several Names annexed

Ordered that Vestry be adjourned   James Kempe

[134]   Princess Anne County ⎫ At a Vestry held the 17th December 1777
         Lynhaven Parish   ⎭

Present Col: Edward Hack Moseley & Capt. Dennis Dawley, Churchwardens
         Col: Thomas Reynolds Walker, Capt. John Ackiss,   ⎫
         Col. Edward Hack Moseley, Junior, Capt. William   ⎬ Vestrymen
         Nimmo & Mr. Anthony Walke Junior   ⎭

Edward Moseley is Appointed Clerk of the Vestry who qualified according to Law

Lynhaven Parish   Dr. Lbs N^t Tobo:

To Charity McCaul for her support		270
To Frances McKeal for cleaning the Church	270	
& for support of two children	230	500
To Col. Edward Hack Moseley Junior by Account		400
To Anthony Fentress by Account	144	
To Ditto for cleaning Pungo Chappel	270	414
To the Churchwardens for the use of Sarah Axtead a poor Widdow		300
To Stephen Deer for takeing care & burying Anne Knight a poor Woman		600
To Mary Whitehurst (widow of Samuel)		200
To Mary Whitehurst (widow of Lemuel)		500
To Elizabeth Whitchard for keeping Susannah Deniston the ensuing Year		360
To Doctor Lewis Price by Account		600
To Mary Moore for keeping & supporting Jemima Berry Orphan of Thorowgood Berry		360
To Caleb Ward for keeping & supporting Abigail Millerson the ensuing Year		660
To George Broughton for keeping & supporting Annis Dearmon by Account		1680
To Elizabeth Power for support of her two Children		500
To Jonathan Whitehurst (son of Solomon) for keeping & supporting Ruth Smith		600
To Thomas Kinsey for keeping & supporting Salley Sharwood Orphan of James Sharwood		360

[135]
To Mary Murphey for support of her three youngest Children	750
To Charles Harvey for keeping & supporting Nancy Pasley Orphan of Joshua Pasley the ensuing Year	250

To Frances Harrison for support of an infirm Child		500
To Col: Thomas Reynolds Walker for Elements at the Eastern shore Chappel	240	
for cleaning the same	270	510
To Mr. Jonathan Bonny Sr. for Elements at Pungo Chapel		240
To Constantine Duffy for his support		360
To the present Churchwardens for the Use of the Poor &ca:		2000
To Edward Moseley Clerk of the Vestry		500
		13414

Ordered that the late Collector of the Parish Levy pay Sarah Hartley three pounds, Col: Edward Hack Moseley twenty five Shillings, Capt. Dennis Dawley nine pounds eleven Shillings & sixpence, Henry Capps Fifty Shillings, Charles Harvey forty one Shillings & eight pence, into the Hands of Mr. John Kenline for the Use & support of Amos Tinion the ensuing Year six pounds, Mr. Anthony Walke twenty Shillings and that he pay the Ballence in his Hands due the Parish to the present Churchwardens

[136] Ordered that the Churchwardens Rent out two thirds of the Land & Plantation whereon the late Reverend Robert Dickson Lived, also the Glebe and Parish Land for the ensuing Year to the highest Bidder

Ordered that the Churchwardens sell Sundry Articles brought from the Parish House

On the motion of Col: Thomas Reynolds Walker Leave is granted him to enlarge his Pew in the [Eastern Shore] Chapel, provided he don't discommode the Communion

Capt. Dennis Dawley & Mr. Anthony Walke Junior are appointed Churchwardens for the ensuing Year

Capt. Edward Cannon is appointed Collector of the Parish Levy for the ensuing Year, he giving Bond & Sufficient Security to the Churchwardens for the due performance of the same

Ordered that Mr. William Keeling Administrator of Thomas Abbott deceased pay the Ballance of his Sallary from the time of his Death which was the nineth Day of March last, to Mr. William Benthall the present Clerk of the Eastern Shore Chapel

Ordered that the Money ariseing for the Rent of the Parish & Glebe Land for the present Year be paid into the Hands of the present Churchwardens

To amount of N^t Tobacco brought over	13414
Collector's Commissions on 14805 lbs Tob^o at 6 per Ct.	888
Fraction to be accounted for by the Collector next year	503
	14805

Lynhaven Parish   Cr:

By 2115 Tithables at 7 lbs Tob^o per Poll is 14805

Ordered that Capt. Edward Cannon do Collect from each Tithable person in this Parish seven pounds of Neat Tobacco and pay the same to each Claimant as is herein before directed.

Ordered that the Vestry be adjourned.

Test: Edward Moseley Clerk Vestry   Edward Hack Moseley

[137] Princess Anne County / Lynhaven Parish — At a Vestry held the 17th Day of November 1778

Present: Capt. Dennis Dawley and Mr. Anthony Walke Junior — Churchwardens

Mr. John Ackiss, Mr. Thomas Reynolds Walker, Mr. William Nimmo, Mr. Edward H. Moseley Jr. and Mr. George Durant Corprew — Vestrymen

Mr. Peter Singleton is appointed a Vestryman in the room of Mr. Anthony Lawson, he having resigned, and Mr. Joel Cornick in the room of Mr. Jacob Ellegood, he being out of the County.

Lynhaven Parish	Dr. Lbs. Tobo:
To George Troughton for support of John Wilebour Orphan of John Wilebour the ensuing Year £10	1200
To Martha Fentress for her support the ensuing Year £6	720
To David Huggins for support of Tully Brinson the ensuing Year (son of Aleph Brinson) £10	1200
To Keziah Barns for support of her four Children the ensuing Year £25	3000
To Elizabeth Power for support of her two Children the ensuing Year £15	1800
To Doctor John Hodgson's Estate by Account £11:12:6	1395
To George Broughton by Ditto £5	600
To Frances Harrison for support of an infirm Child the ensuing Year £10	1200
To Frances McKeal for support of one Child the ensuing Year £6	720
To Charles Harvey for takeing Care & cleaning the Church the ensuing Year £3	360
To Mary Murphey for support of three Children the ensuing Year £18	2160
To Willis Givin for support of Jemima Berry Orphan of Thorowgood Berry the ensuing Year £10	1200
To Thomas Kinsey for support of Salley Sharwood Orphan of James Sharwood £8	960
To Sarah Brown widow of Henry for support of her three Children the ensuing Year £20	2400 |//
[138] To Rebecca Flanakin for support of her Children the ensuing Year £20	2400
To Mary Cox widow of William for support of three Children the Ensuing Year £15	1800
To Margaret Philips for support of two Children the ensuing Year £15	1800
To Amos Tinion for the ensuing Year £10	1200
To Rachel Knoaks [Nokes] for support of two Children the ensuing Year £10	1200
To Sarah Axtead for the ensuing Year £9	1080
To John Woodland's Estate £12	1440
To Caleb Ward for support of Abigail Millerson the ensuing Year £25	3000

To Mary Dobbs for support of an Orphan of John Miller's the ensuing Year £10	1200
To Anthony Fentress for takeing care and cleaning Pungo Chappel the ensuing Year £3	360
To Thomas R. Walker for Ditto Easternshore Ditto the ensuing Year £3	360
	34755

Ordered that the Churchwardens apply to the Executors of the Reverend Mr. Robert Dickson deceased to have the Deceedant's Estate Audited, and prepare for a settlement at the next Vestry.

Ordered that the Vestry be adjourned.

Test Edward Moseley C. V.   Dennis Dawley

[139] Princess Anne County } At a Vestry held the 23rd Day of February 1779
Lynhaven Parish

Present Mr. Anthony Walke Junior Churchwarden

Mr. James Kempe, Mr. John Ackiss
Mr. Thomas Reynolds Walker, Mr. Edward H. Moseley, Jr. } Vestrymen
Mr. George Durant Corprew & Mr. Joel Cornick.

The folowing Persons are appointed to procession the Lands in this County agreable to an Order of the Court of the said County passed the 12 Day of June 1778 Vizt: Thomas Ewell & Henry Collins in Little Creek Precinct, William Thorowgood Junior & James Tenant in the lower Precinct of the Westernshore, William Hancock & Enoch Whitehurst on the south side of the Eastern Branch Precinct, James Moore & Tully Robinson on the north side of Eastern Branch Precinct, Joshua Whitehurst & Jeremiah Land in the upper Precinct of the Westernshore, Horatio Cornick, Jacob Keeling, Joseph White, & Edward James in the lower Precinct of the Easternshore, Capt. William Woodhouse, John James (son of Edward), Dennis Dawley & Charles Waterman in the middle Precinct of the Easternshore, John Cason Junior, Tully Barnes, Nathan Munden, & Nathan Cornick in the upper Precinct of the Easternshore, William Reade & Caleb Old in Blackwater Precinct.

Edward Moseley is appointed Collector of the Parish Levy for the present Year.

Mr. James Henley is appointed a Vestryman in the room of Mr. Dennis Dawley deceased.

Mr. Anthony Walke Junior & Mr. Peter Singleton is appointed Churchwardens for the present Year.

Resolved that it be recommended to the Delegates of this County to endeavour at the next Assembly to obtain a Law for obligeing the Parish of Lynhaven to support a Minister by Assesment, as formerly, adequate to his Duty, the Parish having been for some time past Vacant, owing to the want of a Power of Levying a Sallary, and the People being desireous of having a Clergyman among them.

[140]

Lynhaven Parish	Dr: lbs. Tobo:
To amount of Tobo. Levied the 17th November 1778	34755
To Col. Thomas Reynolds Walker by Account £19:7:6	2325
To George Gasking by Ditto £50	6000
To James Senaca for support of an Orphan of Anne Moore 'til the next Vestry £20	2400
To Elizabeth Doudle for support of her Children this present Year £30	3600

To George Gasking for support of Charles Norris 'til the next Vestry £40	4800
To David Huggins by Account £3:10	420
To Rhodom Grindal for his support this present Year he being a Cripple £5	600
To James Johnson for support of an Orphan Child this present Year £10	1200
To Dinah Caton for support of her Children this present Year £24	2880
To Margaret Williams for support of two Children this present Year £10	1200
To Frances McKeal for cleaning the Church last Year 45/	270
To the Churchwardens for support of the Poor £41:13:4	5000
To Edward Moseley Clerk of the Vestry £10	1200
Commission to the Collector on 70983 lbs Tobo. at 6 per Ct.	4258
Fraction to be accounted for by the Collector next Year	578
	71486

Lynhaven Parish

By 2151 Tithables at 33 lbs Tobo.	70983	
By Fraction in the Hands of the Collector	503	
		71486

Ordered that the Collector receive from each Tithable in this County 33 lbs Tobo. and pay the same to Claimors as herein directed.

Test Edward Moseley C. V.   James Kempe

[141]   Princess Anne County } At a Vestry held the 3rd Day of October 1779
         Lynhaven Parish
             Present

James Kempe, Edward Hack Moseley Sr.
Thomas Reynolds Walker, Edward Hack   Gentlemen
Moseley Jr., William Nimmo, Anthony   of the Vestry
Walke Jr., and Joel Cornick.

Resolved that it is the Opinion of this Vestry that the Manner Plantation which the Reverend Robert Dickson Devised to be sold, Rented, or otherwise Apropriated for the Benefit of Educating poor Male Orphan Children, be retained for the said Purpose, and call'd and known by the Name of Dickson's Free-scool; Resolv'd that it is the Opinion of this Vestry that the Slaves, named Harry, Lewis, Gefford, and Lydia, that were set apart for the said Robert Dickson's Widow's Dower, and after the expiration of which, as happening at her Death, were Devised to be sold, be Purchas'd for the Use and purpose aforesaid, the Vestry conceiving that their Labour and Service at this Time, will be more Advantadious [sic] than the Interest of the Money ariseing from the Sale thereof, and better promote the good Intention of the Testator, and that Mr. Anthony Walke Jr. is appointed to Purchase the said Slaves; Resolved that, if it shou'd hereafter be found, or thought to be more for the Benefit of promoteing the Purpose's of the said Will, that the Land or Slaves shou'd be sold, the above Resolves shall be no Barr thereto; Edward Hack Moseley Jr. and Anthony Walke Jr. is appointed to endeavour to procure a Teacher agreable to the said Will, and Choice of this Vestry.

Ordered that the Vestry be Adjourned till Tuesday the 19th Instant.

Test Edward Moseley C. V.   James Kempe

[142]   Princess Anne County } At a Vestry held the 22nd Day of November 1779
         Lynhaven Parish   }
                              Present

James Kempe, Thomas Reynolds Walker,   }
John Ackiss, Edward Hack Moseley Jr.,   } Gentlemen of
Anthony Walke, George Durant Corprew   }   the Vestry
and Joel Cornick.   }

Mr. Anthony Walke inform'd the Vestry that he had not comply'd with their Order in Purchasing the Slaves belonging to the Estate of the Reverend Robert Dickson, deceased, because, he found on peruseing the Will that the Vestry was not impowered to make such an Order; Resolv'd that the Vestry approves of the same.

Lynhaven Parish   Dr.   Lbs Tobo:

To George Troughton for support of John Wilebour
    (an Orphan) for the ensuing Year £10   1200

To William Sorey for support of Salley Parsons
    (an Orphan) the ensuing Year £10   1200

To Ditto for supporting Ditto to this Day £21   2520

To Kiziah Barnes for support of three Children the ensuing Year £25   3000

To Mary Murphey for support of two Children the ensuing Year £16   1920

To Frances McKeal for support of one Child the ensuing Year £8   960

To Elizabeth Doudle for support of four Children
    the ensuing Year £32   3840

To Mary Dobbs for support of Anne Miller her Grandchild
    the ensuing Year £15   1800

To Elizabeth Power for support of two Children the ensuing Year £16   1920

To Charles Harvey for takeing Care of the Church the
    ensuing Year £20   2400

To Col. Thomas Reynolds Walker for takeing Care of the
    Eastern Shore Chappel the ensuing Year £20. To
    Ditto by Account £6   3120

[143] To Anthony Fentress for takeing Care of Pungo Chappel
           the ensuing Year £20   2400

To Sarah Brown for support of three Children the ensuing Year £24   2880

To James Johnson for support of John Tucker (an Orphan)
    the ensuing Year £8   960
         Harrison
To Frances/for support of an Infirm Child the ensuing Year £10   1200

To Dinah Caton for support of her Children the ensuing Year £24   2880

To Edward Hack Moseley Jr. for a Copy of the List of Tithables   800

To Margaret Salmons for support of one Child the ensuing Year £8   960

To Mary Marsh for support of two Children the ensuing Year £16   1920

To John Ackiss Gent. by Account £20   2400

To Amice Tinny [Amos Tinion] for his support the ensuing Year £10   1200

                                                                          41480

Mr. Francis Land is appointed a Vestriman in the Room of Mr. Anthony Walke, Sr., deceased.

Mr Anthony Walke Jr. and Mr. Joel Cornick is appointed Churchwardens for the ensuing Year.

Ordered that the Vestry be Adjourned

Test   Edward Moseley Clerk [of] Vestry   James Kempe

[144]   Princess Anne County } At a Vestry held March the 20th Day 1780
         Lynhaven Parish
                    Present

James Kempe, John Ackiss, William Nimmo,   } Gentlemen
Anthony Walke, George Durant Corprew,   } of the
Joel Cornick, James Henley, & Francis Land } Vestry

Lynhaven Parish	Dr.	Lbs Tobo:
To Amount of Tobacco Levied last Vestry		41480
To Mary Land for her support this present year £60		7200
To Elizabeth King for support of two of William Pead's Children this present Year £40		4800
To Caleb Ward for keeping Abigail Millerson two months (past) £33:6:4		3998
To William Dolby for keeping Ditto 13 Days past £13		1560
To James Senneca for keeping & supporting an Orphan of Anne Moore's this present Year £60		7200
To Joseph Grimstead for support of an Orphan of Sarah Grimstead this present Year £30		3600
To the Churchwardens for support of the Poor &ca: £300		36000
To William Bell for his support £30		3600
To Edward Moseley Clerk of the Vestry £30		3600
		113038

[145]   The Vestry being inform'd by Anthony Walke that Col. Moseley and himself had Advertised for a Master to take Charge of Dickson's Freschool according to an Order for that Purpose; and that no Body had offered, came to the following Resolutions viz:

Resolv'd that a Master be imploy'd to keep Dickson's Freschool, for the present Year, and be allowed the Use of the Plantation of the late Reverend Robert Dickson and the use of Six Thousand Pounds, as a Compensation for his Trouble, He giveing good Security for the said Sum,

Resolv'd that the Vestry shall have the Previledge of sending to the said School any Number, not exceeding fifteen, of poor Male Orphans, who have not Estates, sufficient to Educate them, and that Mr. Anthony Walke, Mr. Francis Land, and Col. Edward Hack Moseley Jr. are appointed to send such Orphans as they shall Judge to be incapeable of giting Education elsewhere;

Resolv'd that the said Master shall be intitled to the Priveledge of takeing under his Care, eight Gentlemen's Sons, besides the Orphans before-mentioned, by way of further incouragement to the said Master;

Resolv'd that the preference shall be given to a Clergiman;

Resolv'd that the above named three Members of this Vestry shall apply to the Reverend Mr. William Selden to know whether he will undertake the Management of the said School, and if he declines, be impowered to employ any other Master that they may approve. Ordered that the Vestry be Adjourn'd.

Test   Edward Moseley   Clerk [of] Vestry   James Kempe

[146] Princess Anne County } At a Vestry held December 28th 1780
Lynhaven Parish

Present

James Kempe, Thomas Reynolds Walker, } Gentlemen
Edward Hack Moseley Jr., Anthony Walke, } of the
George Durant Corprew, Joel Cornick &   } Vestry
Francis Land

Resolved that George Stephenson be imployed to keep Dickson's Freeschool for the ensuing Year and be alowed the Use of the Plantation of the late Reverend Robert Dickson, as a Compensation for his Trouble, Provided that he don't plant more than one half of the cleared Land with Indian Corn,

Resolved that the said Mr. George Stephenson shall teach six poor Male Children, and that he be alowed to take into the said School seventeen Children to teach on his own Account, and that Colonel Edward Hack Moseley Jr., Mr. Anthony Walke and Mr. Francis Land be impower'd to superintend the School and send such Children as they think were intended to be Educated by the Will of the late Reverend Robert Dickson deceased.

Ordered that the Vestry be Adjourned.

Test Edward Moseley C. V.   James Kempe

November 7th, 1783.

[147]
Sheriff's Return of the New Vestry

The Sheriff of the County of Princess Anne by Virtue of an Act of Assembley for Dissolving the old Vestry of Lynhaven Parish and Directing a new one to be Chosen, This Day made return that by Virtue of the said Act of Assembly to him Directed he had Summoned the Freeholders and housekeepers in the said Parish and a Majority of them Met and made a Choice of the following Gentlemen to Serve as Vestrymen, to wit, John Ackiss, Anthony Walke, John Thorowgood, James Henley, Joel Cornick, Edward Hack Moseley, George Durant Corprew, William White, Charles Williamson, John Cornick, William Robinson, and Peter Singleton.

Parish of Lynhaven   } At a Vestry held the 7th November 1783
County of Princess Anne

Present

John Ackiss, Anthony Walke, James Henley, }
Edward Hack Moseley, William White,   } Gentlemen of the Vestry
John Cornick, William Robinson,   }
and Peter Singleton.

Thos. Walker appointed Clerk

Thomas Walker is appointed Clerk of the Vestry and qualified According to Law.

Dr. Lynhaven Parish   lbs Tobacco

To Keziah Barnes for support of two Children of about }
  Seven and Nine Years old for this Year   }   240

To James Seneca for keeping & Supporting Ann Moore an }
  Orphan of Anne Moore from March 1780 to March 1784 }   960

To Joseph Grimstead for keeping & Supporting William }
  Grimstead about 4 Years old for 3 Years @ £2   }   720

To John Dyer for keeping and Supporting Anne Stranhorn}
  till November 1784   }   480

[148] To Rachel Stranhorn for Burying Sally Stranhorn &c.   240

To Mary Wellins, for her Support 'till November next   240

To Sarah Axtead for her Support 'till November next   240

Levy To Joab Dauge for keeping Jamima Cooper 2 Months   120

VESTRY BOOK OF LYNNHAVEN PARISH   115

To Anthony Fentress for keeping Pungo Chaple till this time	480
To Thomas Reynolds Walker for keeping Eastern Shore Chaple till this time	480
To William Morris Junior for keeping & supporting Frances Lofland, aged about 5 Years till November next	1200
To Mary Dauly for keeping & Supporting Mary Dauly, about 4 Years old, 'till November next	480
To Thorowgood Land for keeping & Supporting William Jobson 'till November next	300
To Daniel Franklin Senior for keeping & Supporting Abigal Millerson 'till November next	720
To Tully Barnes for keeping & Supporting Mary Cason 'till her Death	480
	7740

The following Persons are appointed to Procession the Land in this County agreeable to an Order of Court pass'd the 9th Ultimo vizt:

For Little Creek Precinct, Thomas Ewell & John Hunter, for the North Side of the Eastern Branch Precinct James Moore & Natt Hoggard, for the South side of Ditto Hillary Moseley, John Murray & John Hopkins, for the Lower Precinct of the Western Shore Simon Stone & George Gaskings, for the upper Precinct of Ditto Erasmus Haynes & Joel Simmons, for the lower Precinct of the Eastern Shore Henry Keeling & Thomas Keeling, for the Middle Ditto of Ditto Dennis Dauley & John James Junior, for the upper Ditto of Ditto Tulley Moseley, Jonathan Roberts, Francis Ackiss & John Whitehead, for Black Water Precinct, Henry Woodard & George Ives.

Ordered that the Vestry be adjourned.

Teste Thomas Walker Clerk [of the] Vestry   John Ackiss

[149]   Princess Anne   } At a Vestry held November 25th 1783
        Lynhaven Parish }
                Present

John Ackiss, Anthony Walke, Joel Cornick, Edward Hack Moseley
George D. Corprew, William White, Charles Williamson,   } Gent. Vestry
John Cornick, William Robinson, & Peter Singleton

Dr: Parish of Lynhaven   lbs. Nt. Tobacco

To Ann Hudgins for the Support of herself & one Child till Nov. next 360

To Betty Dowdle for support of herself & one Child 'till Nov. next   420

To Auston Brumbly for keeping John Dowdle till Ditto   180

To Ebenezer Craig for keeping & Supporting Lydia Glasgow three Months 300

To Sarah Bromage for her Support 40/. Ordered that She apply to
    Joel Cornick for the above but he is not to advance it unless
    he is satisfied from Circumstances, She is about to leave the
    Parish and be no longer a burthen to it

To Anne Land for the keeping & Supporting of Charles, Peter and   720
    Mary Land 'till November next

To the Widow of Edward Gisburn in Black Water for the Support   600
    of herself & Child 'till November next

To Mary Randolph for keeping of Richard Bery's Son from his Deth   240
    'till this Time

VESTRY BOOK OF LYNNHAVEN PARISH

To Betty Moseley for keeping the Brick Church till November next	240
To Thomas Reynolds Walker for keeping the Eastern Shore Chaple till Ditto	240
To William Kays for keeping Pungo Chaple till Do.	240
To the Church Wardens for the use of the Parish	1200
To Thomas Walker as Clerk of the Vestry	600
To the Amount of Tobacco Levied November 7th 1783	7740
To Six per Cent. to Collector on Said Tobacco	784
	13864
Cr: By 2373 Tithables @ 6 lbs Tobacco each 14238	
Balance to be accounted for by the Collector 374	13864

Jacob Vallentine appointed Collector — Ordered that Jacob Vallentine receive from each Tithable person within this County 6 lbs of Neat Tobacco & pay the Several Claimers above mentioned According to Law.

Church Wardens Chosen — [150] James Henley & William White is appointed Church Wardens for the ensuing Year

Church Wardens to Receive the Parish Money — Ordered that the Church-Wardens receive the rents, or What ever part thereof may be now due, and other Monies due the Parish, and Rent the Gleeb & Parish Lands if no Minister is chosen before.

Ordered that they Advertise for a Master to Keep Dickson's free School, & be empower'd with the Advice of the Vestry, to rent the Plantation to the Said Master, in Consideration of his teaching as many Boys as the Church Wardens & Vestry Shall think reasonable. And if no Master can be procured before the Second day of January next, that they rent the said Plantation to the highest bidder, reserving the use of the School House & one room in the Dwelling House, in case a Master Shou'd be got afterwords. And if a Master Should offer, or be procured, that any Interest Money which may be collected on Bonds due to the Estate of Robert Dickson may be also paid to the said Master for his Services according to Contract.

Ordered that the Vestry be adjourned.

Teste   Anthony Walke
Thomas Walker   Clerk [of] Vestry   John Ackiss being absent

[151]   Princess Anne County } At a Vestry held the 29th of October 1784.
        Lynnhaven Parish   }
                Present

                        James Henley   } Gentlemen Church Wardens
                        & William White }

            Joel Cornick, Edward Hack Moseley,   }
            Charles Williamson, William Robinson,   } Gentlemen of the Vestry
            and Peter Singleton.   }

The Parish of Lynhaven   Dr.   lbs. Tobacco

Levy

To John Dyer for keeping Anne Stranhorn from the 25th of November 1784 to the 25th of November 1785	600
To Anthony Frisel for keeping Frances Lofland from Ditto to Ditto	240
To Rachel Noaks for keeping Mary Dawly from Ditto to Ditto	240
To Sarah Axtead for her Support 'till November 25th 1785	240

VESTRY BOOK OF LYNNHAVEN PARISH

To Anne Scott for keeping William Holmes Son of Robert Holmes & Elizabeth Scott 'till Ditto	480
To Anne Land for keeping Charles, Peter & Mary Land untill Ditto	600
To Elizabeth King for keeping Elizabeth Peed 'till Ditto	240
To Sarah King for keeping her son Thomas Gall 'till Ditto	120
To Dinah Caton for keeping a Child 'till Ditto	240
To Mary Wellens for her Support 'till Ditto	180
To Henry Capps (son of Richard) for his support 'till Ditto	360

Ordered that the Vestry be adjourned 'till the 25th of November next & that the Clerk give publick Notice thereof, and that he inform the Members by Letter a few days before.

Teste   James Henley   Church Warden
Thomas Walker   Clerk [of] Vestry

[152]   Princess Anne County } At a Vestry held the 25th of November 1784
           Lynhaven Parish

                Present

              James Henley & } Gentlemen { Church
              William White   Wardens

Anthony Walke, Joel Cornick, Edward Hack Moseley, } Gentlemen
George Durant Corprew, Charles Williamson, John   } of the
Cornick, William Robinson & Peter Singleton.   } Vestry

Clerk Chosen   Charles Moseley is appointed Clerk of the Vestry during the Abscence of Thomas Walker, who qualified according to Law.

	Dr. lbs. Tobacco
The Parish of Lynhaven	
To Amount of Tobacco Levy'd last Vestry	3540
To Mrs. Murphey Widow of Patrick for her Support for 12 Months to come	600
To William Ackiss per Account	108
To Michael Eaton per Account	1575
To be paid to Rhode Woodland's Estate	480
To Keziah Barnes for keeping Henry Barnes	180
To be paid for the Support of William Grimstead Son of Amy Grimstead	360
To be paid Frances Jobson for the Support of William Jobson	600
To be paid William Senaca for the Support of Anne Moore, from March 1784 'till November 1785	400
To Capt. George D. Corprew, to be paid to any Person that will take the son of Richard Bery as an Apprentice, a poor Crippled Boy	720
To the Widow of Edward Gisburn in Black Water	480
To the Widow Purde in Black Water for the Support of herself & Children	720
To the Widow Cannon in black Water for the Support of her Children	360

Levy (margin)

Church Wardens pay Wellens   Ordered that the Church Wardens pay immediately to Winefred Wellens the Sum of Forty Shillings for the Support of William Grimstead Orphan

[153]

Levy	Ordered that William Battin be paid for the Support of the youngest Child of Willis Gibbs	240
Church Wardens pay Batten	Ordered that the Present Church Wardens pay William Batten three Pounds immediately for past Services	
pay Ackiss	Ordered that the Present Church Wardens pay Col. John Ackiss Forty Shillings	
Collector appointed	Josiah Vallentine is appointed Collector of the Levy laid this Year given Bond and Security to the Church Wardens for the Tobacco and Money Levied	
C. Wardens appointed	Capt. Charles Williamson & John Cornick are appointed Church Wardens for the ensuing Year	
Levy	To be paid to Martha Fentress for her support the ensuing Year	720
Dickson's Houses to be repaired	Ordered that the *last Year's rent of the Plantation Given in trust by the late Reverend Robert Dickson to the Vestry be Applyed in repairing the Dwelling House & Barn and other necessary repairs on the said Plantation by the Church Wardens of the next Year	
C. Wardens to receive the Parish Money	Ordered that the Church Wardens receive all the rents due to the Parish.	
	To Betty Moseley for keeping the Brick Church untill November 1785	240
Levy	To Thomas Reynolds Walker for keeping the Eastern Shore [Chapel] untill November 1785	240
	To William Kays for keeping Pungo Chaple till Ditto	240
	To Thomas Walker as Clerk of the Vestry	600
	To 6 per Cent for Collector on said Tobacco	744
		13147

The Parish   Cr:

By 2387 Tithables @ 5½ lbs Tobacco each   13128½
Balance to be accounted for by the Collector   18½

                                              13147

Collector ordered to receive	Ordered that Josiah Vallentine receive from each Tithable Person within this County 5½ lbs of Tobacco & pay the Several Claimers above Mentioned According to Law.

Ordered that the Vestry be adjourned

Teste   Anthony Walke
                               John Ackiss being absent

*Note, Supposed to be 1784.

[154]

Princess Anne County } At a Vestry held the 16th of March 1785
Lynhaven Parish

Present

Charles Williamson } Gentlemen { Church
& John Cornick   Wardens

Anthony Walke, James Henley
Joel Cornick, Edward Hack Moseley } Gentlemen of the Vestry
William White & Peter Singleton

Whereas at a Meeting of a Majority of the Members of the Vestry, Vizt. Joel Cornick, Edward Hack Moseley, George Durant Corprew, William White, Charles Williamson, John Cornick, William Robinson, and Peter Singleton Gent. to deliberate on a Letter received by the said Peter Singleton, from the Reverend

Charles Pettigrew, relative to his wish of becoming the Minister of this Parish & Master of the School agreeable to the late Reverend Mr. Dickson's Will. It was agreed unanimusly that he should be received in both capacities, & ordered that the Church Wardens Signify the same to him in the most expressive manner as soon as possible; in consequence of which William White has lately received a Letter from the said Pettigrew, informing that he intends and expects to be an inhabitant of this Parish about the first of April and intends to undertake all the Duties incumbent on a Minister and a Tutor. It is therefore Resolved that the Present Church Wardens send the following Letter to Mr. Pettigrew Vizt.

Reverend Sir

On the 16th Instant a Vestry met at Kempesville, and, having deliberated on the Subject of your letter to Mr. White, determined to receive and imploy you as Minister of the Parish of Lynhaven, & Master of the Free School.

At the Last Session of Assembly an Act was passed dissolving the Vestries through the State, & directing new Vestries to be elected on the 28th Instant; in Consequence Whereof a new one will be Chosen here. For what may be done by that Body in future the present Vestry cannot answer.

That you may receive more particular Information on this Matter, we have enclosed you a copy of the Act of Assembly.

[155]

P. S. Unless you are here on the 1st Day of May next, the Vestry will consider themselves Absolv'd from their Engagement.

We are Respectfully
Reverend Sir
Your most humble Servents

Charles Williamson   Church Wardens
John Cornick

[Editor's Note: When numbering the pages, the Clerk omitted Nos. 156 & 157]

Ordered that the Vestry be adjourned.

Teste
Thomas Walker   Clerk [of] Vestry

Charles Williamson   Church Wardens
John Cornick

[158]

Lynhaven Parish
Princess Anne County   14th April 1785

Vestry Subscribe to the Church

We the Subscribers being legaly chosen by the Majority of the People, this day Subscribe in Vestry to be Conformable to the doctrine, discipline, and Worship of the Protestant Episcopal Church.

Anthony Walke
Edward Hack Moseley
John Ackiss
James Henley
William Ahite
John Cornick
Joel Cornick
Frances Land

Clerk appointed

Thomas Walker is appointed Clerk of the Vestry Who quolified According to Law

An Account of Property belonging to
Lynhaven Parish   April 14th 1785

About 200 Acres of Land as a Glebe, With an old Dwelling House and a few out Houses, all in bad Repair.

About 50 Acres of Land with an old House built for the Reception of the poor, & a Kitchen, both wanting Repair.

Property belonging to the Parish

Belonging to the Mother Church
{ A large Silver Tankard, & a Silver Salver
A cup wash'd with Gold
3 pewter Plates, 1 Pulpit Cloth, & a Broad Cloth Covering for the Communion Table

3 Setts of Secker's Sermons 7 Volumes each
Volumes of Tillotson's Sermons
3 Good Bibles and 2 old Ditto
3 Common Prayer Books (larg)

Belonging to the Eastern Shore Chaple
{ A Silver Tankard, A Silver Cup & a small Silver Salver
3 Pewter Plates, 1 Pewter Bason,
1 Diaper Table Cloth & one Napkin for the Communion Table }

[159] Belonging to Pungo Chaple
{ A Pewter Tankard, 2 Glass Tumblers
2 Pewter Plates, 1 Table Cloth and 2 Napkins for the Communion Table }

A few old Cushions at the Mother Church & the Eastern Shore Chapel.

Revenue

Rent of Glebe Land in 1785:   £8:0:0
Rent of Parish Land in 1785   £7:5:0

         Anthony Walke
         John Ackiss
         Edward Hack Moseley
         James Henley
         John Cornick
         Joel Cornick
         Frances Land

Ordered that a coppy of the above be delivered to the Next County Court.

Church Wardens Chosen   Charles Williamson and John Cornick is appointed Church Wardens for the ensuing Year

Ordered that the Vestry be adjournd.

Teste
Thomas Walker Clerk [of] Vestry   John Cornick

[160] Princess Anne County } At a Vestry held the 6th May 1785
Lynhaven Parish

         Present

         John Cornick   Church Warden

Anthony Walke, Edward Hack Moseley
James Henley, Joel Cornick   } Gentlemen of Vestry
William White, & Francis Land

Vestry Subscribe to the Church   We the Subscribers being legaly Chosen by the Majority of the People, this day Subscribe in Vestry to be Conformable to the Doctrine, discipline, & Worship of the Protistant Episcopal Church.

         Charles Williamson
         John Hancock

         Present

       Charles Williamson, Church Warden
       John Hancock, Gentleman of the Vestry

A Minister Canvis'd for   It was determined this day by a Majoraty of the Vestry Vizt: John Hancock, Charles Williamson, John Cornick, Francis Land, Edward Hack Moseley & Anthony Walke that they Should immediately proceed to induct a Minister.

Rev. Mr. Simpson inducted   The Reverend James Simpson is inducted Minister of this Parish he promising to produce his Episcopal Letters of Ordination to the Church Wardens within ten days, by a Majority of the Vestry Vizt: Anthony Walke, Edward Hack Moseley, John Hancock, Joel Cornick, Charles Williamson and Francis Land.

C. Wardens to Write to the Rev. Mr. Petigrew   Ordered that the Church Wardens Write immediately to the Reverend Mr. Pettigrew informing him that in consequence of his delaying coming on or before the first of May the Vestry have made Choice of the Reverend Mr. James Simpson as their Minister.

Dickson's Donation Rented   The Reverend Mr. Dickson's Donation is rented to Mr. William White 'till New Year's Day for £25:0:0

VESTRY BOOK OF LYNNHAVEN PARISH

[161] The Reverend Mr. James Simpson is appointed Master of Dickson's Freeschool.

Ordered that he teach Nine Boys from this time 'till the first day of January 1786, the Arts of reading Writing & Arithmetick for the Sum of £25

The Reverend Mr. James Simpson Minister & Anthony Walke Gentleman a member of the Vestry of Lynhaven Parish are appointed Deputies to meet in Convention at Richmond on the 18th of this Month.

I James Simpson being inducted Minister of this Parish do hereby promis & agree to Act in the Capacity of Minister Agreeable to the Doctrine & Dicipline of the Protestant Episcopal Church.
                                                  James Simpson

Ordered that the Church Wardens be Authorized to send Nine Orphan Boys to be instructed by the Reverend Mr. Simpson, who have not Estate Suffient to educate them agreeable to the Will of the late Robert Dickson.

Ordered that the Vestry be Adjourned.

Teste   Charles Williamson ⎫ Church
Thomas Walker Clerk [of] Vestry   John Cornick   ⎭ Wardens

[162] I John Thorowgood being Legally Chosen by the Majority of the People this day Subsgribe in Vestry to be Conformable to the Doctrine, Discipline, & Worshipe of the Protestant Episcopal Church.
July 27th 1785   John Thorowgood

Princess Anne County ⎫
Lynhaven Parish   ⎭ At a Vestry held the 27th of July 1785.

                        Present

                        The Reverend Mr. James Simpson Minister
                        Charles Williamson Church Warden

         Anthony Walke, John Hancock   ⎫
         Joel Cornick, William White,   ⎬ Gentlemen of the Vestry
         John Thorowgood, & Francis Land ⎭

The following Persons are appointed to Procession the Lands in this County agreeable to an order of Court held the 14th Instant, to witt:

For Little Creek Precinct William Nimmo (son Garshum) & John Hunter,
For the North Side of the Eastern Branch Charles Sayer & Nat. Hoggard
For the South Side of Ditto John Hopkins, John Murray & David Scott
For the lower Precinct of the Western Shore Simon Stone & George Gasking
For the Upper Ditto of Ditto Erasmus Haynes & Joel Simmonds
For the Lower Ditto of Eastern Shore Thomas Keeling & William Woodhouse
for the Middle Ditto of Ditto Dennis Dawley & John James Jr.
for the Upper Ditto of Ditto or Pungo ⎧Tully Moseley, John Whitehead,
                                      ⎩Jonathan Ackiss & Jonathan Roberts
for Black Watter Henry Woodard & George Ives

[163] And that they begin the 1st of October to Procession the lines in each Precinct & make there return at the next Meeting of the Vestry after the last of March next.

Ordered that the Reverend Mr. Simpson take Charge of the Parish Register.

On the Motion of Mr. Charles Sayer leave is given him to cut a Window opposat to his pew in the Brick Church.

On the Motion of Thomas Walker leave is given him to Cut a window in the end of the Eastern Shore Chaple to give lite to his pew.

Ordered that the Church Wardens do repare the Damage done by the Lightning to Pungo Chaple.

Ordered that the Vestry be adjourned.

Test Thomas Walker Clerk [of] Vestry   James Simpson Minister

Princess Anne County } At a Vestry held the 13th September 1785
Lynhaven Parish

Present

    Mr. James Simpson Minister

    Charles Williamson } Church Wardens
    John Cornick

Anthony Walke, Joel Cornick
William White & John Thorowgood } Gentlemen of the Vestry

Ordered that Thomas Kempe be appointed Clerk for the present.

Ordered that the Clerk of the Vestry be Directed to write to the following Gentlemen and request the favour of them to Ascertain the Number of the Protestant Episcopal Church above 16 Years old both Male & Female that may be in the different Precincts of Lynhaven Parish, in order that it may be reported to the next Convention of the Clergy. Vizt:

[164]
Thomas Lawson & thomas Wishart in Little Creek Precinct.
William White, John Hopkins, & Thomas Kempe Eastern Branch Precinct.
Francis Land & William Haynes lower Precinct Western Shore.
Joel Simmonds & Erasmus Haynes Uper Ditto [of] Ditto.
Adam Keeling & Thomas Walker lower Ditto of Eastern Shore
Cason Moore & John James Junior Middle Ditto of Ditto.
John Ackiss & Dennis Dawley Upper Ditto of Ditto or Pungo.
George Durant Corprew & Caleb Old Black Water Precinct.

Ordered that the Church Wardens be requested to apply to a Gentleman in each Precinct of Lynhaven Parish in the name of the Vestry and request him to present a Subscription paper to each Member of the Protestant episcopal Church to raise a Salery for Mr. Simpson the incumbent of said Parish annually, untill ample provision is made by the Assembly for the Support of the Clergy.

Ordered that Mr. Simpson the incumbent, & Mr. Peter Singleton layman be appointed to attend the Convention of the Clergy of this State when ever Called, & that the Clerk furnish them with a certificate of there appointment.

Copy
Test Thomas Walker Clerk [of] Vestry J. Simpson Minister

[165] Princess Anne County } At a Vestry held the 24th September 1785.
   Lynhaven Parish

    Present

    Charles Williamson } Church Wardens
    John Cornick

Anthony Walke, John Hancock
Joel Cornick, William White } Gentlemen of the Vestry
and John Thorowgood

Ordered that William Robinson be appointed Clerk for the Day

Ordered that the Church Wardens do put or place into the hands of the same Gentlemen Who may be appointed to present Subscriptions for the Minister, papers likewise to Subscribe for readers to the Church & Chapels.

Ordered that the Reverend Mr. Simpson for & during the term of Six Years do hold & enjoy the donation of the Reverend Robert Dickson Deceased so far as relates to that of Land use, on the following terms to wit that he shall educate as many Latin Scholars at ten Pounds each, or as many English Scholars at four Pounds each as at that rate will amount to Forty Pounds per Annum, but the different Classes of Scholars to be at the discretion of the Vestry, And it is Ordered that no Waste be Committed on said Land, but the said Simpson hath full power to make use of any Timber for fencing & firewood or for the use of the plantation the said Simpson is not to Cultivate or cause to be Cultivated the land in Indian Corn two Years Successively.

    Agreed to on my part James Simpson.

Copy Test   Thomas Walker   Clerk [of] Vestry   Charles Williamson } Church
                                                        John Cornick   } Wardens

[166]   Princess Anne County } At a Vestry held the 23rd of November 1785
        Lynhaven Parish   }
                        Present

                The Reverend Mr. James Simpson   Minister
                        John Cornick   Church Warden

            Edward Hack Moseley, John Hancock, George D. Corprew } Gent. Vestry
            Joel Cornick, William White & John Thorowgood   }

Absent William White Gentleman.

This day William White Gentleman one of the Executors of the Estate of the Reverend Robert Dickson Deceased rendered an Account of his Executorship of the Estate of the said Robert Dickson to the 8th of August 1782 and their appears to be the sum of £7663:1:11½ in Paper Money due the said Estate which was put into the Treasuary & for which he has this day produced the Treasurer's Certificates dated the first of June 1783 which agreeable to the Scale of Depreciation of this State amounts to £10:4:10 in Specie, it is therefore Ordered that the said Certificates be received of the said William White in full for the Above Ballance & is also exclusiv of the Bonds & Bills to the Amount of £1100:1 in Specie one half of which is due to Dickson's Estate and the other half to the Widow of the said Dickson who renounced his will.

Ordered that the Clerk take care of the abovementioned Certificates & that he give William White a receipt for the same.

Copy Test
Thomas Walker Clerk   James Simpson Minister

[167]   Princess Anne County } At a Vestry held the 27th April 1786
        Lynhaven Parish   }
                        Present

                    The Reverend Mr. James Simpson   President

                        Charles Williamson } Church Wardens
                        & John Cornick   }

            Edward Hack Moseley, George D. Corprew } Gentlemen
            Joel Cornick & John Thorowgood   } of the
                                                   } Vestry

Thomas Walke Gentleman is elected as a Vestry man in the room of Francis Land Deceased

Jonathan Park is appointed Clerk for the Brick Church
Thomas Reynolds Walker is appointed for the Eastern Shore Chaple
Cason Moore is appointed for Pungo Chaple

The Reverend Mr. James Simpson Rector of this Parish and Thomas Walke Gentleman are appointed Deputies to represent this Parish at the next meeting of the Episcopal Convention at Richmond.

Ordered that the Church Wardens advertise that the Subscription papers for the Minister & Clerk be delivered to the Reverend Mr. Simpson on or before the 22nd of May next.

Ordered that the Vestry be adjourned.

Copy Test
Thomas Walker   James Simpson Minister

[168] Princess Anne County } At a Vestry held Thursday 28th December 1786.
Lynhaven Parish

Present

John Cornick Church Warden

Anthony Walke, Edward Hack Moseley } Gentlemen of
John Hancock, Joel Cornick   the Vestry
William White & Thomas Walke

Ordered that the Church Wardens make out a state[ment] of there Accounts and deliver the same to the Overseers of the Poor at there next meeting, together with all the money that may be in their hands at the Time.

Ordered that the Vestry be Adjourned.

Copy Test   John Cornick
Thomas Walker Clerk

Editor's Note:

Following this meeting of 28th December, 1786, which definitely marks the termination of the parish vestry's handling of funds raised by public taxation for support of the poor, a new vestry was elected at a meeting held at Kempsville on 27th December 1787, in accordance with an act of assembly and an ordinance of the diocesan convention of that year. At this meeting, the new vestry received the resignation of the Reverend James Simpson, effective 6th May, 1788, and he was succeeded as rector of Lynnhaven Parish by the Reverend Anthony Walke, who obtained ordination as a minister in that year and served until his resignation on 10th October, 1800.

During his incumbency, the vestry minutes were almost entirely devoted to the members' proceedings as trustees of Dickson's Free School, and do not have the same interest as the records included in this publication. The vestry book continues until 16th November, 1892, with complete lapses from 1814-1821 and 1860-1865, as the result of war. A photostatic copy of the complete vestry record of the parish, extending from 1723 to 1892, is available for research, at the Virginia State Library, Richmond, Virginia, and has been transcribed by the Editor in the preceding pages of this publication, through the year 1786.

APPENDIX

1. MINISTERS - LYNNHAVEN PARISH

William Wilkinson [?]	1639-1644	Solomon Wheatley	1702
Robert Powis	1645-1651	James Tenant	1714-1726
[Vacancy]	1652-1655	Nicholas Jones [Supply]	1726-1728
Philip Mallory	1657	Richard Marsden [Supply]	1729
George Alford	1658-1662	Henry Barlow	1729-1747
James Porter	1678-1682	Robert Dickson	1748-1776
Jonathan Saunders	1695	James Simpson	1785-1787

2. CHURCHWARDENS - LYNNHAVEN PARISH

Ackiss, John	1774-1776	Lawson, Anthony	1773
Boush, Maximilian	1723-1727	Lucas, William	1646-1647
Cason, Thomas	1644-1645	Martin, John	1645-1646
Cornick, Joel	1780	Moseley, Edward Hack	1777
Cornick, John[1]	1724-1726	Newton, Nathaniel	1755-1757
Cornick, John[2]	1785-1786	Singleton, Peter	1779
Dawley, Dennis	1777-1778	Stratton, John	1640-1641
Ellegood, Jacob[1]	1736-1752	Todd, Thomas	1640-1641
Ellegood, Jacob[2]	1775-1776	Walke, Anthony[1]	1728-1750
Hall, Edward	1645-1646	Walke, Anthony[2]	1772, 1778-1780
Handcocke, Simon	1642-1643	Walke, Thomas	1751-1752, 1755-1756, 1758-1760
Henley, James	1784	Walker, Thomas Reynolds	1763-1765, 1767-1771
Keeling, William	1753-1755, 1760-1761	White, William	1784
Kempe, James	1753-1755, 1761-1771	Williamson, Charles	1785-1786
Land, Francis[1]	1646-1647	Williamson, Roger	1646-1647
Land, Francis[2]	1727-1735	Woodhouse, William	1772-1774
Land, Francis Thorowgood	1758-1759		

3. VESTRYMEN - LYNNHAVEN PARISH

Ackiss, John	1772-1785	Martin, John	1645-1646
Bolitho, John	1724-1728	McLenahan, David [Never served]	1773
Bonney, John[1]	1728	Moore, Henry	1733-1739
Bonney, John[2]	1733-1760	Moseley, Anthony	1744-1760
Boush, Maximilian[1]	1723-1727	Moseley, Edward	1723-1730
Boush, Maximilian[2]	1733-1736	Moseley, Edward Hack[1]	1739-1779
Bullock, Thomas	1640-1641	Moseley, Edward Hack[2]	1770-1786
Burrowgh, Christopher[1]	1640-1641	Moseley, Francis	1732-1737
Burrowgh, Christopher[2]	1724-1736	Moseley, John	1723-1738
Cason, Thomas	1640-1645	Newton, Nathaniel	1739-1766
Chapman, Henry	1723-1732	Nimmo, James	1732-1752
Condon, James	1739-1742	Nimmo, William	1773-1780
Cornick, Joel	1778-1786	Old, Thomas	1760-1776
Cornick, John[1]	1724-1726	Robinson, Tully	1769-1773
Cornick, John[2]	1783-1786	Robinson, William	1783-1784
Corprew, George Durant	1776-1786	Saunders, Jonathan	1760-1764
Dawley, Dennis	1760-1779	Sayer, Arthur [Not elected]	1752
Ellegood, Jacob[1]	1733-1752	Sayer, Charles	1723-1739
Ellegood, Jacob[2]	1773-1778	Singleton, Peter	1778-1785
Ellegood, William	1723-1725	Spratt, Henry	1727-1736
Gasking, Job	1739-1753	Stratton, John	1640-1641
Gornto, John	1733-1749	Thorowgood, John	1783-1786
Hall, Edward	1645-1646	Todd, Thomas	1640-1641
Hancock, John	1785-1786	Tooly, Adam	1739-1760
Handcocke, Simon	1642-1643	Vaughan, Robert	1724-1732
Hayes, Robert	1640-1641	Walke, Anthony[1]	1724-1779
Haynes, Thomas	1727-1733	Walke, Anthony[2]	1765-1786
Henley, James	1779-1785	Walke, Thomas[1]	1744-1760
Hoskins, Bartholomew	1640-1641	Walke, Thomas[2]	1786
Hunter, John	1739-1752	Walker, Thomas Reynolds	1762-1779
Keeling, Thomas	1640-1641	White, Solomon[1]	1724-1725
Keeling, William	1752-1767	White, Solomon[2]	1727-1729
Kempe, George	1728-1733	White, William	1783-1786
Kempe, James	1736-1780	Whitehead, John	1744-1764
Land, Francis[1]	1646-1647	Whitehurst, John	1739-1773
Land, Francis[2]	1723-1735	Williamson, Charles	1783-1786
Land, Francis[3]	1779-1786	Williamson, Roger	1646-1647
Land, Francis Thorowgood	1752-1759	Windham, Edward	1640-1641
Lankfield, John	1640-1641	Wishart, George	1739-1760
Lawson, Anthony	1769-1778	Woodhouse, Henry	1640-1641
Lucas, William	1646-1647	Woodhouse, William	1753-1774

APPENDIX

4. PRESIDENTS OF VESTRY - LYNNHAVEN PARISH

Jacob Ellegood	1744
Anthony Walke[1]	1747-1768
James Kempe	1769-1780
John Ackiss	1783
Rev. James Simpson	1785-1786

Note: The following senior vestrymen signed the minutes in the absence of a president. G.C.M.

John Whitehurst	1773	
Thomas Old	1776	
Dennis Dawley	1778	
Anthony Walke[2]	1783	[Noted: "John Ackiss being absent".]
James Henley	1784	[Signed as Churchwarden.]
John Cornick[2]	1785-1786	[Signed as Churchwarden.]

5. SHERIFFS - PRINCESS ANNE COUNTY

Ackiss, John	1765
Boush, Frederick	1766-1767
Boush, Maximilian	1734
Condon, James	1742
Cox, William	1745
Ellegood, Jacob	1733
Hancock, John	1772
Haynes, Thomas	1728
Hopkins, Jonathan	1770-1771
Keeling, William	1749-1751
Kempe, James	1739-1740
Malbone, Charles	1738
Moseley, Francis	1730-1731
Newton, Nathaniel	1741
Smyth, Charles	1744
Walke, Thomas	1743

Editor's Note: The above lists were made up mainly from the vestry book, and none of them is claimed to be complete, except to the extent that they are covered by the vestry minutes, as published herein. The superior figures attached to similar names are merely intended to show relative order of vestry service and do not necessarily indicate the order of direct family descent. The names of early vestrymen were taken from isolated references to them in the Lower Norfolk County records, and therefore do not show their service.

INDEX

Abbott, Thomas 92, 94-96, 98, 99, 102, 103, 105, 108
Absalom, Edmond 36-38, 45, John 42, William 66
Absolum, see Absalom
Ackiss, 42, Francis 7, 15, 33, 115, George 58, John 66, 75, 82, 86, 89-91, 93, 94, 98-101, 104, 105, 107, 109, 110, 112-116, 118-120, 122, Jonathan 121, William 45, 53, 117
Adams, Richard 31, 32, 35-38, 40
Aerie, Sarah 13, 17, 22, 23
Airie, Airy, see Aerie
Aires, Airs, see Ayres
Alanson, see Alderson
Albin, Sarah 47, 49
Alderson, Elizabeth 66, 68, 69, Worsell 31, 32
Algrove, Elizabeth 32
Allen, Mrs. 29
Ancel, John 5
Ashby, John 31, 32, 34, 36-38, 40-42, 44, 46
Ashley, James 39
Avers, Sarah 23
Axtead, Sarah 34, 97, 101, 107, 109, 114, 116
Ayres, John 40, 41, Ruth 89, 96, Willoughby 48, 51, 53, 57

Back Bay xxiv
Baily, Robert 44, 46, 48, Rev. Thomas 8, 9
Bald, see Ball
Ball, George 58, Richard 62, 64
Baly, see Baily
Banks, Harrison 75, Thomas 38, 44
Bannister, James 10, 19
Barber, James 35
Barington, 27, 29-31
Barlow, Rev. Henry 11-13, 15-22, 24-29, 31-35, 37, 38, 55
Barnes, Anthony 59, 72, Daniel 15, Frances 59, 61, 63, 64, Francis 73, Henry 117, John 63, Jonathan 71, 73, 74, 77, 79, 81, 84, 87, 90, 92, Keziah 109, 112, 114, 117, Mary 71, 73, 74, 77, 79, 81, 84, 87, 90, Tully 96, 101, 104, 105, 110, 115
Barns, see Barnes
Barrington, see Barington
Batten, William 51, 118
Battin, see Batten
Bell, Richard 42-44, 46, 48, 53, William 113
Benthall, William 108
Bery, see Berry
Berry, Anne 59-61, 63, 65, Jemima 107, 109, Richard 56, 115, 117, Thomas 31, 32, 34, 36, Thorowgood 107, 109, William 97, Willoughby 99
Bew, Richard 51
Bibles for churches 12, 119
Biddle, John 45, 53, 55, 69, 75, William 6, 64, 74, 77, 79

Bishop, Mrs. John 77, John 2, 4, 6, 8, 9, 11-13, 16, 17, 19, 20, 22, 24, 25, 27, 28, 30, 73, 75-78
Blackwater River xx
Blair, Anne 44, Dr. James 32, 36, James 39
Bly, Harald 9
Bodman, William 30
Bolitho, John 2, 3, 5, 7-9
Bonney, Jonathan 62, 81, 83, 86, 93, 95, 99, 103, 105, 108, John 2, 3, 15, 17, 20, 21, 25, 28, 29, 33, 38, 45, 52, 54, 57, 58, 62-64, 67, 68, 71, 73, 75, 76, 78, 96, Nathan 88, William 51
Booth, John 39
Bornden, William 64
Boush, Frederick 62, 77, 79, 87, Maximilian 1-8, 14, 15, 17-22, 66, Samuel 9, 19, 68
Bowser, Dr. John 82, 84, 86, 87
Boyd, Jane 43, 44, 46, 49, 51, 54, 58
Braithwaite, James, & Co. 81, 84, 86
Brand, Andrew 41, 43, 44, Elizabeth 66, 68
Brewer, James 96, 99, 103, 105, Mary 51
Brian, Milburn 58-61, 63, 66, 67
Briggs, Sarah 59-63
Brinson, Aleph 109, Hillery 79, Thomas 1, 5, 6, Thorowgood 14, 15, Tully 109
Brock, Iliff 29, James 27, William 72
Bromage, Sarah 115
Brook, Ezra 18-20, 22-25, 27-29
Brooks, Patrick 44
Brosier, Owen 43
Broughton, Betty 92, 95, 97, Charles 79, 81, 82, 84-86, 92, 93, 95, 98, 100, 105, Dorcas 2, Edward 33, Elizabeth 100, George 104, 107, 109, Mary 26, 27, 41, 46, 48, 50, 51, 53, 57, 59, 61, 63, 65, 67, 69, 71-74, 76, 78, 81, 84, 86, Thomas 79
Brown, Edward 11, 12, 34, 54, Henry 109, John 54, Mary 24, Pembrook 96, Richard 45, Sarah 109, 112
Brumbly, Auston 115
Bryan, see Brian
Buchanan, James 43, 45, 46, 48, 51, 52, 54
Bulman, John 71, 72, 74, 76, 78, 81, 83, 85, 88, 90, 92, 95, 97, 99, 102, 105
Burfoot, John 33, 46, Robert 61, 62, 64
Burges, Elizabeth 59-61, 64, 66
Burgess's xxii
Burke, Patrick 23, Eleanor 54, 55, 57, 59, 61, 63, 65, 68
Burkett, Mrs. 58, Elizabeth 59-61, 63

Burrough, Burroughs, see Burrowgh
Burrowgh, Barbara 24, Benjamin 20, 23, 24, 34, 38, 44, 46, 47, 49, 51, 53, 57, 62, Christopher 2-5, 7-10, 12, 13, 15-21, Elizabeth 23, William 17, 18
Buskey, John 24
Butler, William 15
Buttery, Mary 30

Calvert, Mr. 59
Campbell, Dr. Arthur 47, Hugh xiv, John 103
Cannon, Widow 117, Edward 84, 106-108, John 7
Capps, Edward 66, 67, Henry 89, 108, 117, Richard 11, 12, 117, Sally 89, William 91, 95
Care, Dennis 20, 22, 24, 25, 27-31
Carraway, James 35, 55, 71, 80
Carrell, see Carrol
Carrington, Elizabeth 1, 2, 4
Carrol, Mrs. 55, Dorcas 61, William 31, 50, 51, 54, 58, 59
Carter, Secretary 4
Cartwright, Mary 52, 54, 58, Robert 43, 49, 54, 55, 62, 70-72, Thomas 9, 15, 24-27, 29-31, 33, 34, 36, 40, 47, William 42
Cason, Charles 72, James 58, 65, 66, 68, 88, John 88, 110, Mary 115, Sarah 68, 84, Thomas 86, 89, William 38, 40, 41, 60, 61
Casteel, John 36
Caton, Dinah 111, 112, 117
Cear, see Kear
Chambers 49
Chapel, Betty 92, George 92, John 92, 95, 96
Chapels of ease xvii
Chapman, Henry 1-13, 15, 33, 35, John 30, 53
Chapman's Creek 35
Chesapeake River xii
Chesopeian River xii
Church Creek xviii, xix
Church converted to school xv, 23
Church Point xii
Churchyard railed in 45
Churchyard washed away xii
Clancy, William 29
Clark, Francis 53
Colerson, see Collinson
Colley, Anne 76, 77, Bridget 77, 78, 80, 81, Margrett 77, 78, 80-82, 84, 86,
Collins, George 10, 80, Henry 110, John 80
Collinson, Joseph 59, 61, 63, Richard 65, 67, 69
Communion table cloth 27, 60, 119, 120
Communion vessels 60, 119, 120

INDEX

Condon, James 9, 23, 26, 29, 31-33, 35
Cone, Mrs. 49
Consaul, William 19, 47
Consaulvo, see Consolvo
Consolvo, Abia 73, 75, 76, 78, 81, Elizabeth 89, 93, 96, 100, 103, 106, Henry 34, John 29
Cooper, Edward xx, Elizabeth 96, Jemima 114
Corbell, W. 4
Cornick, Henry 72, Horatio 110, Joel 10, 12, 15, 44, 80, 84-86, 88, 109-124, John 2-5, 88, 99, 104, 105, 114, 115, 117-124, Lemuel 26, 49, 51, 82, 93, Nathan 88, 110
Cornick family plantation xx
Corprew, George 74, George Durant 86, 88, 105-107, 109, 110, 112-115, 117, 118, 122, 123, John 9, 15
Cotten, see Cotton
Cotton, Abigail 32, 54, 64, 65, Francis 31, 33, 36, James 9, 11-13, 16, 17, Katherine 19, 20, 35
Court-house, Princess Anne County, xiii, xv, xix, xx
Courtney, John 6
Cowper, Amy 99
Cox, Mrs. John 71, George 70, 101, John 71, 73, Mary 109, William 9, 37, 62, 66, 106, 109,
Craig, Ebenezer 115
Craigdellie, Dr. Hugh 39, 93, 97, 100
Creed, Dinah 97, Thomas 2, 4, 6
Creeds Post Office xxiv
Crompton, Mary 9, 11, William 36
Cumberfoot, John 92
Curtis, John 72
Cuttance, Mary 64

Dale, William 30, 40, 41
Dauge, Joab 114, John 9, 15, Josiah 103, Richard 82
Dauley, Dauly, Dawly, Doyley, see Dawley
Davis, John 24, 84, Richard 50, 53, 57, Robert 58, Sarah 62, 64, William 57, 59
Dawley, Dennis 5, 6, 45, 67, 69, 70, 72, 74, 76, 78, 80, 83, 85, 90, 91, 94-97, 99, 100, 102-110, 115, 121, 122, Elizabeth 33, Henry 19, 34, 73, John 7, 96, Lawrence 2, 4, 6-13, 16, 17, 19, 20, 22, 24, 25, 27, 28, 30, Mary 115, 116, Sarah 33, Thomas 7, William 37, 39, 93, 96, 103
Day, Elizabeth 13, 16, 20
Dearmon, Annis 107
Dearmore, Robert 51, 57
Deer, Stephen 107
Denby, Ann 69, Edward 35, 43, 45, 53, 55

Deniston, Susannah 107
Dennie, William 35
Denny, John 77
Deputies to Diocesan Convention 121-123
Dial, Elizabeth 45, 46
Dickson, Mrs. Robert 123, Rev. Robert vii, 38-42, 44-54, 57, 58, 60-63, 65, 67, 69, 70, 72, 74, 76, 78, 80, 81, 83, 85, 87, 88, 90-92, 94, 95, 97-102, 104, 108, 110-114, 116, 118, 119, 121-123
Dickson's Donation 120
Dickson's Free School xvii, 111, 113, 114, 116, 119, 121, 124
Ditcher, John Cox 82, 84
Dividing Line commissioners xxii
Dobos, 22, Mary 110, 112
Dolby, John 79-81, William 113
Dollar, James 7
Donation, Dickson's, 120
Donation Church xiii, xv, xvii, xxv, 17, 21, 23
Donation Farm xvii, 120
Doudle, see Dowdle
Douge, see Dauge
Dough, Josiah 68
Douton, Anne 36
Dowdle, Betty 115, Elizabeth 110, 112, 115, John 115
Dudley, Mrs. 42, Daniel 79, 97, John 48, Mary 32, Richard 43, 45, Robert 7, Thomas 5, William 72
Dudly, see Dudley
Duffe, Thomas 43
Duffy, Constantine 108
Dunn, James 54, 58, 64
Dyer, Elizabeth 42, 44, 46, 48, 51, 53, 57, 59, 61, 63, John 89, 96, 114, 116, Pheby 71, 73, 74, Sarah 46, William xxiv, 12, 28, 32, 34, 36-38, 40, 41, 65-68, 71, 72, Mrs. William 69
Dyson, Francis 47, Mary 67

Earl, Dr. Charles 103
Easely, Sarah 44, 46, 48, 51, 53, 57, 58, 59, 61, 63
East Lynnhaven Parish 1, xi
Easter, John 92, 93, 95, 98, Mary 92, 95, Thomas 61, 64, 66, 67
Eastern Branch, Elizabeth River, xi, xviii, xix
Eastern Branch Chapel (1642) xviii, (1661) xix
Eastern Shore Chapel (1689) xx, 3, (1726) xx, xxii, 3, 6, 8, (1755) xx, xxii, xxv, 49, 50, 54
Eaton, Elizabeth 58, 60-62, 64-66, 68, James 58, Michael 58, 117, W.G. xiv
Edgar, Patience 84
Edmonds, Sarah 66, 67, 69-71, 73, 74, 76, 78, 81, 86, 89, 93, 97, 99

Edwards, Charles 41
Elizabeth City Corporation xi
Elizabeth City County xi
Elizabeth River Parish xi, xx, 47
Elks, Thomas 42, 44
Ellegood, Edmond 22, 24, 25, 27, 29, 30-32, 34, 36-38, 40, Francis 36, Jacob 7, 12, 15, 17-29, 31-35, 37-39, 41-43, 45, 47, 88, 98-102, 105, 109, Matthew 19, Peter Norley 80, 97, William 1-5
Ellis, Thomas 46
Ellit, Margaret 46, Mary 48, Peter 41, 44, 45
Emmanuel Church (1843) xxv, (1947) xxv
Etheredge, Anthony 56, David 56, Eve 20, 22, 24, 25, 27, 29-31, 56, William 104
Ewell, Thomas 88, 110, 115

Fallen, Hannah 97, 101, 103
Fazakerly, Thomas 56
Fentress, Anthony xxiv, 96, 100, 103, 106, 107, 110, 115, Courtney 60, James 27, John 26, 33, 39, 53, 59, 69, Lemuel 39, 53, Lidia 82, Martha 86, 88, 93, 98, 100, 103, 106, 109, 118, Mary 90, Michael 30-32, 34, 36, 37, 69, William 27, 68, 82
Fentris, Fentriss, see Fentress
Ferry Plantation xiii, 17
Fitzgerald, Mary 6
Flanakin, Patrick 54, Rebecca 109, William 54, 57, 60, 61
Flanegin, see Flanakin
Fleer, Anne 77-79, 81, 82, 84-87, 89
Fountain, Elizabeth 77, 78, 81, Margaret 77
Franklin, Daniel 115, Dorcas 81, Simon 24, 25, 27, 29, 30
Free School, Dickson's, 111, 113, 114, 116, 119, 121
Frisel, Anthony 116
Frost, Abigail 81, 84-88

Gall, Thomas 117
Galleries in churches vii, xii, xv, 22, 69, 75, 91
Gardner, see Garnor
Garnor, Thomas 44, 47
Garton, James 63, 65, 67, 82, 90, William 64, 66-68, 69
Gasking, Charles 43, 44, 48-50, 53, 55, 57, 59, 61, 63, 65, 67-76, 78, 80-86, 88, 90, 92, George 110, 111, 115, 121, Job 26-29, 31-35, 37, 37, 39, 41, 48, 54, 55, John 28, Lemuel 82
Gibbs, 51, Willis 118
Gilbert, Thomas 29, 30
Gisbon, see Gisburn
Gisburn, Mrs. Edward 115, 117

INDEX

Gisburn (cont'd), Edward 115, 117, John 81
Gittery, James 14
Givin, Willis 109
Glasgow, Lydia 115
Glebe farm 5, 10, 24-26, 41, 43, 44, 48, 100, 101, 108, 119, 120
Glebe house 2, 9, 13, 16, 21, 22, 25, 38, 39, 41-43
Godfry, Anne 89-91, 93, 96, 98, 102, 103, 106, Matthew 104, Smith 91, 96, 98, William 68
Gold, Dinah 59, 62, 64
Gorden, see Gordon
Gordon, Mrs. Thomas 77, Elizabeth 96, 99, John 96, 99, Thomas 75-78
Gornto, John 15, 17-22, 24-26, 28, 31, 33-35, 37-41, 45
Gough, Ann 27
Gowns for minister 70
Grainger, Thomas 31-38, 40-42, 44-51, 53, 54, 57, 58
Gray, Benjamin Dingly 53, 54, William Gilbert 91, 92, 97, 99, 104
Great Neck xx
Green, Edward 54, George 73, Sarah 69, Thomas 71
Griffen, George 16, 17, 19, 20, James 62, John 19, 20, 22, 24, Mary 20, 24
Grimstead, Argan 79, 82, 84, Amy 117, Joseph 113, 114, Sarah 113, William 114, 117
Grindal, Rhodom 111
Grines, Mary 47
Griskil, Florence 61, 62
Guin, John 50

Hackett, Patrick 22
Hailes, John 86, 90, Jonathan 86
Hancock, George 10, John 62, 94, 98, 99, 120-124, William 20, 23, 26, 35, 110
Handcocke, Samuel xix, Simon xix, William xix
Handly, Charles 62
Happer, Dr. William 13, 17, 22, 24, 27, 29-31, 35, 36, 38, 40
Harman, see Harmon
Harmon, Elizabeth 27, 29-34, Joseph 18, 23-25
Harper, 70, 71, John 24, 27, 35, 39, 45, Jonathan 77
Harrison, Frances 106, 108, 109, 112, Henry 62, Nathaniel xxii
Hartley, Sarah 108
Harvey, Alexander 9, 64, Anne 32, 102, 103, Charles 107-109, 112, Elizabeth 32, 68, 71, 73, 74, 76, 78, 81-84, 87, 89, 93, Francis 59, 62, 68, 81-83, George 32, John 31, Mary 32, Sarah 86, 89, Thomas 82-84, 88, 93, 97, William 17, 23-25, 27, 29, 59

Hatten, see Hatton
Hatton, 71, John 67, Roger 53, 57, 59, 61-65, 67, William 67
Hayes, Adam 26
Haynes, Erasmus 72, 88, 89, 115, 121, 122, John 58, 80, Thomas 2, 4-6, 8-13, 17, 26, 62, William 122
Heath, Elizabeth 95, James 89, Solomon 87, William 105, 106
Henley, Mr. 54, James 110, 113, 114, 116-120, John 19, Nowdinna 69
Hervey, see Harvey
Hewit, Mary 92
Higgins, Abigail 47
Hill, Thomas 30
Hodges, Joseph 44
Hodgson, Dr. John 100, 101, 109
Hoggard, Natt 115, 121, Thurmer 45, 49, 80, 85
Hogwood, see Hoggard
Hollowell, Samuel 39, 40
Holmes, Edward 14, 15, Francis 102, Henry 35, 61, 64, 66, 67, Robert 117, Sarah 15, William 117
Holmes' Creek 35
Holt, John 33, 34, 36-38, 40-42, 44, 46, 48
Hopkins, John 56, 115, 121, 122, Jonathan 62, 87, 90, 96, Joshua 89
Horsey, 20, 22, 24, 25, 27, 29, 30, 31
Horshay, see Horsey
Horsley, William 34, 36
Hoskins' Creek xix
Hough, Daniel 23, 24
Hours of church service 94
Hudgins, Ann 115
Huggins, David 109, 111, Robert 15, 48, 55, 62, 68, 70, 71
Hull, Rev. John G. xv
Hundley, James 80
Hunter, Jacob 45, James 15, 26, John 5, 7, 19, 26-28, 31, 32, 34, 35, 37-41, 45, 115, 121, Thomas 4, 7, 26, 72, William 53
Hutchings, Capt. 42, John 33, 51, Nathaniel 5
Hutson, Jane 43

Ince, John 39
Isle of Wight County xxiv
Indian River xviii
Isdell, 27, 29
Ives, George 115, 121

Jackson, Jonathan 53, 62, 80
Jacob, Vesty 64
James, Charles 72, 82, 84, Edward 110, Henry 43, James xxiv, 28, 31, John 34, 53, 80, 110, 115, 121, 122, Jonathan 53, Ruth 87, 89, 93, 96, 100, 103, William 63, 65

Jameson, Alexander 36, 37, 46-48, 52, 54, 58, 59, 62, 64, 66, 67, George 43, 55, 72, Henry 34, John 81
Jay, John 15
Jenkins, Elizabeth 24
Jimason, see Jameson
Jobson, 40, 42, Frances 97, 102, 117, William 115, 117
Johnson, Henry 66, Jacob xii, James 111, 112
Jones, 41, 42, 44, 46, Cornelius 2, 4, 5, Jane (Jean) 87, 90, 93, 97, 100, Nelly (a mulatto) 36, 37, Rev. Nicholas 7-10, Richard 7, Sarah 53, Thomas 51, 54
Jouslin, James 60
Joynes, Edmond 54

Kaller, Israel 34
Kays, James 54, William 116, 118
Kear, Mary 77-79, 81-84
Keeling, Mr. 59, Adam 39, 105, 122, Alexander 67, 99, Amy 58, 59, Barbara 33, 35-38, 40-42, 44, 46-48, 51, 53, 57, 59, 61, 63, Henry 72, 115, Jacob 110, John 30, 45, 49, 51, 53, 54, 57, 59, 80, 86, Thomas 34, 115, 121, William xxii, 5, 6, 11-13, 16, 17, 19, 20, 22, 24, 25, 27-32, 34, 36-38, 40-42, 44-50, 52, 53, 55, 61-63, 65-70, 72, 74, 76-78, 103, 105, 108
Kelly, Mary 20, 23
Kempe, George 4-6, 8-13, 15-17, James 15, 21-29, 37-43, 45, 47-50, 52, 53, 56-58, 61-63, 65-76, 78, 80-88, 90, 91, 93-103, 105-107, 110-114, Thomas 122
Kempsville, xxv, 119
Kenline, John 92-108, John Michael 75
Key, 57, John 12, 33
King, Christian 58, 59, Duncan 43, 46, 48, 51, Elizabeth 113, 117, Sarah 117
Kinsey, Henry 73, 81, Thomas 107, 109
Kinzee, see Kinsey
Knight, Anne 106, 107
Knoaks, see Nokes
Knott's Island xxiv
Knowland, Katherine 17, 34-38, 40-42, 44, 46, 48, 51

Lamb, James 96, 97, 103
Lamount, Henry 19, 31, 36, James 15, John 31, 32, 35, 36, 38, 49
Land, Capt. 23, Anne 41, 115, 117, Charles 115, 117, Edward 4, Elizabeth 91, 97, Francis 1-13, 15-21, 91, 97, 99, 104, 112-114, 119-123, Francis Thorowgood 47, 48, 49, 52, 53, 60, 61, 62, 63,

INDEX

Land (cont'd), Jeremiah 110, Judah 91, 92, Lidia 91,97, 99, Margaret 23, Mary 113, 115, 117, Peter 115, 117. Thorowgood 115, William 91, 97, 99, 104

Land survey reports 14, 35, 55, 56

Langley, James 7, 12, 20-24, 35, Thomas 26, 97

Latter, Dauley 34, 36. 37,38

Lawrance, Mary 86, 89, William 43, 44, 46, 49, 54

Lawson, Anthony 79, 83, 85, 90, 91, 94, 95, 97-99,109, Thomas 45, 122

Laycock, Dinah 12

Leamont, see Lamount

Leasley, Leefley, see Easely

Legget, Alexander 41, 47,Anthony 72

Leggitt, see Legget

Lester, James 89, 91, 95, Mary 59, 62, 64, 66, 91, 95, 96, 101, 104, 105, Thomas 97

Leversage, 19, Mary 93, 96, 102, 103, 106, William 57

Lewis, Thomas 76

Linkhorn Bay xx

Linten, see Linton

Linton, James 5, 8, Willis 78

Lofland, Frances 115, 116

Logan, George 62

Lovett, Adam 34, 55, James 88, John 34, 71, 72, 88, Thomas 72

Lower Norfolk County xi, xxiv

Ludwell, Philip xxii

Lynnhaven Church (1639)xii, (1692)xii,xv, 3, 23, (1736) iii, 13, 17, 18, 21, 22,23

Lynnhaven Parish formed xi

Lyon, Walter 85

Machipongo Chapel (1692)xx, xxii, 4, 12

Mackie, Rev. Josias xx,William 15

Malbone, Charles 15,26,James 39, John 51, 75, Mary 58, 61, Peter xv,18, 21,26,33, Reodolphus 7, 33, Solomon 33

Manen (?), John 43

Marrener, see Marriner

Marriner, Mary 77, 84-88, John 67

Marsden, Rev. Richard 10, 11

Marsh, Mrs. 37, Alec 38, 40-42, Alice 89, 93, 95, John 37, 38, 40-42, Mary 112

Martin, Bridget 61, William 36, 39

Mason, Abigail 48, 50, 51, Dinah 81

Mathias, Charles 88, John 62, 80, Joshua 80, 90, 93

May, John 90, 93, 93, 102, Lucy 34, William 46, 51, 52, 54, 71

Maye, see May

McBride, Ruth 40, 41, 45, 46

McCaull, Angus 73, 75,77-79, 81, 82, 84, 89, Charity 97, 103, 106, 107, Duncan 71

McClallan, Moses 61

McClenahan, David 45, 55,56, 96, Nathaniel 34, 35, 56

McClary, Mary 40-42, 44, 46, 48, 50, 51, 54, 55, 58,59, 61-63

McKeal, McKeil, see McKeel

McKeel, Anthony 46, 48-51, 61, 64, 68-72, 74, 76, 78, 81, 83, 86, 88, 92, 95,96, Frances 99, 101, 103, 105, 107, 109, 111, 112

McLanahan, John 5, 6

Mearanor, see Marriner

Merchant, Christopher 7,Willoughby 2

Michason, Const. 12

Milason, see Millerson

Miller, Anne 112, John 110

Millerson, Abigail 101, 104, 107, 109, 113, 115, Elizabeth 27, 29, John 58-63, Whiddon 101, 104, 107

Millian, Edward 9

Millison, see Millerson

Mills, Anne 103

Minister, gowns for, 70

Mitchel, Joseph xxii,50,52,54

Moon, James 62

Montgomery, Elizabeth 9, 11, John 43

Moore, Anne 25, 27, 29-31, 104, 105, 110, 113,114,117, Cason 38, 40-42, 44, 46,48, 50, 53, 57, 59, 61, 63,65, 67, 69, 70, 72, 74, 76,78, 81, 83, 85, 88, 92, 95,99, 102, 105, 122, 123, Elizabeth 47, Francis 80, Henry 10, 17-22, 24, 25, 27, 28, 36, James 30, 53, 88, 110, 115, John 39, 87, 89.Jonas 35, Marke 89, Mary 107, Thomas 22, 24, 25, 27, 29-32, 34, 36-38, 40

Morener, Moroner, see Marriner

Morrice, see Morris

Morris, Josias 12, 18, 39, 54, 55, 57, 59, 68,Mary 9, 11, 12, 26, 30-32, 34, 40-42, 44, 46, 48, 51, 53,57, 59, 61, 63,William 26, 115

Morriset, Mary 48

Morse, Barbara 15, Francis xxiv,15, John 10, 15, Thomas 26

Morse's Point xxiv

Moseley, Amos 4-6, 19, Anthony 13, 16, 21, 32, 34,35, 37, 42, 45, 47, 48, 56-58, 62, 63, 67, Benjamin 44, Betty 116, 118, Burrough 99, Charles 117, Edward 1-5, 7, 8,10-12, 18, 21, 43, 53, 59, 75, 77, 79, 100, 104-108, 110, 111, 113,114, Edward Hack xvii, 21,26,34, 39,42,45,60,76,78,80,83,85, 87-91,94,95,97-120,123,124,

Moseley (cont'd), Francis 13, 14, 16-25, 27, 29,30-32, 34, 36, 41, 42, 79, Hannah 12, Hillary xvii,1, 3, 115, John 1-3, 5, 7-13, 16-18, 20, 23, 25, Luke 4, 7, Margret 1, Tully 34,56, 115, 121, William 62, 68, 71, 93, 94, 98

Mosses, Samuel 65

Moy, Richard 9, 15

Munden, John 14, 15, 45, 53, Nathan 110

Mundens xxii

Murphey, see Murphy

Murphy, 83, Mrs. Patrick 117, James 90, 93, Mary 107, 109, 112, Patrick 85, 89, 93, 96, 117

Murray, John 115, 121, Richard 73, 75, 77-79, 81, 82, 84, 89

Murril, John 47

Murry, see Murray

Nansemond County xi,xxiv

New Norfolk County xi

New Town xix

Newton, James Williamson 75, Lemuel 97, Nathaniel 26-28, 30, 32, 33, 37, 39-41, 43, 45, 47-52, 55, 57, 58, 62, 67-71, 74, 76, 77

Nicholas, John 15, 19,35,94, 95, Nathaniel 10, 26, 45, 56, Willis 27

Nichols, James 5-7, Susannah 87, 89, 92, 97, 100

Nicholson, Elizabeth 23, 30, 33

Nicklis, see Nicholas

Nickols, see Nichols

Nimmo, Gershom 55, 56, 121, James 1, 2, 4, 6-9, 11-13, 16-18, 20-27, 31, 33, 35, 38, 39, 45, 53, Martha 92, William 71-73, 75, 77, 98, 101, 102, 106, 107, 109, 111, 113, 121

Noaks, see Nokes

Nokes, Rachel 86, 89, 93, 103, 106, 109, 112

Norfolk, burning of,xix

Norfolk County xi, 43

Norman, Richard 43, 59, 61, 63

Norris, Anne 46, 48, 51, Charles 98, 101, 104, 111, John 71, 96, 99, 103, 105

North Landing (North) River xxii,xxiv

Oakham, Elizabeth 30-32, 34, 36, Sarah 52, William 19, 30-32, 34, 36, 47, 54, 57, 104

Oast, Elizabeth 61, 62, 64, 66

Oharrow, Winney 79

Old, Ann 66, Caleb 110. 122, Cockroft 20, 22, 24,25,27, 28, 35-38, 40-42,44,46,48, 51, Edward 15,Josias 9,10,18,

INDEX

Old (cont'd), Thomas 67, 69, 72-74, 76, 79, 80, 83, 86, 90, 93-95, 98-100, 104, 105, Willoughby 80
Old Donation Church xiii, xv, xvii, xxv, 21, 23
Olderson, see Alderson
Oldner, George 68, Thomas 12, 13, 18, 75, 76-79, 81, 82, 84-86
Olds, see Old
Oliver, Eleanor 59, 61, 64, 66, Elizabeth 51, 57, 59, 61, 64, 66, Mary 51, 57
Omeary (O'Meara), Elizabeth 42, 82, 84, 87, 89, 90, 93, 96, 100
Otterson, Mary 46, 48
Overseers of the Poor 94, 102, 124
Owens, Thomas 43, 44, 46, 47

Pallet, John 62, Matthew 26, 46
Parish property inventory 119, 120
Park, Jonathan 123
Parsons, Noro 74, Salley 112
Partree, James 16
Pasley, Joshua 68, 71, 107, Nancy 107, William 64, 66
Paterson, Dr. Robert 31, 33, 35, 49, 77, 79
Patterson, see Patteson
Patteson, Robert 46, 47, 49
Peacock, Andrew 1, 2, 4, 6, 8, 9, 11-13, 16, 17, 19, 20, 22, 24, 25, 27, 28, 30-32
Pead, Widow 32, Elizabeth 117, William 32, 113
Peetree, see Petree
Peirt, Robert 33
Persons, John 88
Petree, Elizabeth 85-87, 89, 93, 97, Frances 47, James 47
Pettigrew, Rev. Charles 119, 120
Pews, assignment of, 21, 23
Pews, hanging, vii, xii, 3, 21, 75, 76, 85
Pewter communion vessels 60, 119, 120
Philips, Margaret 109, Thomas 20
Pitt, Hillery 50
Platt, Betty 89, 93, 96
Plummer, Jeremiah 104
Pocaty Swamp xxii
Poole, Alexander 56, Richard 10, 12, 15, William 4-6, 12, 16
Poor farm 119, 120
Poor house 60, 69, 87, 93, 98, 101
Porter, Jonathan 69, 71, 79, 81
Powell, Mark 55
Power, Elizabeth 107, 109, 112
Powers, James 72, 89
Powis, Rev. Robert xviii
Prayer books 119

Presbyterian Meeting House (1693) xx
Price, Adam 99, Elizabeth 99, 104, George 79, 82, Dr. Lewis 55, 60-62, 64-66, 68, 70, 72, 73, 75, 107
Princess Anne County formed xi
Princess Anne Court-house (1689) xiii, xxi, (1695) xiii, (1735) xv, (1758) xix
Processioning orders 7, 15, 26, 34, 35, 39, 45, 52, 55, 56, 62, 63, 72, 88, 110, 115
Pungo Chapel (1692) xx, xxii, xxiv, (1743) 27, 29, 30, (1774) xxiv, xxv, 91, 94, 96, 97
Pungo Ridge xxiv
Pungo village xxiv
Purde, Widow 117
Purdy, George 5, 6, 11, 12, John 71, William 71

Ramsay, Dr. 101, 104
Randolph, Mary 93, 115
Rascow (Roscow), Thomas 59
Rea, Samuel 73, 75
Reade, see Reed, Reid
Reading places 4, 7
Red, Redd, see Rudd
Reed, Robert 26, 41, 43, 104, William 110
Reid, Dr. John 103-105
Rice, Ann 78
Richmond, Robert 13
Riggby, Paul 34
Roberts, Jonathan 115, 121, Moses 64
Robertson, Adam 42, John 43
Robinson, Adam 42, 44, 46, 93, 100, Tully 34, 56, 83, 85, 87, 88, 90, 91, 96, 98, 110, William 21, 39, 55, 114-118, 122
Roe, Kitely 26
Rogers, Richard 44
Rouviere, Dr. George 47, 51, 64
Rudd, John 20, 22, 24, 25, 27, 29, 30
Russel, Anne 47, 51, 53, 54, 58, 59, 62, John 9, 10, 34

Saint Bride's Parish 100
Salisbury Plains xx
Salmons, Margaret 112, Rebecca 89, William 93, 96, 97
Saunders, John 15, 16, Jonathan 39, 67, 69, 70, 72, 73
Sayer, Arthur 28-38, 40, 41, 43, 45, 56, Charles 1-28, 121
Scady, Mary 27
School, church converted to, 23
School, Dickson's Free, vii, 111, 113, 114, 116, 119, 121, 124

Scophus, Thomas 77, 79
Scott, Ann 1, 2, 4, 6, 8, 9, 11, 117, Bartholomew 89, 90, 93, David 121, Elizabeth 117, John 39
Seawell's Point xii
Selden, Rev. William 113
Senaca, Senneca, see Seneca
Seneca, James 104, 110, 113, 114, William 117
Sermon's, Secker's, 119, Tillotson's, 119
Services, hours of church, 94
Sharp, Edward 30
Sharwood, see Sherwood
Shepard, Shipherd, see Shepherd
Shepherd, Smith, 62, 86, William 88
Sherwood, Grace xiii, James 46, 48, 51, 53, 57, 93, 107, 109, John 40, 41, Mary 57, Michael 58, Sally 107, 109, Sarah 93, 96, 100, William 46
Shipp, Dinah 61, 63, 65, John 34, William 12, 44
Shurcraft, William 41
Sibsey, John xii
Sills, Robert 6
Silver communion vessels 60, 119, 120
Simmonds, see Simmons
Simmons, Bullock 9, Joel 47, 115, 121, 122, John 34, 39, 62, 65, Malbone 4, Thomas 80, 81, William 10, 72
Simons, see Simmons
Simpson, Rev. James 120-123
Singleton, Peter 92, 100, 104, 109, 110, 114-118, 122
Small, Andrew 59, 61, 63, 67, 86
Smallwood, Charles 55
Smawn, Henry 98, 104
Smith, Charles 7, 11, 13, 15, 17, 26, 35, Frances 91, 92, George 3, 7, James 30, 62, 97, 101, Mary 106, Perrain 80, Ruth 54, 57, 59, 61, 63, 65, 67, 75, 79, 82, 84, 86, 90, 96, 100, 103, 106, 107, Sarah 33, Thomas 106, Tully Robinson 26, 34, 35, William 42, 44, 57
Smyth, see Smith
Snaile, Henry xix, 15, 19, Hillary 72, John 1, 46, 49, 54
Somerton xxiv
Sorey, William 92, 112
Southern, Elizabeth 40, 41, 43, 44, 94, 95
Southern Shore Church xviii
Southern Shore Parish xi
Spann, Elizabeth 36, William 32
Sparks, Ruth 29
Sparrow, Widow 18, George 10, 56
Spinning wheels for poor 90
Spratt, Francis 30, 35, 43, 68, Henry 7, 9-12, 17, 18,

INDEX

Spratt (cont'd), James 19, John 43, Thomas 7, 15, 26, Thorowgood 35.
Standly, Christopher 9, 11-13, 16, 17, 19, 20
Stephenson, George 114
Stewart, Andrew 73-75, 30
Stiring, George 34
Stokes, Love 47
Stone, John 83, Simon 115, 121
Stranhorn, Anne 114, 116, Rachel 114, Salley 114
Suggs, Aaron 30-32, 34, 36, 37
Sullivan, Frances 89, 93, 96, 100, John 41
Sullivant, see Sullivan
Sundials for churches 94
Sweeny, John 44

Tainer, Ann 26, Josiah 23
Taylor, Dr. 101, 104, Widow 103, Ebenezer xii, Robert 36
Tenant, Rev. James 1-4, 6, James 110, Samuel 72
Thorowgood, Adam xii, xix, 34, 55, 69, Argall 39, 44, Francis 29, John 7, 19, 41, 43, 55, 114, 121-123, Lemuel 88, Robert 9, 15, 44, 72, William 110
Threuston, 56
Tinion, Amos 108, 109, 112
Tinny, see Tinion
Tobacco-counting orders 4, 5, 7, 9, 10
Tooly, Adam 4-7, 20, 22, 24-28, 30, 31, 41-44, 57, 67, James 45, 53, 80
Toone, Elizabeth 96, Mark 82, 93, 106
Tripp, Henry 45, 53
Troughton, Mrs. George 69, 70, 83, 87, George 69-71, 82-84, 87, 89, 90, 93, 96, 98, 101-103, 109, 112
Trouton, see Troughton
Trowers, Mrs. John 85, 87, John 85, 87, 89, 112
Tucker, John 112
Tune, see Toone
Turner, Thomas 77, 78
Turton, William 59, 64-66, 68, 79

Upper Norfolk County xi

Vallentine, Jacob 116, Josiah 118
Vangover, Blazen 81, 84, 86, 89, 92, 96, 99, 103
Vaughan, Robert 2, 4-9, 16
Vestry dissolved 114, 119
Vial, Aby 61
Virginia State Library 124
Vowls, Walter 1

Wakefield, Lemuel 82, 83
Walke, Anthony 1-13, 15, 17-26, 28-33, 35, 37-45, 47-54, 57-62, 64-81, 83-92, 94, 96, 97, 100-106, 108-122, 124,
Walke (cont'd), Rev. Anthony 124, Katherine 3, Thomas 3, 21, 33, 34, 39, 41-43, 45, 47-50, 52, 53, 55, 57, 58, 60-66, 68, 69, 123, 124
Walker, Thomas 114-124, Thomas Reynolds 64, 67, 69, 70, 72, 74, 76, 78, 80, 81, 83, 85-88, 90-92, 94, 95, 97-112, 114-116, 118, 121-123
Waller, Hardress xxiv, 95-97
Walstone, Joseph 6, 7
Ward, Caleb 107, 109, 113, Dinah 61, Edward 35, Mary 69, Robert 69, Thomas 26, 64, 65, 79, William 62, 63
Waterman, Charles 110
Webb, Anthony 9
Weblin, George 55
Weddell, Thomas 96
Weldon, Frances 81, 84, 86, 89, 92, 96, 99, 103
Wellens, Mary 114, 117, Winefred 117
Wellins, see Wellens
Wells, John 91, 92, 97, 99, 104, Priscilla 104
West, Willoughby 62
Whitchard, Elizabeth 107, Glode 20, 22, 24, 25, 27, 28
White, Gidion 72, Henry 45, Joseph 54, 110, Solomon 2, 4-10, 12, William 114-124, William & Co. 98, 100, William Sutton 40-42, 44, 46, 48
Whitehead, John 29, 34, 41, 45, 50, 53, 57, 65, 67, 69, 72, 115, 121, Jonathan 80, Thomas 36, William 53
Whitehurst, Anne 86, Arthur 34, 39, Batson 30, 44, 46, 59, 61, 64, Charles 34, Christopher 88, Enoch 55, 110, Hillary 88, James 19, 53, 80, Jonathan 106, John 15, 19, 26, 28, 29, 32-35, 39, 41, 45, 48, 53, 57, 62, 63, 65, 67, 69, 70, 72, 74, 76, 78, 80, 83, 85-90, 93-95, 97, 98, Jonathan 106, 107, Joshua 110, Lemuel 107, Margret 66, Mary 24, 25, 27, 29, 40, 89, 91, 93, 96, 98-100, 104, 106, 107, Oden 35, Rachel 24, 25, 27, 29, Richard viii, 45, 46, Robert 37, 38, 40, Samuel 91, 96, 98, 99, 107, Sarah 33, 36, Solomon 107, William 7
Wickins, Wiggins, see Wiggin
Wiggin, John 13, 73, William 32, 33, 38, 42
Wilbur, Elizabeth 46, John 109, 112, Samuel 51, 53
Wilebour, see Wilbur
Wiles, Thomas 9, 10, 15, 80
Wilkins, John 65, Solomon 66
Willett, Mary 90, 98, Molly 93, 102, William 77
Williams, 45, Anne 31, Elizabeth 33, George 36, James 35, John 36, 38, 40, 41,
Williams (cont'd), Margaret 111, Mary 43
Williamson, Ann 64, 66, 67, Anthony 27, 68, 73, 79, 87, 88, 93, 96, 102, Charles 7, 72, 88, 114-123, George 7, 15, James 35, 43, 44, 46, 51, 56, 57, 82, 83, 85, 86, 89, 92, 97, Richard 57, 82, 83, 85, 86, Thomas 50, 52, 54, 57, 74, 75, 77, 80, Tully 65, 67, 73-76, 78, 81, 84, 86-88, 95, 99, 100
Willing, Mary 96
Willis, Thomas 84
Willoughby, Thomas 106
Willyroye, Lydda 90
Wilson, Rev. John xviii, Solomon 35
Wishard, see Wishart, Whitchard
Wishart, George 26, 28, 30, 31, 33, 35, 39, 43, 45, 48, 50, 52, 53, 57, 58, 60-63, 65, John 4, Mary 11, 16, 17, 19, 20, Thomas 1, 2, 4, 6-9, 15, 24, 122, William 80
Witchard, see Whitchard, or Wishart
Witch Duck Point xiii
Wolfsnare Creek xx
Wood, Catherine 96, 103, Edward 4, Mark 42, Robert 40, 43, Sarah 60, 62
Woodard [Woodward], Henry 115, 121, John 88
Woodhouse, Elizabeth 61, 63, 64, 65, Francis 4, Henry 4, 26, 62, Horatio 5-7, 11, 36, William 45, 48-50, 52, 53, 57, 58, 60, 61, 65, 67, 69, 70, 72, 74, 76-78, 80-88, 90, 91, 94, 97, 98, 101, 106, 110, 121
Woodland, John 104, 105, 109, Rhode 117
Wright, Dr. Christopher 45, 47, 49, 51, 54, 55, 59, 64, 66, Christopher 88

www.ingramcontent.com/pod-product-compliance
Lightning Source LLC
LaVergne TN
LVHW081535060526
838200LV00048B/2090